पुरातत्त्व
पुरातत्त्व
PURĀTATTVA

Bulletin of the Indian Archaeological Society

No. 19 1988-89

Editor
S.P. Gupta

Jt. Editor
Makkhan Lal

D.K. Printworld (P) Ltd.
New Delhi

Cataloging in Publication Data — DK
[Courtesy : D.K. Agencies (P) Ltd. <docinfo@dkagencies.com>]

Purātattva : bulletin of the Indian Archaeological
Society, no. 19, 1988-89 / editor, S.P. Gupta ;
jt. editor, Makkhan Lal.
p. cm.
Includes bibliographical references.
ISBN 8124602948

1. Archaeology — India — Periodicals. 2. India
— Antiquities — Periodicals. 3. India — Civilization
— Periodicals. I. Gupta, S.P. (Swarajya Prakash),
1931 - II. Indian Archaeological Society.

DDC 934 21

First Published in 1990
First Reprinted in 2005
ISBN 81-246-0294-8
Price for volume 19 (1988-89): Rs. 800 US $ 40

Reprint authorised by
Indian Archaeological Society
New Delhi - 110 016

Purātattva is published annually.

Manuscripts (whether in the form of articles or notes or book reviews) offered for publication should be sent to the Editor, Purātattva, Indian Archaeological Society, B-17, Qutab Institutional Area, New Delhi - 110 016.

Published and printed by:
D.K. Printworld (P) Ltd.
'Srikunj,' F-52, Bali Nagar
New Delhi – 110015
Phone : (011) 2545 3975, 2546 6019 Fax : (011) 2546 5926
E-mail : dkprintworld@vsnl.net
www. dkprintworld.com

PURATATTVA

CONTENTS

EDITORIAL PAGES

ARTICLES

1. Archaeology of Thanesar : A Brief Report on Excavations at Harsh-Ka-Tila
B.M. Pande 1

2. Early Farming communities of Kaimur Foot-Hills
Birendra Pratap Singh 6

3. Rgvedic Base of the Pasupati Seal of Mohenjo-Daro
S.P. Singh 19

4 Pollen Analysis and Chemical Examinations of a Prehistoric Lake Site At Damdama
M.D. Kajale and B.C. Deotare 27

5. On Flake-Blade Element in India
Ashok K. Ghosh & Dipankar Chaudhury 31

6. The Date of King Dhanadeva of Kosala : A Re-Examination of the Palaeographic and Historical Evidence
B.B. Lal and K. K. Sharma 38

7. Rakta-Lokesvara in Indian Buddhist Art
Shashi Asthana 43

8. Urban and Palace Water-Works During the Mughal Period
Mohd. Afzal Khan 46

9. Knapping Technique and Craft Specialization : An Ethnoarchaeological Investigation in Gujarat
Valentine Roux and Jacques Pelegrin 50

10. Ethno-Archaeology of the Traditional Ceremonial Pottery of Gujarat
Syed Anis Hashmi 60

11. Exposing and Conserving a World Heritage Monument
A.K. Sharma 64

NOTES & NEWS

12. Excavations of a Vedic Brick Altar At Purola, District Uttarkashi, Central Himalaya
K. P. Nautiyal and B.M. Khanduri 68

13. Some More Copper Objects From Sheorajpur
Suryakant Shrivastava 70

14. Casing Slab From Nagarjunkonda-A Reappraisal
Anamika Pathak 72

15. Archeaological Testimony of Surunga and the Mauryanism of the Arthasastra of Kautilya
Suresh Chandra Misra 74

16. Prehistoric Research In India : As viewed by two senior American Archaeologists
K. Paddayya 77

BOOK REVIEWS

1. Stone Age Hunter - Gatherers by *D.R. Raju*
H. D. Sankalia 80
2. The Cultural History of Goa by *Anant Ram Krishna Sinai Dhume*
H. D. Sankalia 80
3. Iconography of the Hindu Temples in Marathwada by *Deshmukh, B.S.*
Shashi Asthana 81
4. Origins of the Gandharan Style - a Style of the contributory influences by *Lalita Nehru*
M. C. Joshi 82

Executive Meetings of world Archaeological Congress 84
List of Life Members of Indian Archaeological Society 96

PURATATTVA

Number 19 1988-89

Editorial

Prof. H.D. Sankalia passed away on 28th January,1989. It is indeed a great loss not only for the archaeologist of India but for the whole archaeological community. Prof. Sankalia's contributions to the field of archaeology is too well known. Beside his contributions to the academic journals Prof. Sankalia was mainly responsible for bringing archaeology to the masses. Prof. Sankalia's simplicity and straight forwardness was not disariming but also put even the smallest one at ease when confronting him. Though Prof. Sankalia is no more with us, his work, his love and affection to all, his devotion for the duty, quest for knowledge, encouragement to younger colleagues and students will always remain with us. We all pray God that may his soul rest in peace.

We hope all our colleagues have received the letter from Prof. V.N. Misra regarding his efforts to institute lectures, prizes and several other such befitting Memorials for Prof. Sankalia. We appeal to the archaeological community to extend all possible help to Prof. Misra to make his efforts a success.

We hope our colleagues do remember our efforts towards establishing a Centre for Training and Research in History and Archaeology. Because of untimely death of our two great patrons - Prof. D.P. Singhal and Prof. Devahuti - the pace retarded. We have picked up the threads again and hope to move speedily towards the creation of the Centre. Hopefully, when time comes for writing the next editorial we will have some thing to write in detail.

We are very grateful to the Archaeological Survey of India and the Indian Council of Historical Research for the financial assistance which made the publication of this volume possible. we are also grateful to Dr Salahuddin, Dr. Q.S. Usmani, Mr. Anis Alvi and Mr. Ghulam Mujatba for their help in various ways.

Editors

H.D. Sankalia

OBITUARY

H.D. SANKALIA

Hasmukh Dhirajlal Sankalia, the doyen of Indian archaeologists, passed away in the early hours of 28 January 1989 at the ripe age of eighty. With him closes an era in Indian archaeology.

As the late Sir Mortimer Wheeler had rightly observed, Dr Sankalia was a pioneer in every sense of the term. There is hardly any branch of Indian archaeology which he did not illumine. He belonged to the generation of giants like professors P.V. Kane and R. C. Majumdar who had a commendable grasp of the entire discipline besides being specialists in their chosen fields. Prehistory was Dr Sankalia's forte, but his contributions to other branches of archaeology, though less well known, are substantial. In him one witnessed a unique blend of Sanskrit learning and critical Western scholarship. He had amazing courage to expound his views, even though they were sometimes shocking to the traditional Indian mind.

Dr Sankalia was a man of contradictions. Born with a silver spoon in his mouth, he lived a very simple life; a man of extremely frail constitution, he became the greatest field archaeologist; steeped in Sanskrit learning and a devout Vaishnava, his views on the Ramayana and beef-eating annoyed not only the common man but even luminaries like the Shankaracharya; though he had an abounding interest in astrology, he never waited for the right combination of planets.

Dr Sankalia was born on 10 December 1908 at Bombay. At St Xavier's College he came in contact with the late Father Heras, whose paternal care and discipline kindled in him a genuine and keen interest in archaeology. His father was a solicitor and wanted him to join the family law firm. He did LL.B., but he had no interest in law. Instead he wanted to study archaeology and so did Father Heras. Dr Sankalia's father then consulted an astrologer, who read from the Bhrgu-Samhita that Sankalia was destined to become a jima-sodhaka, an archaeologist. He used to admire the author of Bhrgu-Samhita for coining this word. He then went to England to work under Dr. K.de B. Codrington at the University of London and obtained Ph.D. degree in 1937 for his thesis Archaeology of Gujarat. He acquired training in field archaeology in course of Wheeler's excavation at Maiden Castle, Dorset, which constitutes a landmark in archaeology as a model of technical excellence. He also participated in Ernest Mackay's excavation at Chanhu Daro in Sind. Dr Sankalia always acknowledged his debt to F.J. Richards of England from whom he learnt research methodology.

On his return from England, Dr Sankalia joined the Deccan College in 1939 which was then converted into a research institute. Prior to this he was refused the post of Assistant Superintendent by the Archaeological Survey of India, probably because they found him physically too weak to work as a field archaeologist. However, later he proved to be the foremost field archaeologist in India and the only Indian archaeologist to be awarded the honorary membership of the Explorers' Club of the United states.

Dr Sankalia began his research with Stone Age in Gujarat and later covered many parts of the country. His major contribution lies in the field of palaeolithic research and it is only through his and his students' findings that we now know that the palaeolithic man had occupied most of the subcontinent including Kashmir and Assam. Earlier only Lower Palaeolithic was known, but Dr Sankalia's discoveries at Nevasa brought to light the existence of the Middle Palaeolithic phase which was later found to have spread far more extensively in India. so also is the case of Upper Palaeolithic which was brought to light by his pupil M.L.K. Murty in the Kurnool region. His own excavations at Langhnaj defined the Mesolithic.

Equally commendable is Dr Sankalia's contribution in the field of proto-history. The period between the end of the Indus Civilization and the era of Buddha and Mahavira, which was once considered the Dark Age, is no more dark because of his discovery of the Chalcolithic phase in central India and the Deccan. In his college days he was impressed by Lokamanya Tilak's Arctic Home of the Aryans which aroused in him a deep interest in the Aryan problem. He therefore began his excavations at Maheshwar and Navda - Toli (Madhya Pradesh) and identified the authors of the Chalcolithic phase with the Haihayas of Tripuri who figure so prominently in the Puranas. Later he carried on excavations at Nevasa (Maharashtra) and Ahar (Rajasthan) and planned the large scale excavations at Inamgaon. He was the true follower of Wheeler who had advised his Indian pupils that "We now have the time table, let us put some trains". Most of Dr Sankalia's excavations were large-scale horizontal excavations, for his main interest was to learn about the life of man in all its various aspects. He was the only Indian archaeologist who published the reports of his excavations promptly.

Dr Sankalia was always receptive to new ideas, a rare quality among Indians. He had realized the importance of sciences in archaeological research from a very early period. He made full use of Dr. Zeuner's visit to India in 1949 who demonstrated the importance of palaeo-climatic studies. It was only because of his broad vision that we have today almost all the scientific sub-disciplines of archaeology at the Deccan College. The same holds good in the case of New Archaeology. He was fully alive to the revolutionary changes that were taking place in archaeological theory and method during the past quarter century. At a time when most of the Indian archaeologists were blissfully unaware of Processual Archaeology, he delivered lectures on it which have also been published. He introduced such new branches as Ethno-archaeology and Experimental Archaeology at the Deccan College which, even today, are the only ones of their kind in the country.

A charge that is often levelled against Dr Sankalia is that he neglected historical archaeology. Admittedly, he did not pay as much attention to historical archaeology as he did to prehistory and protohistory; even so he excavated a few historical sites such as Brahmapuri (Kolhapur) and Tripuri. His study of personal names and place names is a pioneering work. Although he did not pursue it, his pupils have covered a major part of the country in this respect. What he did was to work in a particular branch and then leave the field to his students.

Dr Sankalia's study of the Ramayana is well-known, especially for the controversy it raised. His views were unpalatable to the traditionalists and he received several threats; he was advised to give up this type of research. But he was a seeker of truth and remained undaunted. We were amazed at his tremendous courage in those days. A similar outcry, through of lesser intensity, was caused by his views on cow slaughter. He was very alive to public issues such as the language problem and he was a vehement critic of the government's policy in this regard. He never minced words and I remember him castigating his Gujarati audience at Veraval Rotary Club for their hankering after money and inadequate interest in scholarship which, he told them, can flourish only in Maharashtra, especially in Poona. In fact this was the most compelling reason why he did not leave Poona and spurned many lucrative offers.

The reason for Dr Sankalia's great popularity lies in his writing for the common people not only in English but also in Marathi, Hindi and Gujarati. He would always remind us of our duty towards the society; that we are using public money and the people have every right to know how we are spending the tax-payer's money. Even if a poor farmer or a school boy wrote to him, he would reply promptly. That is why people from different parts of the country used to inform him about archaeological remains and he would make it a point to visit the place himself or depute a colleague or a student. In our excavations, he would very gladly take the children round the sites.

The honours showered on Dr Sankalia are a legion. He was the first recipient of the Nehru Fellowship (1968) and was awarded the Padmabhushan in 1974, but he cherished more the fellowship of the Explorers' Club of the United states in recognition of his lifelong fieldwork and the Robert Bruce Foote award conferred by the University of Calcutta because he started his research work in the footsteps of Foote. His lasting contribution is the creation of the Department of Archaeology at the Deccan College which he built up from scratch and turned into one of the leading institutions in the world. In his death, we have lost a pioneering archaeologist, a rishi who brightly shone on the horizon of Indian archaeology for half a century. Alas, an era- the Sankalia era-in Indian archaeology has come to an end !

ARCHAEOLOGY OF THANESAR : A BRIEF REPORT ON EXCAVATIONS AT HARSH-KA-TILA

B.M. Pande*

Kurukshetra is adequately known and it is therefore needless to recount details relating to the area wherein is located the Thanesar town and the Harsh-Ka-Tila[1] which was subjected to excavation by the Archaeological Survey of India between December 1987 and March 1988. The site has thrown up interesting material and results which, it is hoped, would provide useful evidence about the lifeways of the historical period at Thanesar, covering a span of almost about two thousand years from about the first century A.D. onwards. At the same time, as the present evidence from the area and the rather limited evidence from the site itself has indicated, the antiquity of the site may go back to still earlier times. Though it is rather premature at this stage to say so, yet it is hoped that the excavations at Thanesar will give important information particularly of the period between the sixth-seventh century and the Late Mughal times. The excavations at the Harsh-Ka-Tila site, therefore may be of interest to the archaeologist and the historian.

Thanesar is an ancient town and is fairly well-known[2]. For students of history, it is important because of its association with Harshavardhana (606-647) of the Vardhana or the Pushyabhuti (Pushpabhuti) dynasty.[3] Association of Harsha with Thanesar has been described in detail by Banabhatta in his *Harshacharita*.[4] While giving a graphic account of Sthanvisvara, Bana mentions the defence wall and the moat, the palace area with a two-storied dhavala-griha, literally the 'white house', which was the palace proper[5]. Sthanvisvara is categorized by Bana as jana-pada-visesha in the Srikantha janapada[6]. Sthanvisvara was an important centre of the Pasupata cult[7], a fact which is also corroborated by descriptions in the Vamana Purana.

Hsuan-Tsang, the Chinese pilgrim, in his brief description of Sa-ta-ni-ssu-fa-lo or Sthanvisvara mentions it to be more than 7000 *li* 'in circuit' with the capital to be 20 *li* or so which was surrounded for 200 *li* by a district called Dharmakshetra[8]. Hsuan Tsang, during his visit to Sthanvisvara, in A.D. 634, found three Buddhist monasteries and some hundred Brahmanical temples; he also mentions about a brick stupa about 300 feet high, of Asoka 4 or 5 *li* to the north-west of the city[9].

The presence of several mounds in Thanesar also attests to the hoary antiquity of the place. This, coupled with the fact that the area under habitation was fairly extensive, the name Harsh-Ka-Tila given to one of the mounds by the local people clearly supports and suggests the veracity of the tradition.[10]

It was this mound-the Harsh-Ka-Tila - which was taken up for excavation by us. Before we summarize the results of our excavation, it may perhaps be appropriate to give brief idea of Thanesar and its milieu.

The Thanesar town is located on an ancient mound which is quite large both in terms of its height and area. The houses that are built on it, covering almost the entire portions from its top to the slopes, represent an admixture of the new with the old. While the new houses, built over the earlier ones, are mainly of brick and cement concrete, fairly large number of houses are quite old retaining some of the original features which suggest that some of them may be over one hundred or more years old. In some of the houses one can also see juxtaposed ancient bricks with the lakhauri ones, the former being, evidently handiwork of brick-robbing. The narrow winding lanes of Thanesar town are also the vestiges of the past treaded over the years by the inhabitants of the town, itinerant traders and pilgrims visiting the Brahma Sarovara, the Sannihita Sarovara, the Sthanvisvara - Mahadeva and stopping here route to Prithudaka or Pehowa etc.

Thanesar must have been visited by many because of its location on the Grand Trunk Road. It seems evident to us that the Grand Trunk Road has been reoriented at several places; in the time of Sher Shah Sur (1540 - 1545) or the Mughals, the Grand Trunk Road must have went past the Thanesar town. This we are suggesting because of the existence of an old bridge and Sarai[11] (adjacent to Shaikh Chaheli's tomb) which are in all likelihood of the time of Sher Shah Sur or slightly later. As is well known, well planned sarais, kos-minars and, where required, bridges were built on or all along the Grand Trunk Road in the time of Sher Shah Sur and the Mughal emperors. In fact, the close contiguity of the sarai and the bridge (not far from the Sthanvisvara Mahadeva temple) to the Harsh-ka-Tila mound suggest that the road went past the mound in Mughal times, if not even earlier. The Grand Trunk Road (now renamed Sher Shah Suri Marg) is about 8 kms. away from Thanesar town and the river Saraswati on the banks of which the town grew and flourished is now extinct.

The Harsh-ka-Tila is not an isolated mound.[12] It is to the west of and adjacent to the ancient mound over which the town of Thanesar is located. To its west, separated by a gulley, is another mound known as Bahari.[13] Evidently, the name Bahari was given to the mound because it was bahar or outside the main town and the name may be a carry over, if we may suggest, from earlier times. In contrast to the Thanesar and Bahari mounds, the Harsh-Ka-Tila mound is now deserted except for a few kachcha houses on its middle-eastern part adjoining Shaikh Chaheli's tomb ; this mound is also not given any appellation or rather sobriquet like the Bahari mounds. Does it, therefore, indicate that the mound comprising the Thanesar town and the Harsh-Ka-Tila grew and prospered together till later times and were integrated units ?

* Archaeological Survey of India, Janpath, New Delhi

Of course, we are not suggesting that the Bahari mound had no connections or relationship with the Thanesar town. In fact it seems that apart from the three mounds comprising - from east to west - the Thanesar mound, the Harsh-Ka-Tila and the Bahari mound, there existed originally other mounds,[14] following almost the same orientation and alignment, which have been levelled in recent times. One such mound which we saw in the course of our probings in the area was the Madrasa mound to the north-west which is now completely levelled. The remains of a partly-extant burnt brick wall, the impressions, left on the surface by brick robbing of a platform and heaps of Kushana and earlier bricks, in our opinion more or less support the statement of Hsuan-Tsang about the existence of an Asokan stupa at Sthanvisvara[16]. In fact, this now destroyed mound also contained material which can easily be called the Late Harappan or Bara[16]. Another important mound in the vicinity and to the south-west of Thanesar is the Raja-Karn-Ka-Kila from where cultural material ranging in date from early historical to late medieval times is reported.[17]

On the basis of the excavated archeological material from several other sites in the area e.g., Balu, Mirzapur, Bhagwanpura, Mitathal, Siswal, etc., it is clear that the earliest settlers of the region were the so-called Late Harappans.[18]

The Harsh-Ka-Tila mound is to the west and north-west of Thanesar (76°49' 40" east; 29°58' 30" north) town and is separated from it by a road. It is an extensive mound and is approximately one kilometre in length, about 750 metres in width. It is between 15 and 18 metres in height, the highest point being about 26 metres from the surrounding plains. The longer axis of the mound is north-south. On the northeastern edge of the mound below it is the *sarai* (popularly called as stables and now converted into a Municipal park) and towering above is the beautiful tomb of Shaikh Chaheli (or Shaikh Chilli) and the *madrasa* ascribed to Dara Shikoh. Close to the western entrance gate leading to the *madrasa* and *Shaikh Chaheli's* tomb is the small Pathar Masjid which is decidedly earlier.[19] Under the shadow of this tomb and the mosque is the small *basti* already mentioned earlier. The mound has been cut to a large extent on the eastern as well as southern sides where *kachcha* houses have been built below along the road; the northern and the southern portions are relatively intact except for scouring by deep rain gulleys. In the exposed sections of the rain gulleys and portions which have been cut on the eastern and southern sides one can see several courses of brick-built structures of sufficiently large dimensions which are decidedly of pre-Islamic times.

Apart from the almost oblong shape of the mound which seems to be divided into three parts on the basis of surface features, the western edges and the northwestern corner of the mound which are much higher than the rest of the mound suggested to us the existence of some kind of fortification[20]. Equally striking is the gap on the western periphery of the mound towards the Bahari village which we surmise represents entrance gateway [21]. The portion of the mound facing this gap is lower than the surrounding area of the mound. This could perhaps mean that there existed a road leading to and connected with the entrance gateway of the settlement. This surmise will be checked in the coming years when more areas of the mound are excavated. Likewise, our surmise about the raised portions as representing fortification or about the bastion was substantiated in the course of our excavations. On the northern side of the mound are to be seen fallen portions of brick structures of the edge which represent remains of fortifications and also small *hammams* which could perhaps be of the same time or slightly later than the *Shaikh Chaheli's* tomb. A brick built platform close to these remains on the surface with lime-plastered sruface also is a clear evidence that it is seventeenth or early eighteenth century structure.

Apart from the profuse quantity of pottery, bricks and brickbats strewn all over the mound which may belong to the periods ranging from the early historical times to the late Mughal and even modern the Harsh-ka-Tila mound and Thanesar have also yielded Brahmanical as well as Jaina sculptures and architectural fragments ranging in date between the sixth and the twelfth centuries A.D.[22] A few terracotta figures are also reported from Thanesar which can be placed between fourth-fifth century and eight to twelfth century A.D.[23] In recent years bricks of the Sunga period, Kushan pottery, Gupta terracotta plaques have also been found. Cunningham has also reported the discovery of a Gupta terracotta plaque and a mud-brick platform near Thanesar. In his Report based on his visit in 1863-64 Cunningham mentions 'an old ruined fort, about 1200 feet square at top, with the modern town on a mound to the east and a suburb called *Bahari*, on another mound to the west. Altogether the three old mounds occupy a space nearly one mile in length from east to west, and abount 2,000 feet in average breadth. But before the inroads of the Muhammadans, it is certain from the number of brick ruins still existing, as well as from the statements of the people themselves that the whole of the intervening space between the present town and the lake, which is now called *Darra*, must have formed part of the old city.'[24]

As already stated above, the surface features of the Harsh-ka-Tila indicate as if it had three almost clearly demarcated divisions. For the purpose of our excavations too, we treated these three divisions as separate though connected areas and the site was accordingly divided into three sectors called TSR-1, TSR-2 and TSR-3 from north to south with a common base line dividing the site into almost equal eastern and western halves.[25]

In the northern sector or TSR-1, apart from the trenches measuring 80 metres x 20 metres in the flat area, some trenches were opened on the slopes and the northwestern corner as well. In TSR-2 or middle portion of the mound, small trenches were opened only on the western periphery. The trenches opened in TSR-3 also covered an area of 80 metres x 20 metres. A small trench was also opened up in the southern slopes of the mound in TSR-3.

The present settlement on a small portion of the mound and abutting it could be termed as the latest phase of occupation at Harsh-ka-Tila. Between this phase and the last phase of occupation which was excavated by us, there is a distinct gap. At the moment we are not concerned about this settlement and houses which are as if suspended in time and can help us in understanding remains of the last phase of occupation excavated by us.[26]

The last phase of occupation at the Harsh-Ka-Tila as excavated in our first season's dig is represented by structures and other material which could be termed as belonging to the Mughal period. Though it has not been possible for us to clearly separate the two, there seem to be two sub-phases - Mughal and Late Mughal. Among the structures unearthed are house-complexes, a hall-like building, entrance staircase leading from a paved street to (an as yet unexposed) building, brick-built entrance with beautiful offset projections, covered and open drains some of which are lime-plastered, bricks-on-edge floors, etc. In one of the excavated trenches, close to the hall-like structures was found a series of shallow pottery basins in a row on a bricks-on-edge floor. Use of lime remmed with earth, flat bricks, or plain rammed mud was also noticed in floors of houses. Use of *lakhauri* bricks of different sizes (21x11x3 cm., 18x10x4 cm., 18x9x3 cm., 17x12.5x3 cm., 17x11x3.5 cm.) and reused bigger-size bricks (25x15x5 cm., 24x14x4 cm.) and brickbats laid in mud mortar (in a few cases lime mortar) is a feature of the structures of this phase. Use of lime plaster was noticed in some drains and portions connected with the hall-like structure. This structure, measuring 10.15 x 8.50 metres, the roof of which was resting on brick-built square-based pillars, had inside it fair quantity of slag, ash, loose greyish earth, *tandoor*-like oven, *kuthla* or storage jars which leads us of the surmise that this building may have been used as some kind of smithy or workshop and not as a dwelling unit. We have also unearthed houses with kitchens with earthenware utensils, pestles and grinders, *chulhas* and other refuse material.

The houses were built along streets with lanes and bylanes evidence of which was clearly seen both in TSR-1 and TSR-3. One of the houses in TSR-1 opened into a 2.40 metre wide street which was paved with bricks and brickbats.

Apart from structural evidence, ceramic evidence also indicates this phase being Mughal as was attested by the presence of fine Mughal wares, both plain and decorated, stone ware and sherds of Chinese porcelain some of which contain inscription in Chinese characters, fragments of green carafe, besides copper coin of Shah Alam II (1759-1806) issued from the Delhi mint, a signet ring with an inscription a terracotta seal with an inscription on both faces, etc. The inscription on one face of this seal read " *Khadim-i-Shar Ibn Muhammad Qadiyan Qadi Muhammad Fadil*" meaning "The servant of the Religious Code (Shari) Qadi Muhammad Fadil son of Muhammad Qadiyan" on one face and on the other "*Nur Muhammad Ahmad Shaikh ibn*" which means " Shaikh Ahmad son of Nur Muhammad".[27]

Incidentally, it may be mentioned that a few East India Company and even modern coins were also found from some pits.

Immediately preceding the Mughal period and without any perceptiable break were found remains of structures and other antiquities which we have placed in the Indo-Islamic period. The pottery of this period is marked by the presence of glazed wares which are comparable with the ones found in several other excavated sites in northern India.[28] Among the structural remains of this period a large sized house, with at least five rooms, is worth mentioning. Evidence of some kind of conflagration towards the end of this period was noticed in the southern sector (TSR-3) of the mound by way of deposits of ash. However, this needs to be more carefully examined and understood.[29]

The remains of the pre-Islamic period comprise the Rajput, post-Gupta and the Gupta and finally the Kushan. Though we did find a few sherds of the Painted Grey Ware and associated wares, we have not been able to excavate in detail clear areas.

The evidence of the Rajput period is comprised of three structural phases of building activity. Evidence of structural remains and architectural fragments of about the tenth-eleventh century (though found from the surface and rain gullies) confirm the evidence from the dig. The more distinct ware of this period are the red ware pots having stamped decoration in the form of concentric circles, floral designs, etc., knife-edged bowl and micaceous red wares. It was noticed that knife-edge bowl was predominant in the upper levels of this phase.

The phase preceding this is what we have termed as Post-Gupta. Apart from the different types of structural remains, significant discovery of the period was the remains of a massive brick building. We were able to trace portions of this building to a length of about ten metres and one of the walls we had exposed 99 courses without reaching the bottommost course. It is apparent that this massive structure was not an ordinary dwelling and was perhaps a public building representing the remains of - if we may hazard a guess - portion of a palace ! It is, of course, premature at this stage to dwell upon this and it is only in the coming years when we excavate it further that we shall be able to understand it more clearly.

The pottery of this period is typically Post-Gupta ware having chocolate brown slip, impressed decorative motifs, bowls with corrugated profile, etc. A very fragmentary stone inscription in seventh century characters,[30] a beautiful torso of Kubera substantiate our contention ascribing the structure to about seventh century. Incidentally, the bricks used in the construction of this structure are of different sizes varying between 39x24x7.5 cm. and 32x21x5 cm.

The distinguishing features of the Gupta period are red polished ware with typical shapes and forms and moulded wares, a fragmentary Vishnu image and other Brahmanical deities, terracotta plaque, a small mould for human head, etc. Since it was not possible for us to excavated clear areas we are not in a position to say anything about structures at present.

The Kushan period at the site is represented by typical terracotta beads, human and animal figurines and a terracotta plaque. In one of the areas we found more than thirty terracotta tablets having in most cases three oblique, vertical or curved lines which are similar to the ones reported from Rangmahal, Sanghol, Sringaverapura, etc. Finally, we may mention discovery of a sealing with the figure of a humped bull with an inscription below having three letters. The inscription has been tentatively read as '*Sri Rudrah*' written in first-second century A.D. characters. Some copper coins and fragment of terracotta votive tank, and copper antimony rods are also worth mentioning.[31]

As already mentioned earlier, sherds of Painted Grey Ware and associated wares have also been found from one of the excavated trenches. On present showing, this represents the earliest phase of occupation at Thanesar. At the moment we are not in a position to say much about this phase.

Before we conclude, we would like to mention about the discovery of the defence wall on the western periphery of the mound and corner bastion on the northwestern corner and another smaller bastion on the north side as anticipated by us. This brick-built defence wall is on an average about 4 metres in width. Apparently, there are several phases of its building beginning with the Mughal period or slightly earlier. The defence wall exposed in a small area on the southern slopes however may date back to an earlier period, perhaps to about seventh-eighth century A.D., if not earlier.

We believe that the results of our excavations at the Harsh-Ka-Tila have unfolded interesting clues, evidence and information about the material culture covering a span of nearly two thousand years or more. To us, the discovery of remains of the period following the Gupta period seems significant and it would also be of interest to the historians and archaeologists. We would, however, reiterate that several of our conclusions, including our classification of periods or phases, are at the moment rather tentative.

Notes And References

1. It is intriguing to note that in none of the early writings on Thanesar, from Alexander Cunningham onwards, the mound is called the Harsh-ka-Tila. Alexander Cunningham had visited Thanesar (Sthaneswara) in 1863-64. In his report he does not mention about Harsh-ka-Tila and calls it Thanesar, or Sthaneswara even though he does allude to the Bahari mound and another mound to the west besides the modern town to the east. With his penchant for recording all available information including even the legends and traditions about sites and places visited by him, it is rather odd that Cunningham did not mention the name Harsh-ka-Tila. In the map also of Thanesar accompaying the text, he does not give the name Harsh-ka-Tila to the mound while he has referred to name of other ancient mounds and places in and around Thanesar, including the mound known as Raja Karna-ka-Tila. See Alexander Cunningham, *Archaeological Survey of India, Four Reports Made during 1862-63-64-65*, Vol.II, Government Central Press, Simla, pp. 212-223, plate LXX. For description of the Thanesar mounds and buildings, pp. 220-223.

   In his book on ancient geography also Cunningham does not mention the name Harsh-ka-Tila. See Alexander Cunningham, *The Ancient Geography of India*, I, the *Buddhist Period*, reprinted Varanasi, 1963, pp. 276-283.

   Daya Ram Sahni, who had carried out excavations at the mound known as Raja Karna-ka-Tila, while briefly describing Kurukshetra, also does not mention Harsh-ka-Tila; see *Annual Report of the Archaeological Survey of India for the year 1921-22*, Government of India Press, Simla, 1924, pp.46-49. In his brief report on Thanesar published in the following year, Daya Ram Sahni mentioned 'an old ruined fort about 1200 feet square at top, with a suburb locally known as the Bahari Fort, i.e., the outer fortification and the modern town, which is also situated on an ancient mound'. He also referred to the tradition, which assigns the construction of the Thanesar Fort to Raja Dilipa, a descendant of Kuru. He further added that the existing remains 'cannot be anterior to about the 7th century A.D.' and 'felt inclined to judge that the fort was most probably founded by Harshavardhana, who ruled over the whole of Northern India from 606 to 648 A.D.' The chief reason for this inference, apart from other considerations, is the fact that all visible structures in the fort are composed of bricks. See *Annual Report of the Archaeological Survey of India, 1922-23, P. 90*. Sahni also does not mention the name Hash-ka-Tila for the mound.

   That the mound is 'popularly known as Harshavardhana-Ka-Qila' is stated by V.N.Datta and H.A. Phadke in their *Hisotry of Kurukshetra*, Vishal Publications, Kurukshetra, 1985, pp.79-80.

   My colleague Shri R.P. Sharma, a member of our excavation team, informs me that the name Harsh-ka-Tila is given in the revenue records. This however needs to be vertified. The local people who were almost thronging our excavations also used to call the site variously as Hars-Ka-Tila and Harsh-Ka-Qila. An eminent scholar, studies, Kurukshetra University who visited our excavations mentioned the site as Harsh-ka-Tila.

2. Cunningham, *ibid*. Vasudevasharan Agrawala, *Bharat Savitri Mahabharata Ka eka navin aur saragarbhita adhyayana, Khanda 2, Udyoga-Parva se Stri-Parva tak* (in Hindi), Sasta Sahitya Mandal Prakashan, 1985, pp 276-277. Agrawala also mentions that during the time of Prabhakaravardhana, Thanesar became a very big centre of Pasupata Saivas who were the followers of Lakulisa. Also see, Amar Singh, 'Sanskrit Sahitya men Kurukshetra' in *Kurukshetra*, published by Director, Public Relations, Haryana, 1987, pp. 1-8, and S.P. Shukla, 'Sthanisvara', in *ibid*., pp.9-12; H.A. Phadke, 'Kurukshetra a historical reconstruction' *ibid*., pp 29-34; Udai Vir Singh, 'Ancient relics from the Kurukshetra region', *ibid*., pp. 35-40.

   Also see, Nundo Lal Dey, *The Geographical Dictionary of Ancient and Mediaeval India*, reprinted, Oriental Books Reprint Corporation, New Delhi, 1971, s.v. Kurukshetra, Kurujangala, Srikantha, Sthanesvara and Sthanu-tirtha.

3. D.Devahuti, *Harsha A Political Study*, Oxford, 1970, pp.56-57. She has referred to the eponymous progenitor of the dynasty as Pushpabhuti; some scholars, however, call him Pushyabhuti. Vasudeva Sharan Agrawala also mentions both Pushapabhuti and Pushyabhuti as the founder of the dynasty. See Vasudeva S. Agrawala, *The Deeds of Harsha [Being a Cultural Study of Bana's Harshacharita]*, Prithivi Prakashan, Varanasi, 1969, pp.11, 78, 79, 86.

4 Bana's *Harshacharita*(ed. K.S. Parab), Bombay, 1912, pp.

88-89. *The Harsa-Carita of Bana*, translated by E.B. Cowell and F.W. Thomas, Oriental Translation Fund, New Series II, London, 1897, pp.79-84.

5 Agrawala, 1969, op.cit., pp. 45-47, 116-118, fig 21. and Appendix I, Skandhavara, Rajakula, Dhavalagriha, pp.239-255.

6 *Ibid.*, pp.77-78; Devahuti, *op.cit.*, p.56 and note 2; Cowell and Thomas, *op.cit.*, pp. 79-81. The discovery of terracotta sealings bearing the legend *'Sthanesvarasya'* in Brahmi characters of fourth-fifth century A.D. from Daulatpur, a site about 15 kilometres from Thanesar, is important. The site has been excavated by the Department of Ancient Indian History and Archaeology, Kurukshetra University. See Shukla, *op.cit.*, p. 10, Udai Vir Singh, *op.cit.*, pp. 38-39.

7 Agrawala, *ibid.*, p. 79-85. Bana also gives vivid account of the visit of Bhairavacharya, a Saivite saint, to Sthanvisvara in the time of Pushpabhuti; Cowell and Thomas, *op.cit.*, pp.83-99

8 Samuel Beal, *Si-Yu-Ki : Buddhist Records of the Western World*, Trubner & Co., London, 1884 (reprinted, Delhi, 1969), pp. 183-184, In Beal's translation it is mentioned as "The land of religious merit" (or "happiness").

9 *Ibid.*, p.185.

10 See above, note 1.

11 These are as yet not protected by the Archaeological Survey of India. We propose to recommend these for protection as Centrally-protected Monuments of National Importance.

12 *Cunningham*, 1873, *op.cit.*

13 Cunningham (*ibid.*, p. 220), Daya Ram Sahni and others have made a specific mention of this mound. See above, note 1.

14 Cunningham also mentions about 'two ruined mounds, of which the larger is known as the *Madrasa*, or "College", and the smaller is covered with Muhammadan tombs'. *Ibid.*, p. 221.

15 Of the two aforesaid mounds, according to Cunningham, 'it is probable that this smaller mound may be the remains of the stupa from which all the larger pieces of bricks have been carried away, and the larger mound may be the ruins of an extensive monastery; *ibid.*, p. 221.

16 This is what my colleagues Ashok Patel, D.N.Dimri, G.S. Gaur, Jag Mohan Thapar and K.C. Nauriyal, who were in our team, also felt.

17 Cunningham, 1873, *po.cit.*; ASIAR *1921-22*, pp.44-49; Udai Vir Singh. *op.cit.*

18 Udai Vir Singh, *ibid.*

19 According to Cunningham, 1873, *op.cit.*, p. 222, 'The *Patharia* or "stone masjid".....is a small building, being only 37 feet long by 11½ feet broad inside, but it is remarkable for its minars which are attached to the ends of the *back* wall instead of the front wall, as is usual. These minars are fluted below with alternately round angular flutes like the Kutb Minar, and as they have a great slope, I think that the building may be assigned with some probability to the time of Firuz Tughlak, or towards the end of the 14th century'. Dr. Z.A. Desai, formerly Director, Epigraphy, in the Archaeological Survey of India, who kindly saw the few photographs of the mosque available with us, feels that the mosque has certain features like trabeate construction, ornamental ceiling, Khalji type of ashlar masonry, etc., which are ascribable to pre-Tughlaq period. The lower fluted portion of the rear corner circular towers is also reminiscent of the Adhai Din-ka-Jhompra at Ajmer.

20 Daya Ram Sahni, *op.cit.*,p. 90 also (see above, foot note 1)ascribed the fort to Harshavardhana. This be inferred from 'the fact that all visible structures in the fort are composed of bricks measuring 14" x 8½ x 2½". The fort is said to have had 52 towers or bastions, some of which are still extant. The number of gates is not ascertainable, on account of late renewals of the fort during the Muhammadan and Sikh periods. I have, however, definitely located one of the original gates on the west side of the fort. It consists of a broad passage flanked by solidly built brick bastions which presumably gave access to one of the main streets of the fort, as remains of buildings are clearly seen for a considerable distance along it. In the gate the passage is paved in brick laid on edge. The right-hand bastion, which was partly excavated, appears to consist of a small chamber with a narrow entrance. The rampart at this point is just eleven feet thick, and this would appear to have been the thickness of the wall on all sides....'

21 *Daya Ram Sahni also refers to his having 'definitely located one* of the original gates on the west side of the fort'. See above, note 20

22 S.P. Shukla, *Sculptures and Terracottas in the Archaeological Museum, Kurukshetra University*, Kurukshetra, 1983, pp. 40-50.

23 *Ibid.*, p. 72.

24 Cunningham, 1873, *op.cit.*, p. 220.

25 This has been done keeping in view the fact that excavations are to continue for several seasons.

26 We intend to document and study these settlements.

27 These are in beautiful Nastaliq Characters. The readings,for the moment, are tentative.

28 Study of the material and its comparison with other sites is already under way.

29 Though we are not suggesting that this conflagration is connected with Mahmud's invasion, it is important to remember that 'Sultan Mahmud of Ghazna had invaded Thanesar in October 1014 and took away from there the idol of Chakrasvamin to Ghazna where it was cast into the public square'. See, Muhammad Nazim, *The Life and Times of Sultan Mahmud of Ghazna*, Cambridge, 1939 (reprinted, Munshiram Manoharlal, New Delhi. 1971) , pp. 103-104. Also see, Phadke and Datta, *op.cit.*, pp. 79-82, with references to Al-Biruni, Utbi, Isami and Firishta. Al-Biruni had accompanied Mahmud during his Indian expedition and has made interesting observations about Kurukshetra and Thanesar in his Kitab ul Hind.

30 The few surviving letters are reminiscent of the characters in the Madhuban inscription of Harsha.

31 Most of our metal objects, including coins, have not been chemically cleaned so far. Likewise, other scientific studies including metallographic examination, analysis of grains recovered by us using flotation method, soil analysis, etc., are yet to be taken up.

EARLY FARMING COMMUNITIES OF KAIMUR FOOT-HILLS

Birendra Pratap Singh*

After the initial discovery of the remains of early farming communities at Chirand in north Bihar, it was desired to obtain details regarding the nature of settlements, distribution pattern of sites etc, in Bihar. The foot hills of Vindhyan range lying within the administrative boundaries of Allahabad and Mirzapur districts, on the other hand, were proved to be very promising for the archaeological remains of the Neolithic period. The vicinity of Kaimur hills in Rohtas district, Bihar, is an extension of the similar ecological zone which retains evidence for the origin and growth of agriculture in Uttar Pradesh. The alluvial plains of the foot-hills of Kaimur were investigated during the years 1985-86 and 1986-87 by the present author under the auspices of the Banaras Hindu University. As a result of these investigations a number of settlements of early farmers of Bihar have been brought to light. It may, however, be mentioned that the work was restricted to district Rohtas alone and no work so far has been done in the adjoining areas of the district. Our picture of the early farming communities of Bihar, therefore, is rather incomplete. Only intensive and systematic field work in the region will provide adequate knowledge about these early farming communities.

The field work was highly rewarding and a number of Neolithic habitation sites have been brought to light. It may be pointed out that these Neolithic settlements are usually superimposed by the deposits of chalcolithic and NBPW culture. Sites with single culture of Neolithic settlement has not been found so far in the region. Besides, no factory site of the pecked and ground stone industry has been found. All the Neolithic settlement ranged in size from small to medium. The location of these sites are not very far off from the hilly range of Kaimur. They are found within a radius of 25-30 km from Kaimur foot-hills. It was also observed that the sites are situated more on the tributaries than on the main river system. Avoidance of the banks of major river as habitational locale presumably was due to the danger from floods. In an instance the site is situated almost at the foot of the hills and the small stream flows approximately 4-5 km away from the settlement. It is comparatively smaller in size. The available evidence thus indicates that Neolithic farmer of this region did not prefer the hilly ranges, they opted for plains and followed river courses. Further, it may also be pointed out that the sites located on or near the river have flourished in comparison to the one which is situated near the foot-hills. It appears that the alluvial plains were occupied for the reasons of the agricultural operations, while the vicinity of the hilly tract was being exploited for the requirement of lithic and faunal resources etc. The evidence for the growth of agriculture based subsistence from Neolithic, Neolithic-chalcolithic to the early historic times (NBPW culture) in this region is well demonstrated. The present paper seeks to highlight the occupational pattern and the techno-cultural details of the early farming communities of the area.

The discovery and subsequent excavation of a Neolithic habitation site of Senuwar in the district Rohtas, Bihar, gave fresh impetus to further research in the region. It may be mentioned that practically no archaeological excavation had been carried out in this region in previous years. Senuwar (Lat. 24° 56'N, long. 83° 56'E) is located 7 km south of Sasaram and situated on the right bank of the river Kudra which flows approximately 1 km away from the site. The ancient mound covers an area of 300 mt. from east to west and 360 mt from north to south, and rises to the maximum height of 9 mt from the ground level. The total areas covered by the ancient mound is 60,000 sq. mt. Proximity to the river Kudra and the rocky hills of Kaimur, which is approximately 10 km away from the site provided all basic needs for the settlement to flourish for longer duration.

Excavations at Senuwar has revealed four cultural periods, which provide a schematic sequence to the entire cultural debris of the region. Periods II, III and IV of Senuwar which belong to the chalcolithic, NBPW culture and the Kushan period respectively fall out side the purview of the present paper. The earliest Period I is important for the present paper. It is divisible into two sub-periods I and IB. IA is metal free and it can be regarded as pure neolithic, while in IB all the basic cultural traits of IA continues with an addition of metal.

Period IA (Pure Neolithic)

This sub-period is represented by 1.5 m thick deposit and characterised by the occurrence of three principal ceramic wares viz., red ware, burnished red ware and burnished grey ware. Occurrence of the rusticated ware and the cord impressed pottery are other noteworthy features of the ceramic assemblage of the sub-period IA. All these have been distinguished mainly on the basis of surface treatment and other technological details. The common pottery shapes recovered during the period consist of wide mouthed shallow bowl, channelled bowl with varying profiles, vases, spouted vessels (figs 2,3,4) .The pottery of this sub-period is mainly wheel-made, although hand made specimens are also found in sufficiently large quantity though perhaps not as frequent as the former.

Red ware is the dominant industry in this sub-period. It is devoid of any kind of slip or wash. The core is gritty and porous. The fabric of pots varies from medium to coarse and the thickness of the core from thin to medium. The pottery is soft and light in weight.

Burnished Red ware is christened mainly after its surface

* Department of AIHC & Archaeology, Banaras Hindu University, Varanasi 221005

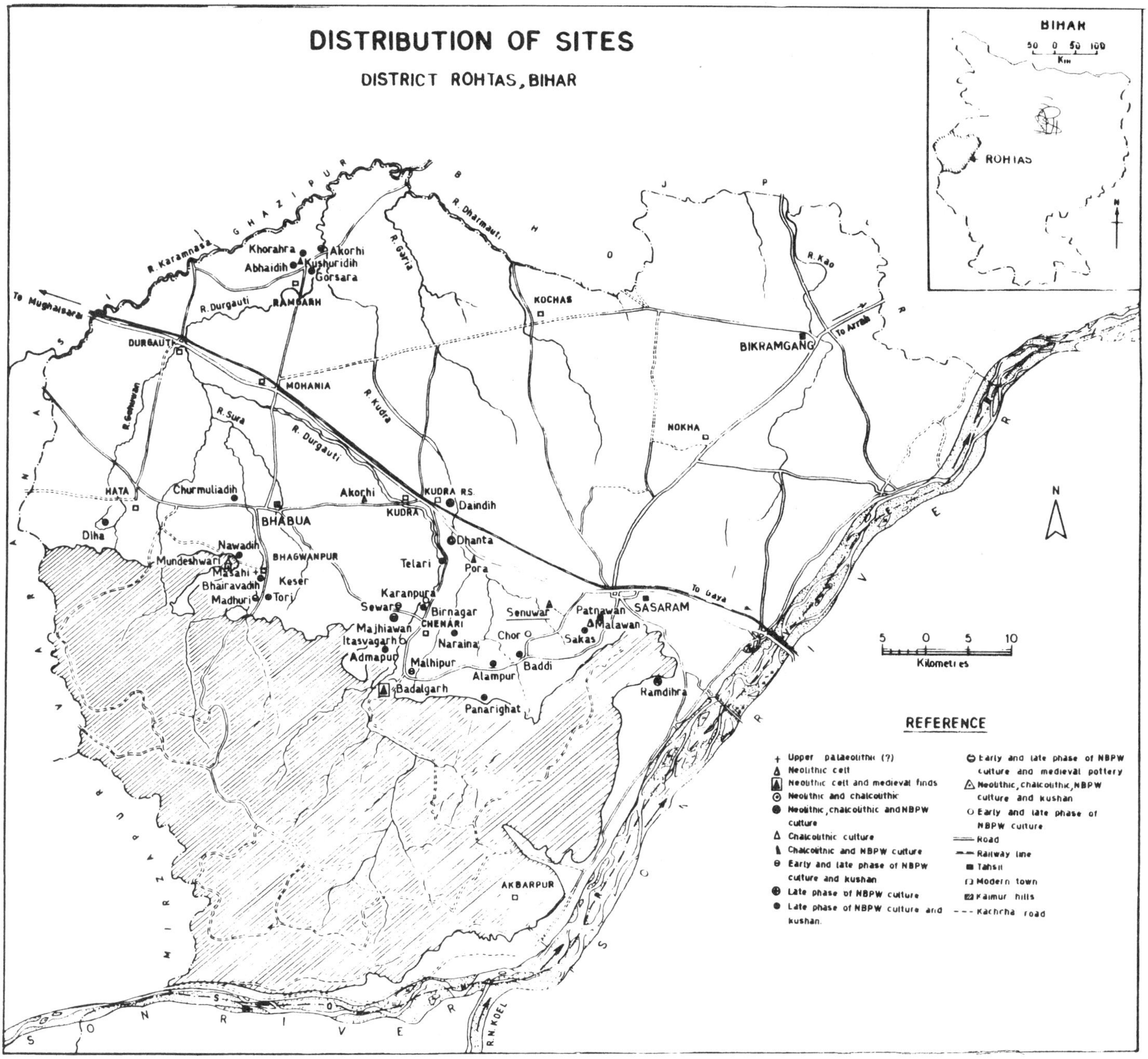
DISTRIBUTION OF SITES
DISTRICT ROHTAS, BIHAR
BIHAR
ROHTAS
Khorahra
Akorhi
Abhaidih
Kushuridih
Gorsara
RAMGARH
KOCHAS
DURGAUTI
MOHANIA
BIKRAMGANG
NOKHA
HATA
Churmuliadih
Akorhi
KUDRA R.S.
KUDRA
Daindih
BHABUA
Diha
Nawadih
Mundeshwari
BHAGWANPUR
Masahi
Bhairavadih
Madhuri
Tori
Keser
Dhanta
Telari
Pora
Karanpura
Sewar
Birnagar
CHENARI
Majhiawan
Itasvagarh
Admapur
Malhipur
Naraina
Senuwar
Chor
Patnawan
Malawan
SASARAM
Sakas
Baddi
Alampur
Badalgarh
Panarighat
Ramdihra
AKBARPUR
To Mughalsarai
To Arrah
To Gaya
R. Karamnasa
R. Durgauti
R. Dharmauti
R. Garia
R. Kudra
R. Sura
R. Kao
R. N. Koel
SON RIVER
Kilometres
REFERENCE
Upper palaeolithic (?)
Neolithic celt
Neolithic celt and medieval finds
Neolithic and chalcolithic
Neolithic, chalcolithic and NBPW culture
Chalcolithic culture
Chalcolithic and NBPW culture
Early and late phase of NBPW culture and kushan
Late phase of NBPW culture
Late phase of NBPW culture and kushan.
Early and late phase of NBPW culture and medieval pottery
Neolithic, chalcolithic, NBPW culture and kushan
Early and late phase of NBPW culture
Road
Railway line
Tahsil
Modern town
Kaimur hills
Kachcha road

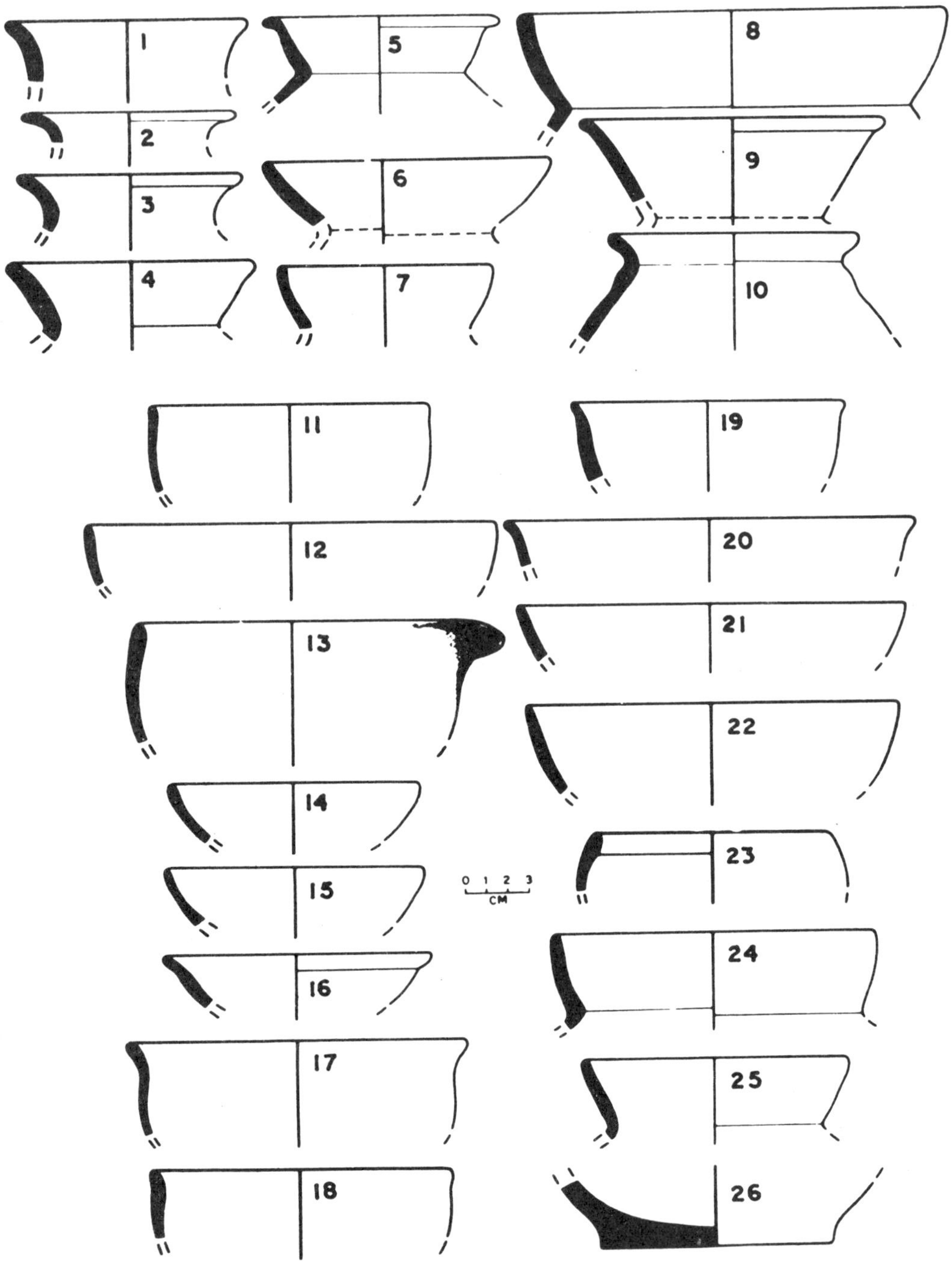

Fig. 2. 1-10 Coarse Red Ware; 11-26 Red Ware Pd. IA.

dressing. The fabric is coarse and range from medium to thick. The pots are usually treated with a thick bright red slip, occasionally the use of dark red slip is also attested. The treated surfaces are smooth and even. The burnishing has been done horizontally, parallel to the rim as suggested by the burnishing marks. Vases with long straight or concave neck and spouted vessels are the types noted in the ware. Small vases with medium fabric are slipped on both the sides whereas the bigger specimens with thick fabric are slipped on outer side and burnished subsequently. Some of the specimens which are highly burnished show glossy surface.

Another important ware is the Burnished Grey ware. Like the preceding ware it is also distinguished mainly on its surface treatment. Barring a few specimens, in majority of the cases it has been noticed that a thin solution of greyish slip containing fine variety of sand is applied on both the surfaces and subsequently burnished. The burnishing is inferior when compared with the burnished red ware. The pottery on the whole is coarse, gritty, porous and heavily tempered. Bowls and vases are the shapes noted in the ware during the sub-period. The former predominate in the ware.

An interesting feature noted in the pottery is the occurrence of painted sherds. The pigment used is red ochre and executed on the rim of the pot. Beside painting the rim execution of band on the neck is also evidenced. The painting is post-firing and hence would wash off if cleaned with water or rubbed. In IA it is found on the burnished grey ware alone.

Rusticated ware has been separated from the remaining wares mainly on the basis of exterior sufrace treatment. The pot sherds recovered under the category are mostly from the red ware, occasionally quite a few sherds of burnished red ware has also been noticed rusticated. The outer surface of the pot is rusticated by the application of clay solution prepared with straw, small stone granules and ground pot sherds. At times specimens are found smeared with ochre colour pigment all over the roughened surface.

Cord impressed pottery is noticed from thin to medium fabric in section. The fomrer is numerically very less. The clay employed in the manufacture is heavily tempered and not well levigated. The core is gritty and porous. External surface is makred by cord impressions. The characteristic feature of the ware belonging to this sub-period is that the impressions of cord are incipient to thin. At times, the cord impression is indistinct. The cording strokes are vertical, oblique or slanting. Bowls are the only identifiable type in the ware. It may be recalled that this pottery is treated as diagnostic trait of the Vindhyan Neolithic culture particularly at sites like Koldihwa and Mahagara.

The microlithic industry shows emphasis on the producing bladelets, next in order of frequency comes flakes and blades. The tool recovered comprised parallel sided bladelet with one edge retouched, backed bladelet with one edge unretouched, partly retouched bladelet, parallel sided retouched backed bladelet, marginal retouched blade, side scraper on flake and partly retouched flake, Besides, a total number of 30 cores have been recovered. It is divisible into three main groups viz : flake core (13), blade core (4) and bladelet core (13). Majority of the specimens are multidirectional and do not show any prepared platform. Flakes have been removed by using natural ridges. In case of unidirectional, striking platform is made by removing a single flake. Along with these worked nodules, debitage etc., have also been recovered suggesting thereby that the tools were locally manufactured. The materials used in the manufacture of these tools consists of chart, chalcedony, agate, quartz and quartzite. Triangular celts of basalt generally of small variety, ground and polished all over the body are found. Some of them still retian sharp edges. The butt-ends are blunt and have bi-facial working edges.

Among other lithic objects recovered during the sub-period, mention may be made of pestle, saddle quern, rubber stones disc, hammer stones and sling balls of varying sizes. Besides, finished and unifinished beads of agate and chalcedony are also found.

Other noteworthy finds are the bone tools which consists of points with use marks at the working tips and a blade (?). The former appear to have been shaped out of long bones or splinters. Animal bone remains have been obtained in large number. Most of these are charred and bear cut-marks revealing the food habits of the Neolithic folk.

Recovery of carbonised grains shows that a variety of crops were grown by these early farming communities of the region. The farmers cultivated the following cereals : The lower most stratum just above the natural soil revealed.

1. Rice (Oriza sativa)

2. Barley (Hordeum vulgare)

3. Field pea (Pisum sativum vararvense)

4. Lentil (Lens culinaris) and some millets.

In the subsequent upper layers in addition to the material of same kind dwarf-wheat (*Triticum-sphaerococcum*), grass pea *(Lathyrus-sativus)*. Kodon *(Paspalum scrobiculatum)* and the seads of Vetch (*Vicis sativa*)which grows as a weed in the winter crop fields have also been encountered. They also practiced even crop rotation, *Kharif* and *Rabi*. The evidence from Senuwar thus provides us a fair picture of the early agriculturel[1]. It appears that rice (*Oryza sativa*) was the principal cereal of the Neolithic people of Senuwar. Rice *(Oryza sativa)* of this variety is also reported from Koldihwa and Mahagara dated to 7th-6th millennium BC in the Belan valley[2]. The flood plains available in the vicinity of the habitation site was suitable land for the cultivation of rice without much extra effort. The variety of crops suggests that agriculture became the chief source of their economy from the very beginning of the period. Equally important means of subsistence would have been animal husbandry as evidenced by the occurrence of large number of animal bone.

Among objects of terracotta, mention may be made of edge ground pot sherds (traingular or rectangular in shape

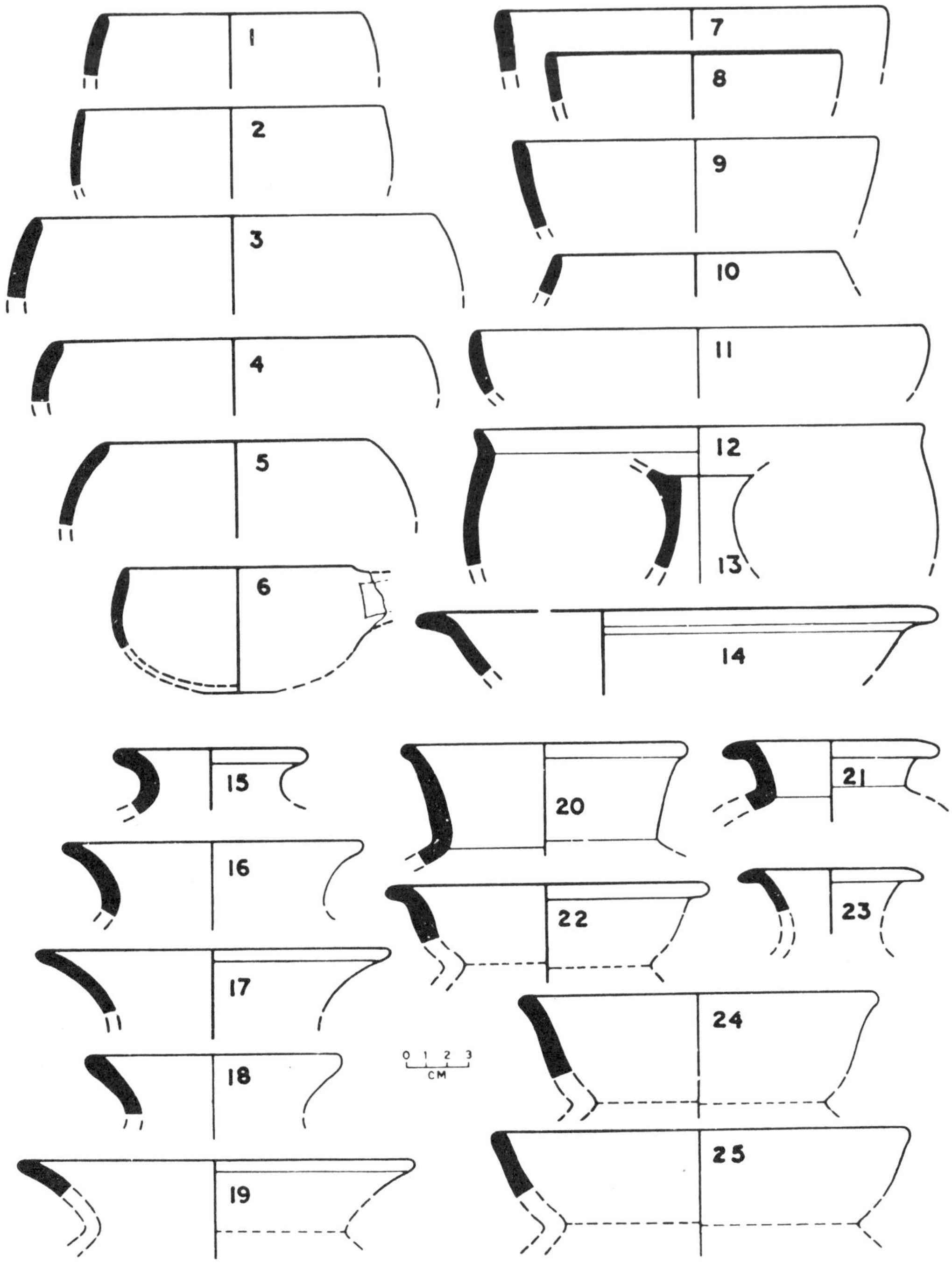

Fig. 3. 1-14 Burnished Grey Ware; 15-25 Burnished Red Ware.

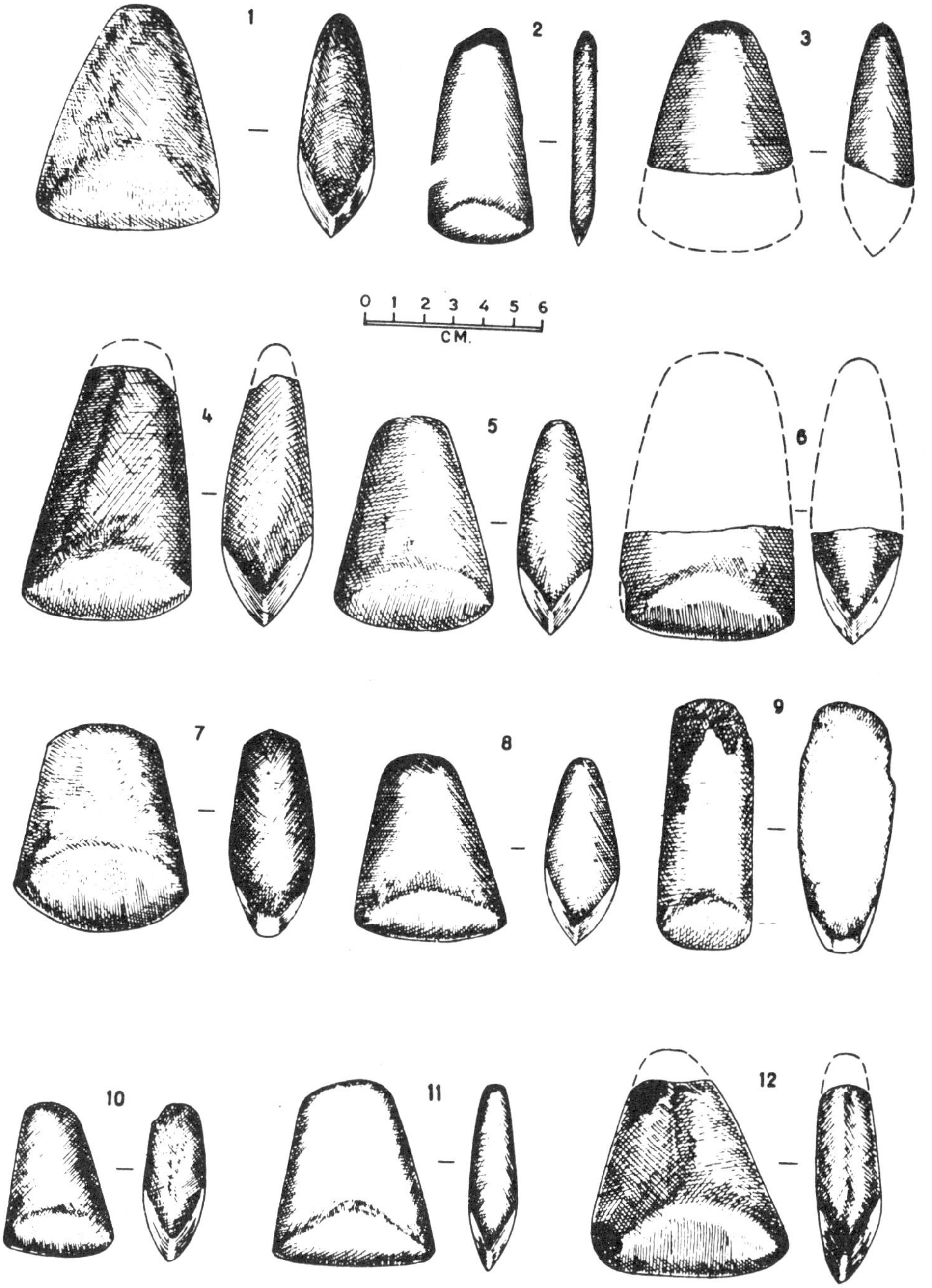

Fig. 4. Stone Celts : 1-3 IA; 4-8 I B; 9-10 II; 11 Surface; 12 unstratified

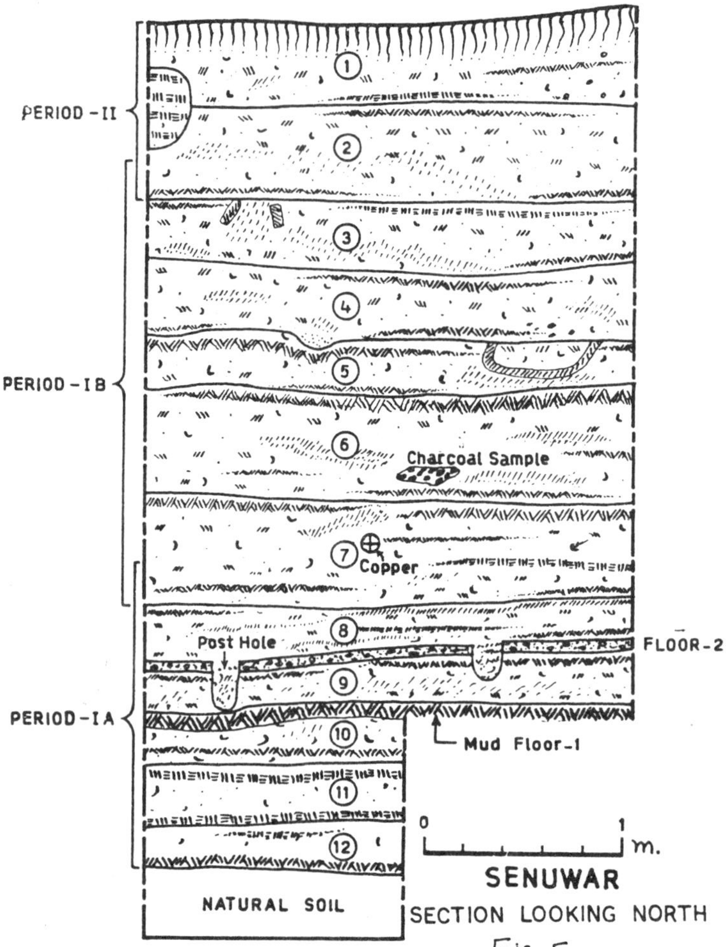

SENUWAR
SECTION LOOKING NORTH
Fig. 5

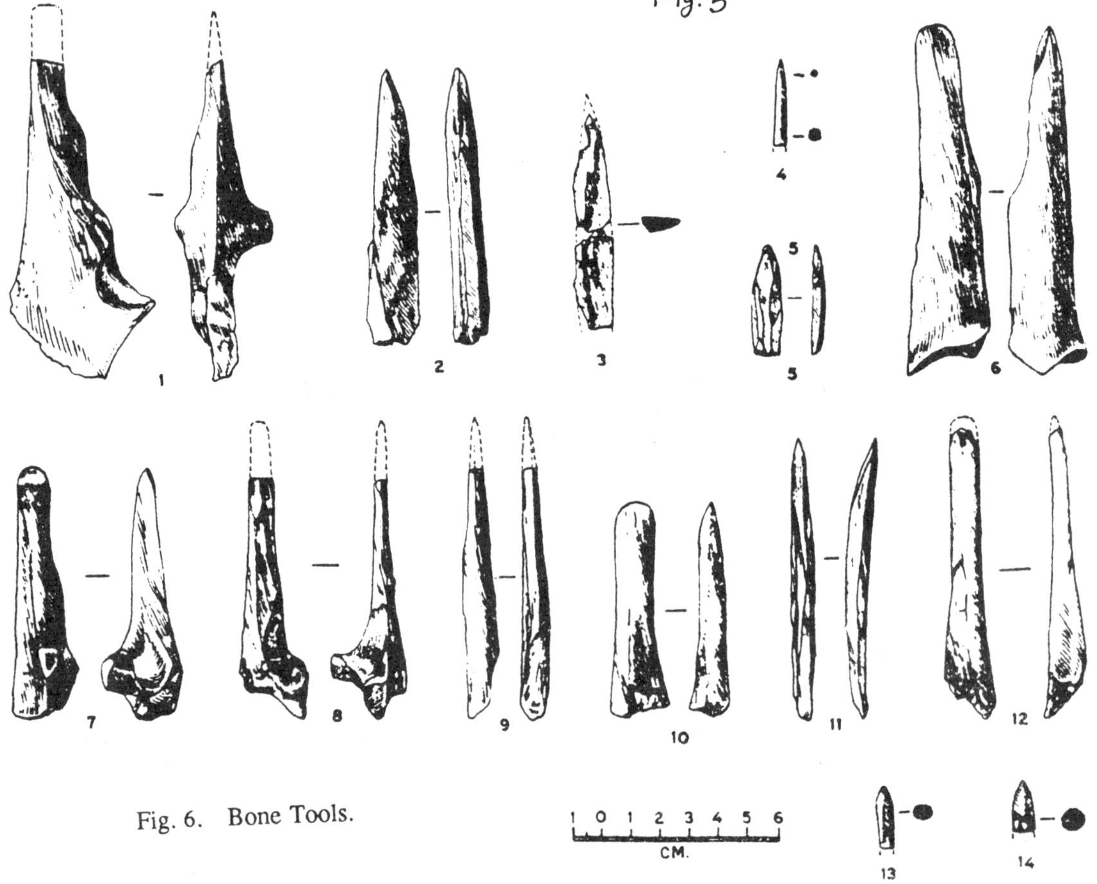

Fig. 6. Bone Tools.

and spherical beads with central perforation. Besides, pottary discs sometimes centrally perforated are also recovered. Due to limited area undertaken for work not much information is known about their house building activity. However, the occurence of burnt clods of clay with reed marks and floors made of rammed earth mixed with pot sherds etc., provided a glimpse of their settlement pattern. Two successive floors belonging to this sub-period have been recovered.

Period IB (Neolithic-Chalcolithic)

Sub-period IA is followed by sub-period IB, without any break. It is represented by 2.02 m.thick strata. In IB, continuation of the features of IA was noticed with an addition of metal. Thus sub-period is marked by the appearance of copper comprising a fishhook, a wire, a needle (?) and an indeterminate object.

Besides, a fragmentary rod of lead rectangular in section is also recovered towards the closing phase of IB. The chemical analysis of a copper wire revealed that it was made of almost pure copper.[3] "Considering other elements present in this object purity comes to around 99%, however, neglecting the presence of oxygen and sulphur in the metal". It is interesting to note that almost all metals analysed in chalcolithic context in Bihar and West Bengal are more or less alloyed with tin or arsenic. "Microstructure indicated that the specimen was in single phase with the total absence of dendritic cast structure. Hence it was not a cast object. There is no evidence of annealing and the wire of Senuwar was manufactured by cold forging alone". Further, on the basis of the trace element present in the object it has been suggested that copper was not extracted either from Singhbum or Rajasthan chalcopyrite. 'Senuwar copper has similarities with Rakha ores with reference to the common presence of silver, zinc, nickel, molybdenum, magnesium, lead and common absence of bismuth, gold, zirconium, tungsten and titanium. Hence it is suggested that there is possibility for getting ore from Rakha mines'.

'The fragmentary piece of lead rod contained high amount of silver (0.20%). The metal was perhaps extracted from argentiferous galena. From Phaga area of Bhagalpur (24° 46'N, 86° 56' 15"E) existence of lead ore is noted which contains silver copper and zinc'.

All the ware of the preceding sub-period along with its common types continued. In IB, a marked improvement in the pottery making is noticed particularly in the surface treatment. The use of fine quality of slip and high grade burnishing provide a striking finish to the vessels. In burnished grey and red wares the slip applied is usually well levigated, fine in texture and rich in adhesion. The application is skilful as the surfaces are generally even, uniform and show no cavities on the surface. Due to nature of slip, smoothening and high grade burnishing the striation marks were obliterated and gloss produced on the surface. However, the study of such sherds which are internally without any surface treatment clearly revealed evidence of finger or plam marks, uneven surface gives indications that some of the vessels were hand made also. The cord impressed pottery recovered during the sub-period IB shows greater variation in impression. The impressions are usually in bold relief. The post-firing ochre colour paintings which was confined to burnished grey were alone in the preceding sub-period have been noted in the burnished red wares also. The painted specimens considerably increased during the sub-period. The painted designs consisted of simple linear pattern, mostly on the rim. This pattern of painting is followed in the remaining wares of the period. In some of the burnished grey were specimens, bands are noted on luting point also, a feature emerging during this sub-period. In one instance criss-cross pattern is noted. Post-firing painting in ochre is an important trait of Senuwar and Chirand Neolithic pottery and not

Table 1. Chemical analysis

Element		% composition of Copper wire	% Composition of lead rod
Silver	Ag	0.05	0.20
Iron	Fe	0.01	0.01
Arsenic	Sb	0.10	-
Lead	Pb	0.05	Base
Nickel	Ni	0.05	-
Silicon	Si	0.50	0.10
Magnesium	Mg	0.10	0.10
Copper	Cu	Base	0.20
Zinc	Zn	0.05	-
Tin	Sn	-	0.002

Table 2. Presence of trace elements in the specimens

	Ag	Fe	As	Sb	Pb	Bi	Cu	Sn	Ni	Zn	Mn	Co	Au	Al	Cr	Mo	Zr	W	Ti	Mg	V	Gd	P.	Si
Copper	+	+	+	+	+	-	+	-	+	+	-	-	nt	-	-	+	-	-	-	+	-	nt	nt	+
Lead rod	+	+	+	-	+	-	+	+	-	-	-	-	nt	-	-	+	-	-	-	+	-	nt	nt	+

Present = +; Absent = -; nt = not tried.

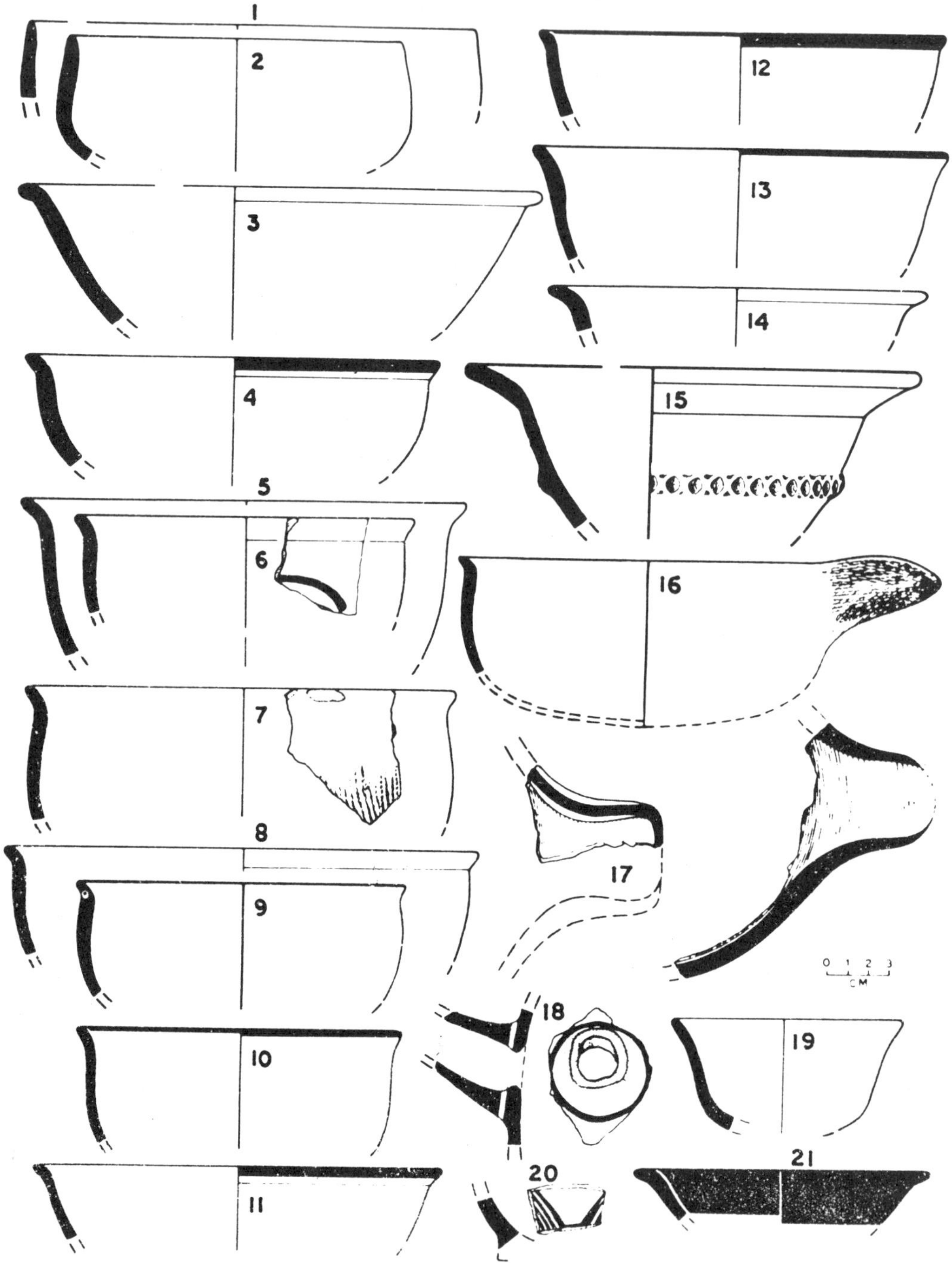

Fig. 7. Burnished Grey Ware.

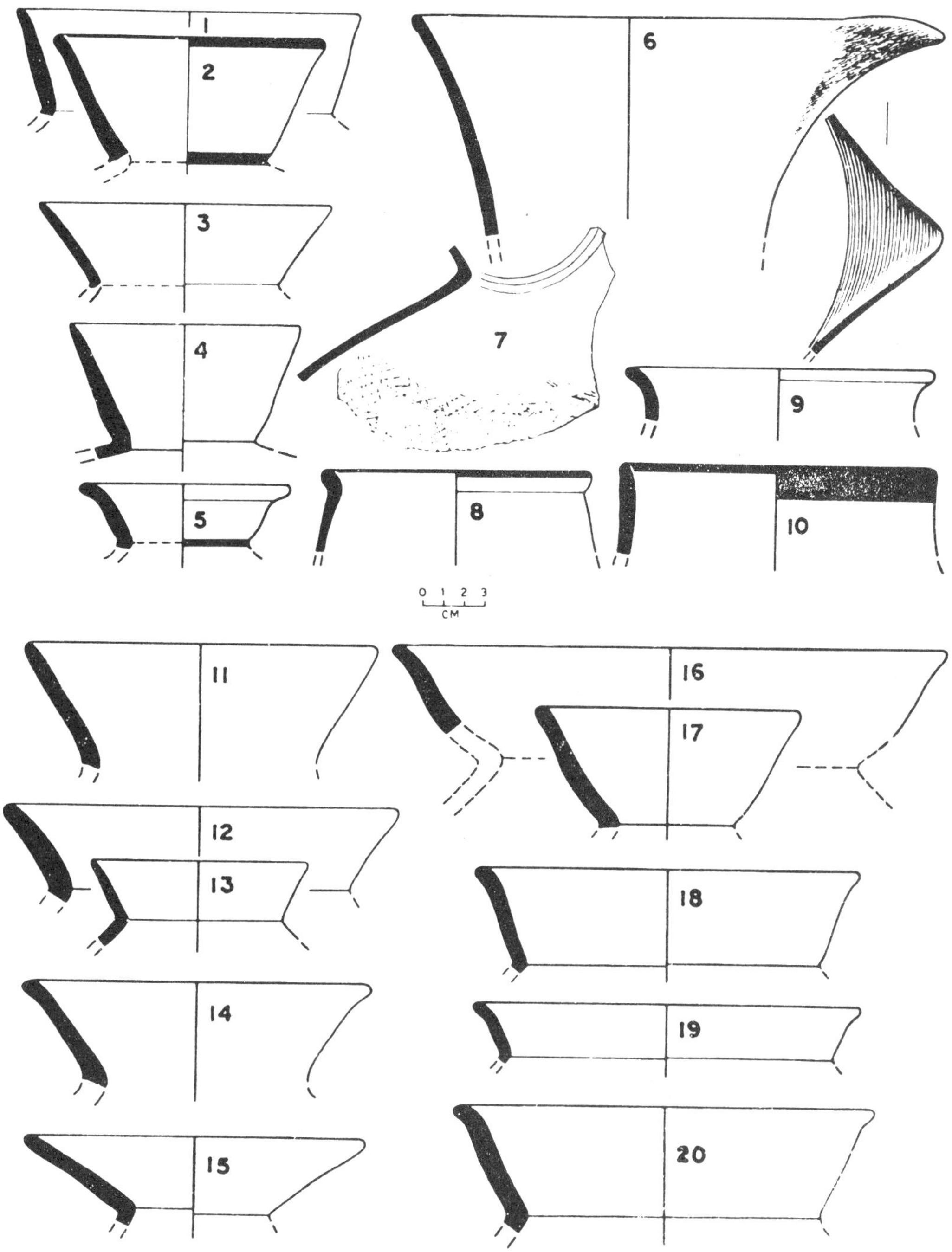

Fig. 8. 1-10 Burnished Grey Ware; 11-20 Burnished Red Ware.

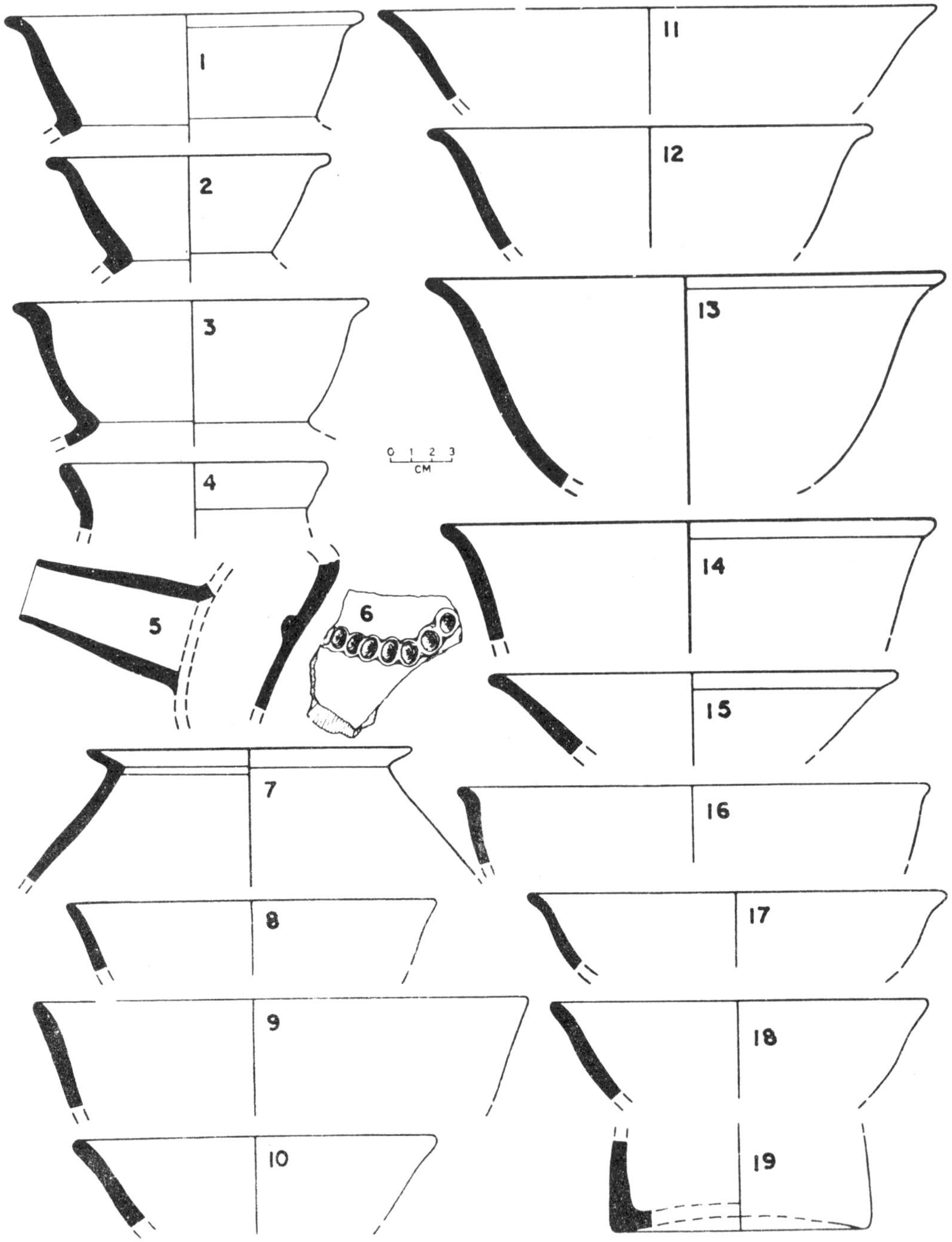

Fig. 9. Burnished Red Ware.

present in Vindhyan Neolithic sites, Its occurrence at several Neolithic sites of south India have also been noted[4].

Thus the painting on pottery appears from the very beginning of the settlement. The pigment used was red ochre and applied on the pottery in post-firing condition in both the sub-periods. However, in some cases its use in pre firing stage is also attested which suggests that painting in pre firing condition had its start from IB. This may be regarded as a technological development in the ceramic industry.

Apart from painted designs, the pottery has also been decorated with thumb or finger impressions, rope, notched patterns etc., on applique bands of clay. Post firing scratched designs are also met with. The scratched surface in same instances are filled with ochre colour pigment.

Although wheel made pottery dominates, hand made pottery is also present. In all the ceramic industries of the period bowls out number the other types. Noteworthy shapes in the wares include deep bowl, hemispherical bowl, lipped bowl, spouted vessels, perforated vessels, storage jars and vases of varying shapes. Most of these pottery types are comprable with those of Chirand. Applique decorations representing rope and notch designs are common to both chirand and Belan valley sites. But incised and punctured decoration on pottery present both at Senuwar and Chirand is absent in the Belan valley. Thus the ceramic assemblage of Senuwar is more developed and shows more nearness to that of the Chirand. However, some shapes in bowls and vases are comparable with that of Belan valley sits. One common feature noted at all these sites is the presence of Burnished ware.

An increased frequency of stone artifacts has been noticed. Polished stone celts have been recovered more in number in comparison to the preceding sub-period. These are usually made of black basalt. The microlthic industry shows little change, except that the frequency of tools increased and geometric foms such as lunate and scalene appeared during the sub-period. But in view of the fact that comparatively much larger area was excavated and varying thickness of strata of IB this may not be overemphasized. Besides, the continuation of earlier tools mention may be made of bladelet point, retouched notched blade with both edge retouched, notched flake, drills, straight sided scraper, convex sided scraper, burin, retouched flakes etc.

The raw material used in the manufacture of tools remained the same as noted in the preceding sub-period. Chert remained the dominat material for fashioning flakes and baldes, while in the case of bladelet chalcedony was the popular material next in order of frequency comes chert, agate and quartz. The occurrence of a large number of waste chips, fluted coures, and lumps of raw material do suggest that the site had a flourishing lithic industry. The characteristic feature of microlithic industry in both the sub-periods at Senuwar is that the majority of the tools are made on bladelet.

Other stone objects such as hammer stones, rubber stones, pestles, saddle querns, sling balls, disc etc. noted in the preceding sub-period continued in varying sizes and forms. The new enterants are sharpener, rectangular in shape, made of black besalt and two specimens of circular stone with plano-convex section. On the upper convex surface approvixmately in the centre a slight depression with several marks of soem sharp pointed instrument around the central depression is evidenced. Presumably these stones were used for perforating stone beads. The beeds were placed in the central depression and then perforated. The marks around the central depression might have been missing marks of the instrument used during the course of perforation. Apart from all the grains continuing from IA, some more cereals were added such as bread-wheat *(T.aestivum)*, chick-pea or gram *(Cicer arictinum)* and green or mung *(Vigna-radiata)*.

Objects of shell were generally used for personal adornment and tools of indeterminate use. It comprised of pendant of different forms and shall cut and edge ground to a traingular shape. These objects of shell form a special feature of Senuwar. Love for ornaments is further suggested by the occurrence of finsished and unfinished beads of agate, carnelian, jasper etc. Of particular mention are twenty five beads of faience (?) introduced only during this sub-period and may have been imported from somewhere else. This suggest the proficiency of the people in the lapidary art.

The occurrence of finished and unfinished bone tools along with waste material is most significant discovery of the sub-period. The finished tools comprised chisels of varying shapes and sizes, borer, points etc. The last being noted in majority. The micro-wear study revealed that waste material were also used as points, borer etc., as suggested by the usemarks[5].

Among other noteworty find of the sub-period is a hand made terracotta figurine of a bull. It may be mentioned here that bull figurine is also reported from Chirand. Oaher terracotta objects include a whistle (?), beads, indeterminate rectangular broken object with two perforations, circular burnt clay, miniature rectangular cake, pottery discs, edgeground pot-sheds etc.

The last being rerovered into various shapes viz., triangular, rectangular, oval etc., and are found from both the subperiods of Senuwar. These are absent at Chirand and Belan valley sites. Their occurrence at other Neolithic sites outside the region are reported from Hallur and Tekkalakotta. Specimens with hollowed or concave surfaces due to grinding have been suggested as sharpner while others have been regarded as skin rubbers by Sankalia.[6] But none specimens of Senuwar bear such marks. Besides, they are small in size also and hence their use either as sharpener or skin-rubber is doubtful.

Specimens which are cercular in shape constitute the majority and popularly known as pottery-discs. They are both of pierched and unpierced variety. Numerically the latter is more in number. Like the preceding group of specimens they are also of an uncertain use. However, pierced specimens are belived tobe either spindle-whorls[7] or toy-cart-wheels. The unpierced specimens have been suggested as gaming counters 'possibly used in hop-scotch game by children.[8]

The excavation revealed remains of successive floors, which were made of well rammed earth mixed with kankar and potsherds. The maximum diemension of the two successive floors exposed in an area measures 7 m. from noth to south and 6.50 m. east to west. The floors with a maximum thickness of 20 cm. where marked by burnt patches. Four post-holes varying in diameter and depath from 10-15 cm and 10-34 cm, respectively were also noticed. It may,however, be mentioned that the position or post-holes does not conform to any specific plan. The recovery of burnt lumps of clay with reed marks on these floors indicated that the houses were made a wooden posts which were further covered by a bamboo screen and then plastered with clay.

The radio-carbon dates available from the lower layers of Neolithic-Chalcolithic phase reading 1770 B.C. ± 120, 1660 B.C. ± 120 (trench 2B, layer (7)) and 1500 B.C. ± 110 and 1400 B.C. ± 110 (trench 2 C, layer (6)) way be taken into consideration. In the light of these dates IB started around 1800 BC and the beginning of IA may be suggested to the beginning of third millenium BC or a littler earlier. It may be mentioned that the early date for the occurrence of copper in this region is noteworthy.

On the basis of the above evidence the following conclusion may be drawn.

It appears that by the beginning of the second millenium B.C. or a little earlier Neolithic folk appeared in the region. The location of the site was most ideal keeping in view the basic needs of the settlement. Plenty availability of farmland, water source provided by the river Kudra, occurrence of raw material , moderate forest etc., would have been suited for the economy of these early farming communities of Senuwar.

The salient feautres of this culture was a microlithic industry which was local in both the sub-periods with an emphasis on the production of bladelets, small polished celts of triangular variety made on basalt, querns, pestles, rubbers, hammer stones, balls, beeds of semi-precious stone and terracotta. The pottery consists of red, burnished red, burnished grey, rusticated and corded wares.

They were leading settled life. The house were used both for living as well as manufacturing tools etc., as finished and unfinished tools along with pots and pans and other materials have been evidenced on the floors of the houses. The subsistance economy of the early farming communities of Senuwar was multibased incorporating farming, domestication of animals, hunting and fishing.

Ceramic industries of both the sub periods of Senuwar closely reasembles with those of Chirand. Both these sites share common features as far as cultrual assemblage, settlement pattern and other details are concerned. It may be mentioned that the material culture of Chirand is comparable with the Neolithic-Chalcolithic phase of Senuwar. Noteworthy comparisons in this regard may be made of faience beads, terracotta animal figurines particularly of bull, incised and punctured designs on pottery etc., which made their appearance at Senuwar in IB. The evidence in the region is nearly everywhere the same exept a few local variation. It is suggetive of the fact that the inter connection between the sites existed.

In view of the advance nature of the culture particularly with reference to well developed agriculture and indication of element of craft specilization, it may be suggested that Senuwar/Chirand complex represent mature or final stage of Neolithic Culture in Bihar which finally transformed itself into the full fledged Chalcolithic Culture.

Acknowledgement

The author is greatful to Prof. K.K. Sinha under whose general supervision the excavation was conducted. The author is indebted to his friends and Colleagues Shri Lalta Misra, Shri J.R. Singh, Shri Ram Badan and Shri J.S. Yadava for their assistance. The line drawings in the paper have been prepared by shri Shiva Kumar and Shri Ram Badan.

References

1. In collaboration with BSIP, represented by Dr. K.S. Saraswat attempt has been made to collect and study the botanical remains from excavation. The author gratefully thanks to Dr. Saraswat for supplying preliminary information of botanical remains of Senuwar.
2. Sharma, G.R. et al., *Beginnings of Agriculture*, P.23.
3. Training Centre, Alloy Steels Plant, SAIL, Durgapur. The author thanks to Sri Pranab K. Chattopadhyay for supplying results of the investigation of Senuwar metals and the two tables connected with it. The entire information presented in the paper is based on the report kindly sent to me.
4. Post firing ochre painting mostly on the rim portion have been found at Piklihal, Utnur, Brahmagiri IA, Sangañkullu, Banahalli etc.
5. Thakur, Nina; Jayaswal, Vidula, et. all., 'Bone Tools from Senuwar' paper presented at the Annual Conference of Indian Archaeological Society held at Santiniketan, 1st-3rd Dec. 1988.
6. Sankalia, H.D., *Prehistory and Protohistory of India and Pakistan* p. 533, (Poona, 1974), also Nagaraja Rao, M.S. *The Stone Age Hill Dwellers of Tekkalakota*, p. 82, pl.XI, B (Poona 1965).
7. Sankalia, H.D., *op.cit.*, (1974) p. 533.
8. Thapar, B.K., 'Maski 1954 : A Chalcolithic site of the southern Deccan' *Ancient India* No. 13, p.110.

RGVEDIC BASE OF THE PA´SUPATI SEAL OF MOHNJO-DARO

S.P. Singh*

Amongst Indus seals, probably the most important is one known as the Pa´supati Seal (Pl Ia). It has evoked great interest since it has been unearthed. It has depicted on it a peculiar human figure wearing a horned head-dress, sitting in *sidhāsana*, legs placed cross-wise and arms resting on knees, eyes turned towards the tip of the nose; three-faced, wearing a meagre loin-cloth with its ends projected slightly from the waist and three big and eight small bangles in each of the arms and having a triangular torque hanging over the chest. The figure is rugged in look and meditative, serene and calm in posture. It is surrounded by a number of animal-figures depicted on the two sides and below the seat. On its right side at the top is an elephant moving outside with his trunk extending ahead. Below the elephant is a tiger, stripped, claws opened out, and growling at the human figure. On the left side at the top is a rhinoceros facing the human figure. It too is in a moving posture with all its four legs visible distinctly. Below the same is another animal looking partly as bull and partly as buffalo. Its horns are almost of the same shape as the head-dress of the human figure, the latter, however, having some vegetation growing in between the horns. Below his seat, which is a little raised from the ground, there is a pair of entelopes with their horns sweeping back and faces raised in awe towards him.

Irrespective of the vast difference of size in the animals in reality, the four bigger animals are depicted more or less as of equal size, with the tiger as a little bigger than the elephant, the bull-buffalo as a little bigger than the rhinoceros, and the human figure matching all of them put together. This deviation from reality is suggestive of the highly idealized nature of the figures. In this ideal scheme of things, the human figure is intended to be most important. This is indicated by his central position as well as the massive size. The four animals, on the other hand, are treated as of equal importance amongst themselves and as subordinate to the human figure. The focal point of the whole depiction is the face of the human figure with its eyes looking round, the eye-brows considerably raised and the face appearing bold and indignant, bearing with perfect equipoise the growling of the tiger on the one hand and the expectant look of the bull-buffalo on the other.

There is a group of six pictorial symbols or scripts at the top of the seal and one in-between the elephant and the tiger. The day these would get deciphered, the curtain of mystery enshrouding this as well as kindred seals of the site would be lifted making all such attempts as ours almost redundant. But until the dawn of that great day every venture of interpretation, even though a sheer guess-work, would have its relevance with the probability of anyone of them happening to touch the core of the problem.

Needless to point out that Sir John Marshal, the excavator of the Indus Valley site, named the human figure of the seal as Pa´supati, the Lord of animals. He did so rightly as the figure bears overwhelmingly the characteristic features of the Saivaite deity. The three-edged head-dress was reminiscent of the trident of ´Siva; his yogic posture went well with the ascetic character of the deity while the animals around him could not but be taken as a sure proof of his being the Lord of animals which ´Siva is believed to be in almost all his forms. But the problem rested with the how of such a form of ´Siva being conceived as early as the middle of the third millennium B.C. by which epoch the Aryans were not supposed to have touched the Indian soil. As an easy way out of this difficulty, Sir John Marshal declared his Paśupati as a proto-´Siva figurine which getting mixed up with the Vedic Rudra resulted, in course of time, in the emergence of the real´Siva of the post-Vedic era. Thus he took his Pa´supati as a wholly non-Aryan phenomenon having little to do with the Vedas and the Vedic Rudra at that stage.

The burden of the present paper is a set of evidence cumulatively suggesting inherence of the motif of the Pa´supati Seal in considerable detail in the Rgveda itself. The evidence is offered by Ṛgveda I.64, a hymn addressed to Maruts. The Maruts are viewed here particularly in relationship to Rudra. This is borne out by their characterization as the 'son of Rudra', 'young Rudras' and 'mortals of Rudra'.[1] These expressions show how, though quite important in themselves, the Maruts are just the sons, younger representives and relatively mortal epiphanies of Rudra. They are his progeny and dependents. As such, they can easily be depicted as a number of children moving or playing around the father sitting in constancy, conscious of their well being and ready to intervene in their strifes and fightings. In view of this relationship obtaining between Rudra and the Maruts, any artist could easily have drawn the former in a human form and the latter as his children surrounding him in some or the other posture but in any case as much smaller in size and after all mobile. In relation to them, Rudra could be represented by a human figure seated in a posture of wisdom, gracefulness, bounty and might,[2] adorned in golden light,[3] benign towards animals, kine and children,[4] having braided hair,[5] strong limbs, bedecked with golden ornaments and looking aggressively mighty.[6]

More or less this is how Pa´supati of the Mohenjo-Daro seal has been depicted. He is as tall and massive as all the animals surrounding him put together. Two antelopes are carved under the pedestal he is seated on. The pedestal is raised from the ground understandably to suggest his divinty. He is towering over the elephant and the rhinoceros. Through his head-dress he appears to shoot up in the boundless space. This is quite in accordance with the Ṛgvedic account of Rudra as

* Department of Sanskrit, Aligarh Muslim University, Aligarh-202001.

'the boar of heaven', bright in colour and having braided hair.

Incidentally if the hair-lock is not visible in this seal, that is due to the head-dress. Otherwise its being there is very much vindicated by another seal in which the same figure is seated with a thick lock of hair hanging off the left shoulder. This is also the case with a third seal in which the same figure is again depicted as standing in-between two branches of a peepal tree, and having a braid of hair hanging off the left shoulder.

Another significant point on which there is peculiar akinness between the Mohenjo-Daro Pa´supati and the Ṛgvedic Rudra is the abundance of ornaments which both are made to put on. As regards Pa´supati, his both arms are laden with bangles from wrists to shoulders. His chest also has a triangular torque hanging over it. Parallel to it, in the Ṛgveda, we get the account how Rudra has adorned himself with pieces of gold.[8]

The third important feature of the figure of Pa´supati is the modelling of the face. It is peculiarly bull-like. In fact, along with the head-dress consisting of a pair of stout horns with a decorative piece in-between the two, his face seems to have been intended to bear the semblance of a bull's. Of course there is no dearth of human images in Mohenjo-Daro or Harappa. None of those images, however, has been adorned with a head-dress of horns nor is anyone of them made bull-faced. If there is any exception to it, that is the image of Pa´supati in all its versions whether squatting on the ground or standing in the midst of a pair of branches of a peeple tree. No doubt, there is variation in these images in so far as the braid of hair is concerned. For out of the four images of Pa´supati of this variety, two have distinct braids and two have not. But in regard to the head-dress of horns, there is perfect uniformity among them. Incidentally there is a fifth image also in which a naked man is moving with bow in one hand and arrow in the other. This man is made to put on a mask of animal head along with a pair of horns and the characteristic face. This mask also has the probability of being a representation of the bull's face. Alternatively, however, it may be taken to represent either deer or dog. This figure also is taken as a variant form of Pa´supati. Being admitted as bull-faced it too confirms Pasupati's close association with bull.

This association of Paśupati with bull is a prelude to the later conception of ´Siva having bull as his ride. This development lies simply in separating the bull-feature of Pa´supati from him and making it fall apart as his ride. But, interestingly enough, what appears as a ride in the later conception of the deity, and as mask in Mohenjo-Daro, the same is found as an inherent attribute of him in the Veda. For in a number of Ṛgvedic mantras he has been addressed as Vṛsabha, bull sometimes simply as 'bull' and sometimes as 'brown bull'.[9] Thus there seems to be a developmental process involved in the association of ´Siva with bull. What was sheer adjectival at the early stage, came to assume the form of a separate entity at the post-Vedic stage. The Indus civilization seems, therefore, to occupy a position intermediate to these inasmuch as here the bull is associated with Pa´supati neither as an adjective nor as an independent being but as his mask.

In view of the above facts, it was but natural that while being depicted as Paśupati the deity was conceived as bull-faced. As such, the animals depicted on the seal could have been shown either as calves or as childern depending on whether the deity was conceived as a human being or as a bull. If he was taken as a human being, the animals ought to have been shown as children playing around him. On the other hand, if he was treated as a bull, his issues should have been sheer calves. But, as we have noted in the beginning, neither of these two alternatives has been followed in the portrayal on the seal. The animals around Pa´supati are neither children nor calves. They are buffalo-bull, rhinoceros, tiger, elephant and antelopes. How could it be so ?

This gets very well explained if we look into the manner in which maruts, the sons of Rudra; have been described in the hymn under consideration. After being proposed for description by Nodhas, the seer, they have at the outset been addressed as bulls, *uksānah*, and men of Rudra, *rudrasya maryāh*. This was perfectly in accordance with the possibilities envisaged right now in view of Rudra's figuring out sometimes as a bull besides his regular human from. In this capacity they are said to have been born of the heaven and be lofty, taintless and mighty. They are pure, purifying and mighty as the sun and at the same time ferocious in look.[11] They are young Rudras, unaging, demon-slayers and irresistibly expanding like mountains. By their might they are capable of making tremble even well settled entities of the heaven and the earth.[12] Possibly bulllike or human in form, these issues of Rudra are represented here by a variety of animals introduced by way of simile. The animals brought in here in this way are buffalo *(mahiṣa)*, elephant *(hasti)*, lion *(simha)*, *pi´sa*, spotted deer *(pṛsati ṛsti)* and serpent *(ahi)*.[13]

As regards the buffalo, elephant, lion and deer, obviously there is perfect agreement between the Rgvedic account and the Indus depiction. If there remains anything of doubtful identity that is the Ṛgvedic *pi´sa*. Sāyaṇa takes it in the sense of a type of deer called *ruru*. He considers the cognate word *supi´saḥ* occuring in the same mantra to mean beautiful. Obviously he comes to this meaning by deriving the word *pisa* from *piṣ*, to adorn. But this derivative meaning is not decisive. Many an animal can come under the purview of this sense. Indeed the *Vaidika Pādanukrama Ko´sa* indicates to the possibility of taking this word in the sense of elephant and bull as well. This is enough to suggest the ambiguity of the meaning of this word since long. In fact the ambiguity is due to the absence of this word in this form in the whole of the Sanskrit literature except here and in a slightly variant form in Ṛgveda VII. 18.2. As a part in *pi´saṅga* and *pi´saṅgaka*, however, it occurs frequently in the Vedic as well as post-Vedic literature. In the Ṛgveda itself it occurs at least a dozen times. Here it has been used in the sense of yellowish and golden as distinct from the reddish. This latter meaning is particularly evident in Rgveda V. 57.4, where *pi´saṅga´svāh* have been recounted as distinct from *aruṇa´svāḥ*. Thus it is obvious that the animal called *pi´sa* must be yellowish in colour as a whole or at least pre-eminently, Such an animal can be the pig. Here it is interesting to point out that the Oxford English Dictonary has noted *picga* as the old English form of pig. About *picga*, it observes that its etymology is obscure and the origin is unknown. In view of the rarity of the Sanskrit word *pi´sa* and the almost total loss of its meaning at an early stage here in India, the puzzle of the lexicographer is quite understandable. Otherwise phonetically *picga* seems to be just a variant of *pi´sa*. Needless to point out that *C and S are* one and the same sound geting differentiated in the Centum and *Satem* groups of Indo-European languages respectively. In view of this as well as the akinness of colour as pointed out above, we can justifiably take the Ṛgvedic *pi´sa* to mean pig. And if we view rhinoceros in the Pa´supati seal in the light of the above fact, we shall possibly not be very much unjustified in taking it as a representation of what in the Ṛgveda is intended by the word *pi´saḥ*, for, in the least, both the pig and the rhinoceros are very much similar in look. To take it other way round, in view of its closeness to the family of pigs, the rhinoceros has a strong case for being signified by the word *pi´sa*. Moreover, Rudra-´Siva has closely been associated with rhinoceros itself as well as with boar. While in the Ṛgveda, as pointed out earlier, he is described as the heavenly boar, *divo varāham*, in the Mahābāarata once he is characterized as *gaṇḍalin*, the Lord of rhinoceros.[14]

Thus the above facts are sufficient to bear out perfect correspondence between the Ṛgvedic account and the Mohenjo-Daro seal in regard to the animals brought in by way of simile in the Rgveda and as the companions of Pasupati in the seal. However, not only in kind but action also the Ṛgvedic animals mentioned above tally very much with those cast on the seal. In the Ṛgvedic account the buffalo is described as miraculously mighty, bright in colour, strong as the mountain and gliding swiftly. So is the case with the bull-buffalo of the seal. Along with its stoutness, it is depicted in a swiftly moving posture. Similarly the Ṛgvedic elephant is characterized as wild and busy in eating up forests. The elephant of the seal also has turned his face outward stretching his trunk considerably ahead with its tip turned to some extent. As regards the tiger there is perfect unanimity of action in the text and the seal. In the text it is described as roaring loudly. In the seal also it is depicted as growling at Pa´supati. The rhinoceros-boar is simply showing the bearing of its form almost equally at both the places.

While the four major animals mentioned above are introduced jn the hymn as similes to Martus, the antelopes are brought in as their rides yoked to their chariot. Interestingly enough, this distinction in the respective status of the two classes of animals is maintained in the seal also. Here while those brought in by way of simile to Maruts are depicted as moving on the two sides of Pa´supati, the pair of dear is placed under his seat with their legs put at considerable distance from one another, heads raised, faces turned half backward and horns coming close to each other's thus suggesting cumulatively a state of movement in diverse directions. It is as if they are trying to drag the seat of the deity in opposite directions but failing to do so on account of his eternal constancy, they are looking behind in utter dismay. This *motif* is akin to the tiger's which though trying utmost to frighten him, fails completely to disturb his peace.

The skin-designs of the antelopes in the text and the seal also bear considerable resemblance with each other. The antelopes in the text are characterized as spotted, *pṛsatiḥ*. In the seal also we find rings of colour around the neck of them suggesting that they are spotted. If any reference to the use of spotted deer as a ride is required, we have the same in Ṛgveda V.57.3, where Maruts, the sons of *Pṛṣṇī*, are said to run over mountains and forests and shake the heaven and the earth riding on their chariot drawn by spotted deer. Rudra, however, is different from the Maruts in this regard. As against his sons, never does he ride on a chariot except at one place in the Vājasaneyi Samhitā (XVI. 26) where also, as is evident from the use of his name in the plural, it is more probably Maruts who are meant rather than Rudra himself. On account of this mythological position as held in the Veda perhaps, the pair of antelopes is placed below his seat just in a state of suspended animation.

As regards the bangles around the arms of Pa´supati, there is an expression in the text which seems to have a close bearing on it. It is *Vṛṣakhādayah* used an epithet for Maruts in the tenth mantra of the hymn.[15] It is used for them after restoring them to their human form, *narāḥ*, from within a cluster of anthropomorphic images. This expression in this compound form occurs only here and hence it has not been possible to assign to it a meaning with a sense of certitude. But the word *Khādi* occurs separately five times in the Ṛgveda. In all these occurrences it has been used in association with Maruts.

In Ṛgveda I. 166.9 and VII 56.13, *Khādi* is said to be on the shoulders of Maruts.[16] In Ṛgveda V. 58. 2, they are said to have *Khādi* in their hands.[17] As against it, in Ṛgveda V. 54.11, they are said to put *Khādi* on their feet.[18] Lastly in Ṛgveda V. 53.4, *Khādi* is enumerated along with *srak* (garland) and *Rukma* (necklace).[19] These details suggest that *Khādi* was an ornament as well as a weapon and that it was put sometimes on the foot, sometimes on the wrist and sometime on the arm near the shoulder. That it was made of gold, is suggested by its enumerations along with **rukma.** A more positive evidence in this respect, though later, is provided by the term *hiraṇyakhādi* used in ´Sāṅkhāyana Srauta Sūtra III. 5.12. Addition of *Vṛṣa* to *Khādi* in the hymn under consideration may be taken to give a twofold meaning to the term depending on whether the latter is used in the sense of weapon or ornament. If it is taken in the sense of weapon, then the word *Vṛṣa* would introduce the image of a bull scratching the ground by means of his horns and hooves, denoting the effectiveness of the weapon. If, on the other hand, it is taken in the sense of ornament, then *Vṛṣa* would add the sense of manliness to it. This interpretation is very much corroborated by Griffith's translation. He translates *Vṛṣakhādayaḥ* as "armed with strong men's rings" and comments on it as follows :

"The meaning of *Vṛṣākhadayaḥ* is uncertain; but the *Khādi* seems to have been a ring worn on the arm and foot. It may also have been used as a weapon".[20]

If we correlate these Ṛgvedic evidences with the seal of Mohenjo-Daro, we cannot negate the possibility of *Khādi* being something akin to the bangles put around the arms of Paśupati from the wrist to the shoulder. On account of *Khādi* being peculiar to Maruts in the Ṛgveda, it was quite easy for the artist of Mohenjo-Daro to transfer the same to the father of Maruts. On account of being depicted as animals when Maruts were not in a position to make use of their *Khādis*, the same were handed over to their father, as it were.

One pertinent point which still remains to be brought to the focus of attention is the personality of Rudra in the Ṛgveda, and the extent of its correspondence with the Pa´supati of the seal. In this connection it is to be kept in mind that a special feature of Pa´supati, if not appearing clearly in the seal under duscussion yet manifest in other three seals depicting him, is his braid of hair hanging off his left shoulder. In the Indus seals, amongst males, the braid of hair is peculiar to him, though amongst females it is quite common. Almost the same is the case with the Ṛgveda. As regards the females, a young lady is said to have as many as four locks of hair in this Saṁhitā. This obviously is meant for beautification.[21] But amongst males, it is peculiarly Rudra, besides Pūṣan, who has been referred to as *Kapardin*. In Ṛgveda I. 114.1, along with the use of the adjective *Kapardin* for him, he is prayed to be peace-giving to human beings and animals and bring prosperity and health to the village.[22] In the fifth mantra of the same hymn he is given the same adjective again along with the characterization as the shining boar of heaven having choicest herbs in his hand and is prayed to bring peace and protection to people.[23] These details are sufficient to show how Rudra in the Ṛgveda keeps a long braid of hair, is peace-giving to animals as well as men, cures diseases by means of herbs and has got a bright, powerful and shining personality. That the braid of hair is associated specially with spiritual *Sādhanā* and that Rudra is a deity characteristically connected with such practices, is evident from Rgveda X. 136, in which *munis* are said to keep long hair, put on yellow garment, keep mute, have access to spiritual knowledge and delight, travel in air and drink poison in the company of Rudra.[24]

If Rudra of the above description happens to be conceived by the ceramic artist in the Mohenjo-Daro seal as a yogin sitting calm and quite in the midst of ferocious animals, self-contented and benign and posing in *sidhāsana* with his gracious palms resting on his knees, naked but bedecked with ornaments made of gold, keeping a braid of hair hidden perhaps under the head-dress, there does not seem to be any improbability in it. On the contrary, such a conception and the subsequent depiction seem to be a natural consequence of what is said about the deity in the Ṛgveda.

In the Yajurveda, however, the yogic character of Rudra is more pronounced. Besides being addressed several times as *Kapardin* he is also conceived as dressed in skin which too is a special feature of yogins. But from out viewpoint at the moment, still more important are certain other accounts of him in this *Saṁhitā*. In the first place, Rudra is described here as having put on a head-dress, *uṣṇiṣin*. This description goes well not only with the seal under discussion but also with other three seals in which the same person recurs in different circumstances. It is particularly important to note that the same head-dress occurs not only in the three seals depicting the deity in an identical way in *siddhāsana* but in the fourth one also where he is standing between two branches of a peepal tree. Moreover, if the seals in *siddhāsana* depict the deity as a perfect yogin, that in the standing pose brings out a meeting-ground between the two apparently conflicting facets of Rudra's personality, the terrific and the benign, as of course described in the *Saṁhitās*. Just as the Ṛgvedic mantras under discussion form the motif of the famous Paśupati seal, even so there is a mantra in the Yajurveda which seems to have provided the basic idea of this fourth seal. In this mantra Rudra is prayed to become most generous and auspicious by placing his weapon on the highest tree and moving around in a skin-dress. [25] Interestingly enough, in Mohenjo-Daro also while on the one hand we have three seals depicting the deity in *siddhāsana*, there is on the other a fourth one bringing out the same deity with bow and arrow in his hands and almost naked throughout the whole body or putting on some skin-dress. This last figure corresponds to the Vedic Rudra having bow and arrow in his hands. The seal depicting him as standing between the branches of tree and as completely disarmed has correspondence with the Vedic idea of Rudra having placed his weapon on the highest tree while the remaining three seals correspond to that form of Rudra which has become ´Siva and Pa´supati. It is also noteworthy that the deity standing between the branches of the tree is being prayed by a devotee sitting in a devout pose nearby with a goat standing behind him. At the bottom of the seal are seven human figures standing in a pose akin to the deity's. What these seven figures represent, is difficult to explain in this context. But one thing is certain that this motif as a whole corresponds to the position of the Yajurveda in which obeisance is made to Rudra by associating him with trees, herbs and animals.[26]

As regards the motif of the peepal tree in the seal, it has a special bearing on the Vedic Rudra. If Pa´supati is standing complete disarmed between the branches of the peepal tree and as attended by the human devotee, the devout animal and the seven human figures as depicted in the Mohenjo-Daro seal, in the Ṛgveda Vāyus are prayed to bring the offering of honey close to the A´svattha tree where victorious people sit, cows procreate without getting thin, and barley is cooked.[27] It shows that if the Aśvattha tree was sacred to the Indus people, it was no less sacred to the Vedic ones. Secondly, if in the Ṛgveda Vāyus, the gods of air, are prayed to bring the offerings of honey to the peepal tree, in Mohenjo-Daro a god intimately connected with them is standing between its branches. In fact, if Vāyus and Maruts are related with the leaves of the peepal tree understandably on account of the latter's getting affected so much by their blowing, it is quite in the fitness of things that Rudra, their father and the god of eternal constancy is standing at its root and is being worshipped by the two-footed and the four-footed alike. He indeed is the eternal constancy lying at the root of perpetual flux. It is on account of this constancy that he is being prayed by the devotee so as to emulate him. Here the fleeting wants to be transformed into the eternal. In the words of Dirghatamas, the delicious fruit of the peepal tree of the cosmos cannot be relished until and unless one knows the Father.[28] It is this Father who is standing at the root of the peepal tree as depicted in the seal. The human devotee is seeking to know and emulate him through self-effacement. The animal with human face standing behind him is perhaps his own animal nature intended to be offered to the deity for self-transformation. This is suggested further by its composite nature wherein it is partly goat, partly bull and partly man. A composite creation like this and particularly when introduced in such a highly figurative context cannot but be deeply symbolic. The human face with the animal body is suggestive of its being basically the man having his animal nature magnified. As bull and goat both are the animals of sacrifice, the combination of them in this figure indicates that it is meant for being sacrificed. The seven human figures depicted at the bottom of the seal may represent the seven sons or daughters of Viśpati, the Father, as the case may be, attending upon him or singing in his praise, as has been conceived by Dīrghatamas.[29]

The above details are sufficient to drive home the idea that there was a close connection between the Ṛgvedic seers and the builders of the Indus civilization and that the builders brought out in plastic form some of the more striking images conceived by the seers. Here it would be interesting to note that this proposition of the borrowal of the Ṛgvedic images by the sculptors of the Indus valley is not anything entirely new. It has already been mooted by certain other scholars, amongst whom of particular interest in this context are T.N. Ramachandran and Buddha Prakash, as they both have sought to trace the imagery involved in the Pa´supati seal in two different contexts of the Saṁhitā. In his Presidential Address delivered in the Ancient India Section of the Indian History Congress held in 1956 at Agra, Ramachandran associated this seal with Ṛgveda IV.58.3 which reads as follows :

Catvāri ´sṛṅgā trayo asya pādā

dve ś–irṣe sapta hastāso asya;

tridhā baddho vṛṣabho rorav–iti

maho devo martyānāvive´sa.

He has tried to relate in particular the image of the roaring bull here in his mantra with the Indus bull with all its mighty appearance along with its characteristic dewlap. He is of the view that the Ṛgvedic idea that the bull does all the roaing to proclaim *dharma-vijaya* is caught up by the Mohenjo-Daro seals and sealings representing the bull with its characteristic dewlap. To quote him further, "That such a bull with its powerful physique bellows for all time to come the advent of a great God (Māho-Devaḥ) is the spirit of a few sealings from the Indus Valley of the third millennium B.C., where the bull is shown with three heads, one of the heads looking back, the second head which is centrally placed looking down and the third head looking ahead or stretched forward. He further observes :

"This seal combined with another seal wherein the anthropomorphic figure of a God supposed to be Rudra as Māhāyogi seated amidst animals such as bull, elephant, rhinoceros, tiger, antelopes, and among men and birds and fish brings out forcibly the ideas contained in the Rigvedic hymns :

"tridhā baddho vriṣabho voravīti

Maho devo martyānāvive´sa".

He takes this hemistich in the sense that "The thrice-bent bull goes on roaring that the great God (is no longer in some invisible heavens put) has actually completely entered the mortals".[30] In conclusion he observes : "The minds of the Rigvedic people and the Indus Valley appear to have thought tout on the same lines, as much in accepting animals, birds and beings as they are in realistic study as in integrating them into *āve´sas* or chimeras'. A pertient example is the Maho-devo seal from Mohenjo-Daro described above." In fine he maintains that "the Ṛigvedic poet and the Indus Valley artist have fancied and fashioned alike."[31]

If we make a review of the above tnesis of Ramachandran's, we cannot but appreciate his effort to see Ṛgvedic images in the Indus seal. Moreover, the Rgvedic image of the *maho-devaḥ* entering into the mortals has a pertinent bearing on the seal as has been made out by Ramachandran. For, as has already been pointed out, the Paśupati of the seal also represents permanence in the flux of life and the world. But excepting this central idea, in other details there is incoherence between the mantra and the seal. His interpretation of the mantra in such a way as to make the entering of the great God into mortals the subject matter of the roaring of the bull and thus the bull and the great God as two different entities, is, though ingenius, uncalled for. In fact, the context of the mantra makes it quite explicit that the roaring bull itself is the *maho-devaḥ* here. Moreover, neither the bull of the seal nor the Paśupati tallies in form any way with the Ṛgvedic account of the bull as having four horns, three feet, two heads, seven hands and three-fold bondage. As against it, the bull of the seal is almost a normal one while the Pa´supati has three faces, two hands, two feet and no bondage whatsoever. If the Ṛgvedic image were there before the Indus sculptor. he could not but have incorporated at least some of these singular details in his carving. So far as the other animals of the seal are concerned, there is no trace of any one of them at all in the mantra. If the *maho-devaḥ* of the mantra were intended to have been depicted in the seal so as to indicate its entry into the mortals, it could very well have been surrounded by any set of mortals and not necessarily by the one which is conspicuous by total absence in this mantra and occurs as a whole in the mantras referred to above. As such, those mantras, rather than the one referred to by Ramachandran, seem to have guided the Indus sculptor in his depiction. Ramachandran associates the iconography of the God in the seal with Ṛgveda IX. 96.6 which reads as follows :

brahmā devānām padavi–i kavīnāṁ

ṛṣir viprāṇām mahiṣo mṛgāṇām;

śyeno gṛdhrāṇāṁ svadhitir v–anāṁ

somaḥ pavitramatyeti rebhan.

Regarding this association he observes, "The same has been described in other hymns of the Ṛigveda as Brahmā by virtue of his possessing more faces and as Mahisha by virtue of his possessing buffalo's horns".[32] Here it is to be noted that the mantra under reference has Soma rather than Rudra or Maho-Devaḥ as its deity. As such, if it has anything relevant to the explanation of the deity of the seal, that is only Soma's being called Brahmā, who later on appears as four-faced, and Mahisa who is supposed to have lent its horns to the deity. But the deity of the seal can be taken to have drawn from the image of Brahmā only if it were proved to be four-faced which is a mere conjecture. As against this, he is obviously three-faced. The same is the case with the horns. They can as well be the bull's.

In sum, therefore, what can be conceded to Mr. Ramachandran at the most is his pioneering effort to associate the different components of the figure on the seal with different images in the Ṛgveda used in different contexts. On this score also his achievement is only scanty as it leaves unaccounted for the specific set of animals such as elephant, tiger, rhinoceros, bull-buffalo and antelopes depicted on the seal.

Buddha Prakash, on the other hand, has made a more vigorous attempt to trace in the Ṛgvedic images figures depicted on the seal. But failing to find out the proper clue, he in his vigour, has confused several irrelevant things together. he identifies the deity of the seal with the three-headed, six-eyed being mentioned in Ṛgveda X.99.6 on the one hand and with Tvāṣṭra Vi´svar–upa recounted in Rgveda II.19 on the other.[33] But the position of Tvāṣṭra Viśvarūpa is doubtful in the Saṁhitā. While in Ṛgveda II. 11.19 he is presented as something divine and welcome, in Ṛgveda X 99.6 he is clearly stated to be a *dāsa*, destructive agency roaring loudly and killed by Tṛta. Tvastra obviously is the son of Tvaṣṭṛ, the architect of the world. Since the world comprises the good and the evil both, Tvāṣṭra, the son of Tvaṣṭṛ is conceived sometimes as a divine and at others as a demonaic being. Hence it is difficult to conceive how such a dubious character could find such a sublime representation as is given to him in the seal. The only point where the Ṛgvedic Tvāṣṭra and the Indus deity meet is three-headedness and six-eyedness of the former and three-facedness of the latter. But though apparently similar, these respective features of the two beings are really not one and the same thing. While three-headedness implies division in fundamentals, three-facedness suggests only aspectual multiplicity. Due to the division while Tvāṣṭra is a God on the one hand and demon on the other, due to aspectual multiplicity in it the Indus deity maintains perfect equipoise even in the midst of bewildering diversity and various kinds of polarities. Thus while Tvāṣṭra represents division and dichotomy, the Indus deity symbolizes unification and harmony. How can the two be one and the same ?

Another difficulty with Buddha Prakash's viewpoint is his interpretation of antelopes lying under the seat of the Indus deity. He associates the pair with the legend of Prajāpati assuming the form of a deer so as to cohabit with his daughter Usas who had assumed the from of a doe. In order to ward Prajaptai off this heinous act, Rudra is said to have aimed his arrow at him but to have been induced to lay down the bow and the arrow by the promise to be made the lord of animals.[34] The anomaly in the interpretation is too obvious to need explaination. How can such a legend involving the father be engraved under the seat of the meditative son ? Moreover, the two antelopes have their faces turned in opposite directions and do by no means betray and kind of infatuation whatever towards each other.

Being more or less conscious of these difficulties in his equation, Buddha Prakash seeks to avoid them by identifying Tvāṣṭra, the son with Tvaṣṭṛ the father himself. But the anomaly involved in this identification apart, it, even if admitted for the time being, does not solve the problem. For, in the first place, when Tvāṣṭra becomes Tvaṣṭṛ, he loses his three-headedness and thus the principal feature by virtue of which he somehow or other happens to have some resemblance with the Indus deity. Secondly, if Tvaṣṭṛ himself is seated as the main deity in the perfectly yogic pose, it would be totally anomalous to engrave him again in the form of a deer showing infatuation towards his daughter turned into a doe. In the third place, there is no doubt that Tvastr has been described in Ṛgveda III, 55.19 as the creator and feeder of his progeny,[35] as is pointed out by Buddha Prakash, yet it is important to note that the progeny of the creator does by no means comprise animals alone. On the contrary, it ought to be represented by a largely mixed variety of creatures which indeed is not the case with the seal in question. Here all the creatures surrounding the deity are exclusively animals. In fact, it is totally erroneous to confuse *prajāpati* with *pa´supati*. The latter is an eipthet which almost invariably goes with Rudra and seldom with Prājapati.

In view of the above it is quite evident that the Ṛgvedic imagery referred to neither by T.N. Ramachandran nor by Buddha Prakash is capable of accounting properly for the Pa´supati seal. They both have concentrated mainly on explaining the three-facedness of the deity but have miserably failed.[36] The rest of their explanations also are hopelessly casual. In fact, when the actual target is missed, all other actions, howsoever well intended, become just a mimicry.

As regards the three-facedness of the Indus deity, this could very well be explained by the word *tryambaka* used for Rudra in the famous *mahāmṛtyuñjaya* mantra.[37] The solitary occurrence of this word in the Ṛgveda and yet its getting perfectly settled as a name of Rudra subsequently bear out the fact that the feature of the deity implied in it was universally admitted even at the time of the Saṁhitā. So far as its meaning is concerned, it has been interpreted in a twofold manner. The Śatapatha Brāhmaṇa takes the word as a combination of *str–i + ambaka*, and considers it to have been given to Rudra on account of the fact that the latter shared oblation in a certain sacrifice along with Ambikā, his sister.[38] Needless to point out how funny this derivation is. The other derivation suggested by Sayana is *tri + ambaka*. Sāyana takes *ambaka* in the sense of father. This is quite plausible as *ambakā* can very well be the masculine form of *ambikā*, meaning 'mother'. Thus Sāyaṇa considers it to mean the father of the three deities, Brahmā, Vishṇu and Rudra. Obviously this explanation is quite late and hence inadmissible in this form. On the basis of a certain text not referred to, Griffith on the other hand takes it in the sense of the deity having three eyes. explanation also is based on the later form of Rudra. Thus, though not admissible precisely in their respective forms, these explanations, however, bear out a definite triplicity inherent in the character of the deity, no matter be it the triplicity of his sons, of his eyes, of his faces or of his aspects. Now when the triplicity was so pertinent as to have given him a particular name, it was but natural that the same was brought out in the form of faces in the Indus seal, for the Indus designer had only to convert *nāma* into *r–upa*, which indeed he had taken upon himself to accomplish in other details of the seal also. He, no doubt, was the greatest artistic genius of the Indus culture and eminently capable of giving shape to even abstract ideas, not to say of nomenclatures.

Adorning the deity with a pair of horns may be viewed as another example of the tendency of plastic representation of abstract ideas. To give horn to a man-like figure is obviously ludicruous. To some it may look demonic too. But, as a matter of fact, horn belongs originally to animals which, if deified, may easily lend the same to the ensuing deity. An instant example of it is the image of the divine bull with four horns as referred to earlier.[39] If a 'great god' *(maho devaḥ)* may be conceived as having horns and even as many as four in this Ṛgvedic instance, there is nothing devilish in giving the same to the Indus deity. In fact the horns of the latter are very well explicable in terms of the present assumption. When Rudra's sons would have come to assume the form of animals in the imagination of the Indus sculptor on the basis of the similies used by the Ṛgvedic seer, it would have been but in the fitness of things to accord some semblance of animality to the father also. Addition of horns to the head was perhaps the easiest way to that end. Moreover, being associated with animal, horns are symbolic of powers and ferocity which indeed are characteristic features of Rudra. As such, the feature of horns on his head might have come to be extended to other Paśupati seals also where he figures even all alone. The extension may partly be due to the analogy of the prominent seal and partly due to the inherent symbolic sense of the horns.

FOOTNOTES

1. *Rudrásya s–unúm Ṛgveda I. 64.12.*

   yúvāno rudrāḥ. Ibid., I 64.3.

   rudrásya máryāḥ. Ibid., I. 64.2.

2. *kād rudrāya prácetase mīḷhúṣṭamaya távyase vocéma śántamaṁ hṛdé. Ibid., I. 43.1.*

3. *yáḥ 'sukrá iva s–uryo híraṇyamiva r'ocate śréṣṭho devānāṁ vaśuḥ. Ibid., I. 43.5.*

4. *yáha no áditiḥ kárat páśve nṛ́bhyo yáthā gáve yátha tokā́ya rudriyam. Ibid., 43.2.*

5. *kapardíne. Ibid., 114.1.*

6. *sthirébhirángaiḥ purur–úpa ugró babhrúḥ sukrébhiḥ pipiśe híraṇyaiḥ. Ibid., II 33.9.*

7. *divó varāhámaruṣám kapardínam. Ibid., I. 114.5*

8. *Ibid., II. 33.9.*

9. *Ibid., II. 33.4,6,7,15.*

10. *rudró yád vo maruto rukmavakṣaso v'ṛṣājani p'ṛśnyaḥ 'sukrá –udhani. Ibid., II. 34.2. See also V. 60.5.*

11. *Ibid., I. 64.2.*

12. *Ibid., I. 64.3*

13. *mahiṣáso māyínaś citrábhanavo giráyo ná svátavaso raghuṣyádaḥ.*

    mṛgá iva hastínaḥ khādatha vánā yádārúṇīṣu táv–iṣīr áyugdhvam.

    siṁhá iva nānadati práceasaḥ piśá iva supíso ví 'svávedasaḥ.

    kṣápo jínvantaḥ p'ṛṣatibhir ṛṣṭibhiḥ sámít sabādhaḥ

    'śávasāhimanyavaḥ. Ibid., I. 64. 7-8.

14. *Mahābhārata XIII. 17.91.*

15. *ástāra íṣum dadhire gábhastyor anantá'suṣmā v'ṛṣākhādaya nárah. Ibid., I. 64.10.*

16. *ámseṣvā vaḥ prápatheṣu khādáyaḥ. Ibid., I. 166.9. ámseṣvā marutaḥ khādáyo vo vákṣaḥsu rukmā upaśiśriyānāḥ. Ibid., VII. 56.13.*

17. *tveṣáṁ gaṇáṁ tavasáṁ khādihastam. Ibid., V. 58.2.*

18. *áṁseṣu vaḥ ṛṣṭáyaḥ patsú khādáyo. Ibid., V. 54.11.*

19. *sraksú rukmésu khādísu. Ibid., V. 53.4.*

20. R.T.H. Griffith, *RV. I 64.10 (his note on)*

21. *cátuskaparda yuvatíḥ supésā ghṛtápratika vayúnāni vaste. Ibid., X. 114.3.*

22. *im ā rudrāya tavási kapardíne ksayádvīrāya prá bharamahe matīḥ.*

yáthā śámasad dvipáde cátuspade víśvam pustám grāme asmínnanāturam. Ibid., I. 114.1.

23. *divó varāhámarusám kapardínam tvesám rūpám námasā ní hvayamahe. háste víbhrad bhesajāváryāṇi śárma várma cchardír asmábhyam yamsat. Ibid., I.114.5.*

24. *Ibid., X. 136.*

25. *mṛ-ilhustama śivatama śivó nah sumánā bhava. paramé vrksé āyudham nidhāya k'ṛttim vásana ā cara. Vajasaneyi Samhita XVI. 51.*

26. *námo vrksébhyo hárikeśebhyo. Ibid., XVI. 17. vṛksānām pátaye námaḥ. Ibid., XVI. 19. óṣadhīnām pátaye námaḥ. Ibid., XVI. 19.*

paśūnām pátaye námaḥ. Ibid., XVI. 17.

27. *átrāha tád vahethe mádhva āhutim yámaśvatthámupatísthanta jāyávo' smé té santu jāyávaḥ.*

sākám gāvaḥ súvate pácyate yavo ná te vāya úpa dasyanti dhenávo nāpa dasyanti dhenávaḥ. RV. I. 135.8.

28. *yásmin vṛksé madhvádah suparnā niviśánte súvate cādhi víśve.*

tásyéd āhuḥ píppalam svādvágre tánnónnasad yáḥ pitáram ná véda. Ibid., I. 164.22.

29. *átrāpaśyam viśpátim saptáputram. Ibid., I. 164.1.*

saptá svásāro abhí sám navante.

yátra gávām níhitā saptá nāma. Ibid., I. 164.3.

30. T.N. Ramachandran quoted by S.R. Rao, *Lothal and the Indus Civilization* (1978) pp. 137-8.

31. *Ibid., pp. 138-9.*

32. *Ibid., p. 138.*

33. Buddha Prakash, *Ṛgveda and the Indus Valley Civilization* (Hoshiarpur, 1966) pp. 24 ff.

34. *Ibid., p. 29.*

35. *devás tvásta savitā visvárūpah. pupósa prajāh purudhā jajana. RV. III. 55.19.*

36. Buddha Prakash, *Ṛgveda and the Indus Valley Civilization.* pp. 29-30.

37. *tryambakam yajāmahe sugándhim pusti várdhanam*

urvārukámiva bándhanān mrtyór muksīya mām 'rtat. RV. VII. 59.12.

38. *ámbika ha vai nāmāsya svása. táyā syaisá sahá bhāgas tad yádasyaisá striyā sahá bhāgas. tásmāt tryambako nāma. Satapatha Brāhmaṇe II. 6.2.9*

39. *RV. IV. 58.3.*

POLLEN ANALYSIS AND CHEMICAL EXAMINATIONS OF A PREHISTORIC LAKE SITE AT DAMDAMA

M.D. Kajale and B.C. Deotare*

Abstract

The paper embodies results of pollen analysis and microfossil preservational potentials of a prehistoric lake site in the immediate vicinity of a Mesolithic occupational site of Damdama in Pratapgrah district of Uttar Pradesh. It also accounts for poor preservation of microfossils in minerogenic and intermittently anaerobic (seasonally exposed) deposits in terms of chemical factors such as Hydrogen Ion Concentration (pH), Oxidation-Reduction Potential (EH) and organic carbon content. Further, It also helps us to know the palaeoenvironmental conditions during the course of deposition of the lake sediments.

Introduction

In tropical climatic zones of India, most of the archaeological sites are associated with the minerogenic alluvial sediments and have been subjected to limited pollen analysis (Kajale & Rajaguru, in press; vishnu Mittre & Gupta 1978) for understanding local vegetational environment witnessed by Prehistoric Man. Unfortunately, the sites ideal for pollen analysis are not necessarily archaeologically promissing. And archaelogically fertile deposits in many cases are not highly suitable for preservation of microfossils. The lakes and swamps developed in anaerobic environment with acidic pH are supposed to be congenial for pollen preservation. At the site of Damdama, luckily we have had a Mesolithic occupational site belonging to c. 10,000 to 5000 B.C. (Verma et al. 1985) adjacent to an ancient lake bow swamp representing a defunct river course. Hence it was thought that his area might offer an ideal situation for pollen analysis and could provide vegetational sequence correlatable to the mesolithic occupation. Similar earlier attempts of pollen analysis by Gupta (1978) of horse shoe lake in the Ganga Valley in the vicinity of Sarai Nahar Rai in Pratapgarh district were successful. He deduced four phases of vegetational development in the last 8,000 years and inferred arable and pastoral economy chiefly based on the cereal pollen to have begun around 4500 bp. Pant & Pant (1980) have reported a few microfossils from the horse shoe lake with reference to the archaeological sites of Chopni-Mando and Mahadaha in the Ganga valley and indicated grassland vegetation in the past.

The Site and the problem

The Mesolithic site of Damdama (26 °10' N and 82 °10' 36" E) is situated on a terrace formed on the confluence of two branches of Tambul nulla (Fig. 1). The habitational deposit is 1.5 m thick and the pollen site is about 50 m. north of the highest point on the habitational mound. The habitational mound is roughly roundish in shape and the adjoining lake is now partially silted and also under cultivation. It forms a dry lake bed during non - rainy seasons. During monsoon, the habitational site gets completely surrounded by lake waters giving an appearance of an island. From the trenches dug for stratigraphic in the vicinity of the habitational site indicate that during prehistoric times the entire settlement must have been surrounded by rich biological resources besides providing suitable ecological niche to the prehistroic Man.

Verma et al. (1985) have brought to notice non-agricultural subsistence strategy adopted by microliths using communities practising systematic burial of the dead during early Holocene times, besides exploitation of wild animals, like antelope, pig, stag, deer, rhinoceros, elephants, gaur, neelgai, various birds, fishes, tortoies, etc. Kajale (1988, in press) has thrown light on the palaeobotanical evidence for Mesolithic plant Economy belonging to nearly ten wild plant species representing broad-spectrum exploitation of vegetal food. It is against the background of the previous works that the pollen analysis of the adjacent lake deposits had aroused great interest.

The Methods

The sample were collected from a freshly dug trench of 3 x 3 x 2 m in the dried lake bed. At the bottom, yellowish alluvial silt (locally known as 'Khadar') is present. It occurs from 1.6 to 2 m from the top. It is overlain by silty clay (0.3 to 1.6 m from the top) with yellowish red patches formed due to limonitisation of the lake sediments. It is overlain by 0.3 m thick modern soil with humus (Fig. 2) Total depth of 1.8 m. was sampled at an interval of 10 cm each from bottom (1.8 m) to top. All the sample were treated with few drpos of carbolic acid to prevent post -collection fungal growth.

The samples were processed using 40% hydrofluoric acid and as per the methods given by Faegri and Iversen (1964). However, no acytolysis was done. Since most of the samples were clayey, they used to remain in suspension for a very long time. Such samples were left undistrubed for 24 to 72 hours for proper settling, thus avoiding dependence on ultra-centrifuge. In order to appreciate the chemical nature of the sediments, they were also analysed for Hydrogen Ion

* Deccan College Postgraduate and Research Institute, Pune - 411006

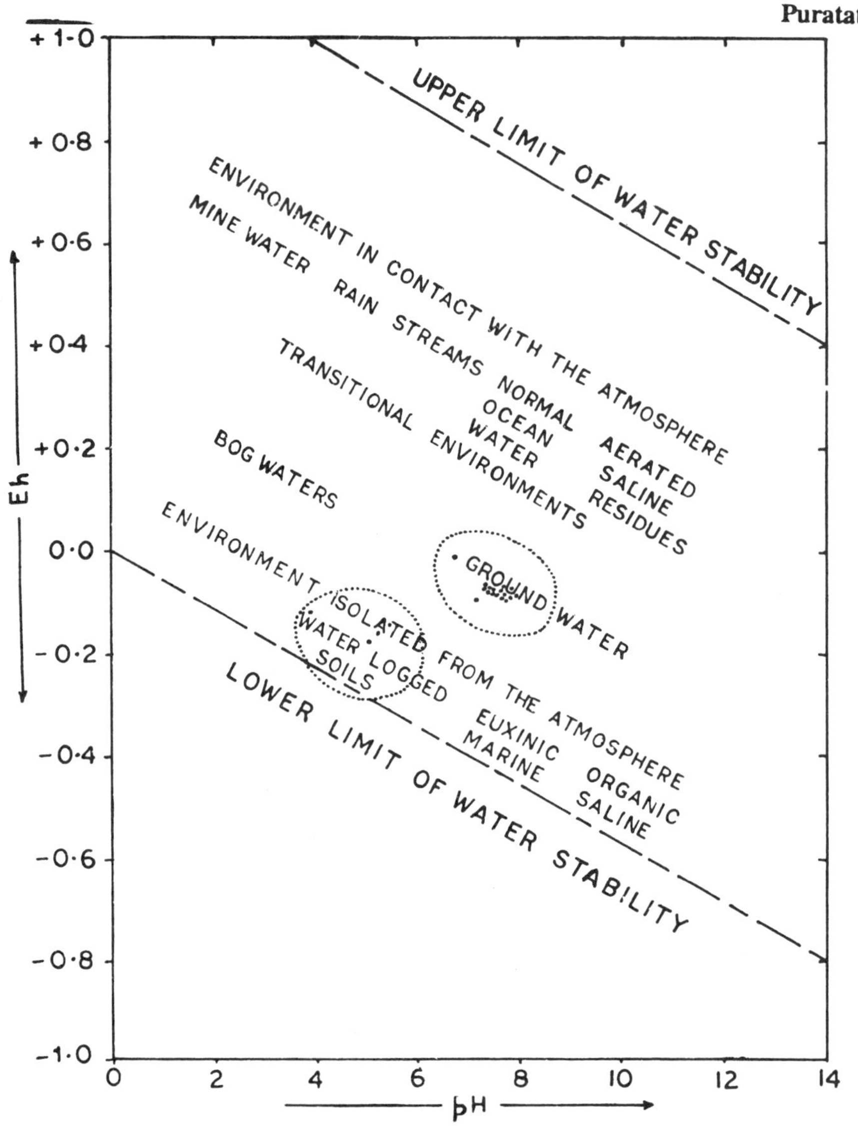

FIG. 3 APPROXIMATE POSITION OF SOME NATURAL ENVIRONMENTS IN TERMS OF Eh and pH USING GARRELS'S (1960) MODEL

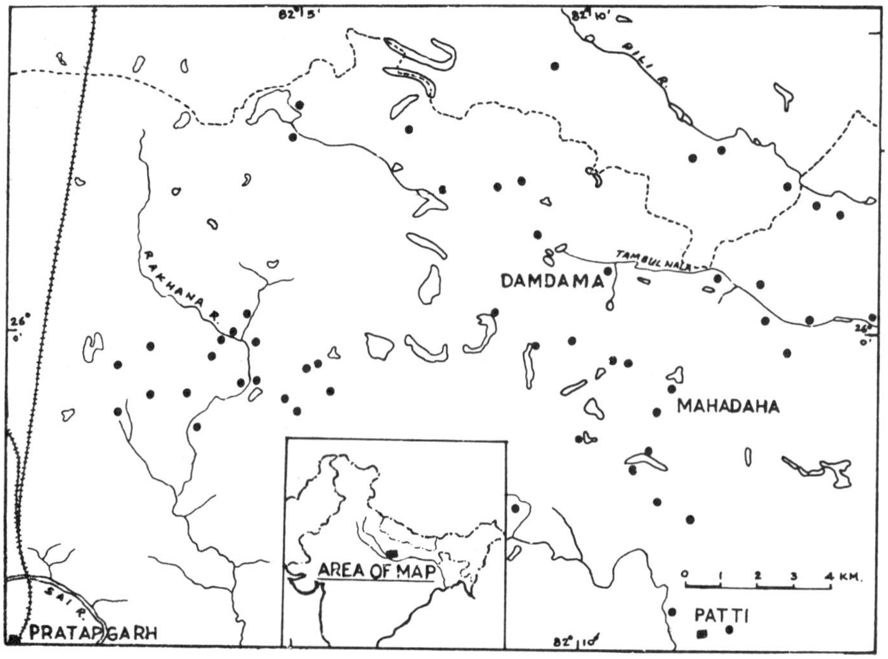

FIG. 1 MAP SHOWING LOCATION OF THE SITE (AFTER PAL, 1985)

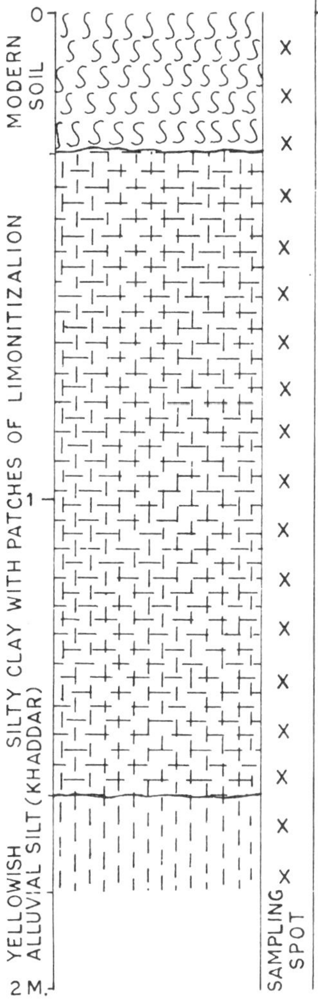

O.C. %	pH	Eh
1·01	6·8	-0·093
0·35	7·2	-0·09
0·30	7·5	-0 05
0·18	7·6	-0·06
0·14	7·8	-0·07
0·24	7·7	-0·07
0·11	7·5	-0·07
0·07	7·6	-0·04
0·08	7·5	-0·06
0·08	7·8	-0·07
0·08	7·5	-0·07
0·09	7·5	-0·05
0·22	7·4	-0·05
0·24	7·7	-0·04
0·07	7·8	-0·08
0·10	7·6	-0·08
0·12	7·9	-0·09
0·24	8·2	-0·02

FIG. 2 STRATIGRAPHY AND CHEMICAL NATURE OF THE SEDIMENTS FROM DAMDAMA

Concentration (pH), Oxidation - Reduction Potential (Eh) and organic carbon content. The pH was determined with the help of a pH meter using 1:1 prporation of sediment to water. Eh has been determined using null balance potentiometer with glass and platinum electrodes in suspension of equal proporation of sediment and water as given by Langmuir (1971). The organic carbon content has been determined by using sulphuric acid-dichromate oxidation followed by colorimetric determination as per Datta (1962).

Results

Of eighteen samples proceesed, the fifteen from the lower levels were found to be extremely poor. The upper three samples yielded a few pollen representing surfical incorporation. A few fungal spores are present in the lower level samples. Eventhough this disappoints us palynoloically, the chemical nature of the sediments in terms of pH, Eh and organic carbon content (Fig.2) is extremely significant from the viewpint of understanding causes for their poor preservation. pH of all the samples are within the rang of 6.8 to 8.2 Lowermost and topmost sampels show 6.8 and 8.2 pH respectively indicating neutral to alkaline nature of the sediments. The organic carbon content is in general very low except the top three samples which contains 1.01, 0.35 and 0.30 percent organic carbon. The organic carbon content varies within the range of 0.06 to 0.2 per cent in case of remaining samples. The oxidation - reduction potential of the eighteen samples is very low and range from - 0.02 to - 0.09.

Discussions

Despite lacustral nature of the deposits analysed, there is hardly any preservation of the pollen and this needs to be explained in terms of chemical factors and depositional palaeoenvironment. The alkaline sediments are in general low in organic carbon content. It speaks for high probability of oxidation during and after the deposition of the sediments. Krumbein and Garrels (1952) studied chemical nature of the sediments from three distinct evironments, i.e. normal marine open circulation environment, restricted humid (euxinic) environment and restricted arid (evaporite) enivronment. They concluded that pH and Eh afford two basis controls and determine the chemical nature of the end products fromed by the inorganic and biochemcial reactions. Baas Becking et al (1960) gave the limits of natural environment in terms of pH and oxidation-reduction potentials. They established that the Eh-pH- limits of biological systems and of the natural acqueous environment coincide. Gerrel (1960) constructed diagrammtic representation of some natural environment in terms of Eh and pH. Taking hints from these basic principles, we have applied this methodology to the pollen analysed deposits and the results have been expressed in figure 3. Most of our samples fall in the zone of partially oxidising depositional environment. Secondly, limonitised patches in the sediment profile clearly indicate intermittent exposure of the sediment and this may be because of groundwater fluctuations during wet and dry seasons as it happens even these days. Similar view have also been expressed by Tschudy (1969) who have suggested that the lack of palynomorphs in the calcareous deposits is not a function of the alkalinity alone but is a function of the relatvely long period that they have been in contact with the oxygenated environment or of the original lack of the availibility of palynomorphs to be preserved. Eventhough this appears to be a familiar fact, it has been substantiated here at the site of Damdama with the help of analytical data from chemical factors.

To have a cross check on this methodology, we selected a few samples from a know depositional environment of the humid tropical anaerobic swamps in Manipur area. The samples are distinctly acidic (pH ranging from 3.9 to 5.5) and relatively high oxidation - reduction potential (Eh ranging from -0 .128 to - 0.148), thereby suggesting oxygen free depositional conditions during sedimentation. This is quite unlike sediments from Damdama where we infer intermittent seasonal exposures due to ground water fluctuations resulting in limonitisation and unfavourable chemical factors attributable to extermely poor preservation of pollen.

Acknowledgement

Grateful thanks are due to prof. V.D. Misra of the Department of Archaeology, Allahabad University for kindly inviting one of us (MDK) to undertake botanical investigations on the Mesolithic site of Damdama. Sincere thanks are also due to Dr.J.N. Pande and Dr. J.N. Pal for all the help in the field. The authors are grateful to Prof. M.K. Dhavalikar and Prof. S.N. Rajaguru for the encouragement and general academic facilities.

References

BAAS BECKING, L.G.M., KAPLAN, R.M. & D.MOORE (1960). Limits of the natural environment in terms of pH and Oxidation-Reduction Potentials. *Journal of Geology*, 68 : 243-284.

DATTA, N.P. (1962). A Rapid Colorimetric Procedure for the Determination of Organic Carbon in Soil. *Journal of Indian Society of Soil Science*, 10 : 67-74.

FAEGRI, K. & J. IVERSEN (1964). *Textbook of Pollen Analysis*, Blackwell Scientific Publications, Oxford.

GARRELS, R.M. (1960). *Mineral Equlibria at low Temperature and Pressure*. Happer & Brothers, p. 254.

GUPTA, H.P. (1978). Holocene Palynology from meander lake in the Ganga valley, District Pratapgarh, Uttar Pradesh. *Palaeobotanoist*, 25 : 109-119.

KAJALE, M.D 1988. Palaeobotanical Evideence for Mesolithic Plant Economy from Exacavations at Damdama, District Pratapgarh, Uttar Pradesh (Paper presented at the National seminar of Indian Society for Prehistoric and Quaternary Studies, held at Visvabharati, Santiniketan during 1st to 3rd December 1988)

KAJALE, M.D. AND S.N.RAJAGURU (1989). Quaternary Gomorphological and Pollen Analytical observartions around Nirgudsar in the Ghod valley, Upland Maharashtra : Some Preliminary Observations (In press).

KRUMBEIN, W.F. & R.M. GARRELS (1952). Origin and Classification of Chemical sediments in terms of pH and Oxidation - Reduction Potentials. *Journal of Geology*, 60 : 1-33.

LANGMUIR , D. (1971). Eh-pH Determination. In *Procedures in Sedimentary Petrology*, Carver, R.E. (Ed.), Willey Interscience, New York, pp: 597-634

PAL, J.N. (1985). Some New Light on the Mesolithic Burial Practices of the Ganga Valley : Evidence from Mahdaha, Uttar Pradesh. *Man and Environment*, p. 28-44

PANT, D.D. & REKHA PANT (1980). Preliminary Observations on Pollen Flora of Chopani Mando (Vindhyas) and Mahadaha (Ganga Valley). In *Beginnings of Agriculture* by Sharma, G.R., Misra, V.D., Mandal, D., Misra, B.B. and J.N. Pal, Abinash Prakashan, Allahabad, pp. 229-230

TSCHUDY, R.H. (1969). Relationship of Palynomorphs to Sedimentation. In *Aspects of Palynology*, (Eds.) Tschudy, R.H. and A. Scott, Wiley Interscience, New Yorks, pp : 79-96.

VERMA, R.K., MISRA, V.D. PANDEY, J.N. AND J.N. PAL (1985) A Preliminary Report on the Excavations at Damdama (1982- 1984). *Man and Environment*, 9 : 45-65.

VISHNU MITTRE & H.P. GUPTA (1976).Pollen Analysis of fossil soils along the bank of river Ghod, Inamgaon, Maharashtra. *Palaeobotanist*, 23 (1) : 72-77.

ON FLAKE-BLADE ELEMENT IN INDIA

Ashok K. Ghosh*
Dipankar Chaudhury*

Preamble

In the scientific study of any kind, the problem of terminology is indeed important because it serves the purpose of communication. This is due to this reason, the terminology would be such that it would be devoid of any ambiguity and must be understandable to all concerned.Terminology, again is an expression with connotation, and care should be taken to develop meaningful terminology. This is well explained in the context of terminology and its change with regard to Palaeolithic culture complex of the Old World. The three-fold division of Palaeolithic culture, lower, middle and upper first emerged in the European context. From the circumstantial evidences the above terminology was found to be apt. But the problem aroseo when the same scheme of terminology was extended further under different context. In Africa, for the Palaeolithic culture, the concept of European terminology was extended further under different context. In Africa, for the Palaeolithic culture, the concept of European terminology was in vogue for a long time. But at times it was difficult to explain the period and the industrial component of Palaeolithic Africa in the light of European counterpart. Naturally, new and appropriate terminology was sought for, and finally the total scheme of terminology in africa was changed and gave rise to three broad periodization, viz. Early Stone Age, Middle Stone Age and Late Stone Age. These three periods cover the entire stone age in Africa. Later, modification was made for the improvement and in due course two more minor periods were suggested, viz. First Intermediate and Second Intermediate, which were placed between Early and Middle Stone Ages, and Middle and Late Stone Ages respectively.

The condition in South Asia is somewhat different, and here south Asia is represented by the sub-continent of India, and other parts are excluded. Since 1863 palaeoliths are being discovered from Indian sub-continent (Foote, 1866). Through this very long span time period, which covers more than a century, the terminological nomenclatures went on changing. Foote (1866) followed the European concept, and the same concept was continued until 1930 when new terminologies were suggested on the basis of typological features and technological peculiarities of an industrial assemblage found from the Kurnool (Burkitt and Cammiade, 1930). This is more on a classificatory system of tool series than the periodization of industrial complexes, and the division was made into four series, as I, II, III and IV. The same series concept again reappeared after a quarter of a century, and emphasis was given on broad typology of tools. In this classification, the tendency of over simplification is very marked, and it was proposed to classify the palaeolithic industries in terms of three Series, I, II and III (Sankalia, 1956). In fact, the classification is merely of tools and their typology in very broad way, but in no way the same classification can be used for ascertaining the industries, because the stratigraphic implication is completely devoid of. Under such circumstance, the tool typology can hardly be classified in the same scheme.

It was felt that none of the terminological nomenclature which was being used is satisfactory, and the seeking for ideal terminology was continued. In 1958, a new suggestion was made and Early Stone Age, Middle Stone Age and Late Stone Age came into use (Subbarao,1958). In the truest sense of the term this terminology can not be considered as new, but it may be explained as the influence of African terminology. Endeavours were made to get rid of the influence, but instead of European influence this time it came from Africa. The inevitable result was the reappearance of problems and difficulties. To avoid these, some scholars used this terminology with minor change (Allchin, 1959; Mohapatra, 1962; Misra, 1967) but the total problem could not be eradicated. Some more proposals were made by scholars, and either they are of the similar nature as mentioned above or the terms were local in nature, as found in the Soan sequence (De Terra and Paterson, 1939). The terms of the second category can not be used in the pan-Indian context.

MATERIALS

The industries belonging to Flake-Blade element has a considerably wide distribution in India. But due to lack of precise data on this element, at times some proportions of màterials from the Flake element have been included. Most of the information on the typology are of surface finds, without any information on the geological context, and as such the types of the Flake-Blade element are hard to be separated. Under the circumstance, the selection of materials was made with great care and precaution. Types which can easily be identified as belonging to Flake element on the basis of nature of technology, neatness in the typology, raw materials, etc. have been intentionally excluded.

The selected materials reveal a more or less representative picture for the whole of Indian sub-continent. In this work, the coverage is made on five major geographical regions. The total sample comprises 2094 pieces. The regionwise breakup of samples is shown in Table-1. It may be said that within the total sample, a fraction (100) has been included from Pakistan.

* Department of Authropology, Calcutta University, Calcutta

Table - 1

REGIONWISE BREAKUP OF SAMPLES UNDER STUDY

I. India : 1769		
1. Northern region	96	
a. Himachal Pradesh		82
b. Uttar Pradesh		14
2. Western region -	305	
a. Gujarat		10
b. Maharashtra		272
c. Rajasthan		23
3. Central region -	379	
a. Madhya Pradesh		379
4. Eastern region -	496	
a. Bihar		475
b. West Bengal		03
c. Orissa		18
5. Southern region -	493	
a. Andhra		72
b. Mysore		154
c. Tamil Nadu		267
II. Pakistan - 100		
a. West Punjab		100
III. Miscellaneous -		225
(Without specific location of site, but all from India)		
Total :		2094

In the total population, there is some amount of disparity. This primarily Includes unequal number of specimens. From northern region the sample is relatively little (96). In rest of the regions, despite the difference in number the sample size is sufficient, varying between 305 and 493. For Pakistan, especially of West Punjab for obvious constrains, the size of the sample is restricted to 100. A total number of 225 specimens have also been included on regional identity. In spite of the fact, these have been included for this study. At least, in the present case the comparison on regional basis has not been taken into account. Work along this line may be continued further with bigger samples, covering more sites. In such case areal comparison may also be made.

Out of this total sample of 2094 pieces, further subdivision has been made on the basis of tools with form of raw materials and pieces which are not tools (Table - 2).

Table - 2

DISTRIBUTION OF SPECIMENS, TOOLS AND NOT TOOLS, ACCORDING TO FORMS OF MATERIAL

	Frequency	%
Tools on core	162	7.73
Tools on flake	1448	69.14
Tools on blade like flake	205	9.79
Tools on blade	137	6.54
Blank	76	3.63
Core chips	50	2.39
Unidentified	16	0.76
	2094	

The assemblage within the sample shows that there is conspicous domination of tools made on flakes (69.14%). Tools on blade like flakes (9.79%) and on blades (6.54%) are minimum. Though when these two forms of material are taken together (16.33%) the presence of the same turns higher. On the other hand, tools made on core are quite less (7.73%). The above result points to the fact that the industry is basically on flake with the addition of blades and of intermittent blade-like flakes. Above all, a few tools are still there which could not be fabricated other than core.

The sample, pulled and under consideration, has been examined in necessary details. With a view to achieving utmost precision and accuracy on-spot work was carried out in the Department of Ancient Indian history, Culture and Archaeology of Punjab University, Deccan College, Department of Anthropology of Calcutta University and Indian Museum, Calcutta.

Extension of the work was further made with the help of available reports. Areawise references include Himachal Pradesh (Mohapatra, 1966, 1973), Uttar Pradesh (Sharma, 1969; report made by Sankalia, 1962), Gujarat (Ansari and Pappu, 1970-72), Maharashtra (Todd, 1939; Sankalia, 1952, 1956; Malik, 1959), Rajasthan (Misra, 1967; Allchin et al, 1972), Madhya Pradesh (Ghosh, 1961; Khatri, 1961, 1962; Sen and Ghosh 1963), Bihar (Ghosh, 1966, 1970), West Bengal (Ghosh 1962; Sen, Ghosh and Chatterjee, 1963), Orissa (Mohapatra, 1962; Ghosh and Basu, 1969), Andhra Pradesh (Murty 1968, 1970), Mysore (Joshi, 1955), Tamil Nadu (Foote, 1966), Aiyappan and Manley, 1942) and West Punjab (De Terra and Paterson, 1939).

METHODOLOGY

The main aim of the present study is to find out the standardized tool typology on the basis of the clustering of characters. It is indeed essential to establish a well recognized type list which comprises the major types and their classification. This is needed for the purpose of necessary communication through approval vocabularies. the typological terminology primarily serves two functions, one, for communicating complex series of observations, and secondly, it helps to formulate the structure on methodology.

For the purpose of precision in methodology and studying the materials objectively, the major features of the tools have been considered in terms of attributes. Each attribute has been subdivided into a number of values which are mutually exclusive and cover the entire range of variation of specific attributes. The selection of relevant attributes is made on the basis of morphological, technological and assumed functional implications.

The attributes are the main component of the present study, and for the purpose of clarity the major attributes along with their vlaues have been included here. The attribute is taken as the field. In the same way the vlaues are termed as categories. Along with values the numerical proportion in terms of frequency and percentage for each attributes and their vlaues have been tabulated here (Table-3).This will also indicate the total population of samples on the one hand and the numerical preponderance of each value on the other. In other words, the data part is more important for the purpose of understanding the characteristic features of the specimens. Here the data have been presented in necessary detail.

It requires to be mentioned that the attributes, expressed as field and the sub-attribute or the category have been selected from a large number of attributes with a view to find out only the relevant points which form the characteristics of the types. The selection of the same has been made on the basis of a trial analysis. In course of this exercise, the irrelevant parts have been excluded.

Table - 3

LIST OF THE FIELD WITH CATEGORY SHOWING FREQUENCY AND PERCENTAGE

Sl. No.	Field	Category	Frequency	%
01.	Raw material	Quartzite	537	25.64
		Quartz	80	3.82
		Flint	2	0.10
		Agate	64	3.05
		Jasper	400	19.10
		Chalcedony	106	5.06
		Chert	892	42.59
		Others	13	0.62
02.	Types of material	Core	162	7.73
		Flake	1448	69.14
		Blade like Flake	205	9.79
		Blade	137	6.54
		Blank	76	3.63
		Core chip	50	2.39
		Unidentified	16	0.76
03.	State of preservation	Fresh	90	4.30
		Slightly weathered	769	36.72
		Moderately weathered	1101	62.57
		Heavily weathered	133	6.35
		Unidentified	1	0.05
04.	General shape	Rectangular	231	11.03
		Roughly rectangular	409	19.53
		Rounded	249	11.89
		Oval	395	18.86
		Triangular	278	13.27
		Trapezoidal	164	7.83
		Semi-circular	76	3.63
		Amorphous	292	13.94
05.	Transverse Cross-section	Triangualr	829	39.58
		Trapezoidal	318	15.18
		Biconvex	398	19.00
		Plano-convex	433	20.67
		Concavo-convex	48	2.29
		Others	12	0.57
		Amorphous	56	2.67
06.	Longitudinal Cross-section	Biconvex	379	18.09
		Plano-convex	377	18.00
		Concavo-convex	134	6.39
		Triangular	258	12.32
		Trapezoidal	857	40.92
		Others	50	2.38
		Amorphous	39	1.86
07.	Striking platform	Unworked	316	15.08
		Simple worked	364	41.25
		Detailed worked	318	15.18
		Unidentified	369	17.62
		Absent	227	10.84
08.	Nature of bulb of percussion	Positive	1506	71.91
		Negative	30	1.43
		Flat	1	0.05
		Absent	557	26.59
09.	Angle at the striking platform	More acute	5	0.24
		Less acute	16	0.76
		Right angle	186	8.88
		Less obtuse	480	22.92
		Medium obtuse	516	24.64
		More obtuse	144	6.87
		Not measurable	251	11.98
		Absent	496	23.68
10.	Bulb of percussion	Prominent bulb	767	36.62
		Bulbar Scar	438	20.91
		Bulbar area worked	167	7.97
		Indistinct	140	6.68
		Broken	7	0.33
		Absent	575	27.45
11.	Location of bulb of percussion	Distal	99	4.73
		Proximal	1033	49.32
		Lateral (Left)	111	5.30
		Lateral (Right)	67	3.20

		Corner (DL)	15	0.72
		Corner (DR)	15	0.72
		Corner (PL)	95	4.53
		Corner (PR)	64	3.05
		Absent	595	28.41
12.	Centrical surface	All over	2	0.10
		Mostly present	40	1.91
		Partially present	500	23.87
		Slightly present	142	6.78
		Absent	1410	67.33
13.	Area of butt	Small	549	26.21
		Medium	1150	54.91
		Large	379	18.10
		Absent	16	0.76
14.	Thickness of butt	Thin	459	21.92
		Medium	1422	67.90
		Thick	197	9.40
		Absent	16	0.76
15.	Location of cutting edge	Lateral (one side)	1067	50.95
		Lateral (both side)	281	13.42
		Distal	379	18.10
		2 adjoining sides	231	11.03
		3 adjoining sides	106	5.06
		All round	30	1.43
16.	Profile of cutting edge	Straight	456	21.77
		Broad wavy	82	2.91
		Medium wavy	112	5.35
		Narrow wavy	208	9.93
		Sinuous	1037	49.52
		Denticulated	199	9.50
17.	Shape of cutting edge	Straight	687	32.80
		Convex	968	46.22
		Concave	97	4.63
		Concavo-convex	59	2.82
		Pointed	168	8.02
		Notched	18	0.86
		Round	36	1.72
		Flat (Burin)	13	0.62
		Straight pointed	4	0.19
		Convex pointed	26	1.24
		Straight convex	16	0.76
		Straight concave	2	0.10
18.	Nature of marginal retouch	Fine	1116	53.29
		Medium	388	18.53
		Heavy	57	2.72
		Scaled	1	0.05
		Flat	5	0.24
		Denticulated	164	7.83
		Absent	363	17.28
19.	Location of the marginal retouch	Right lateral side	318	15.18
		Left lateral side	596	28.46
		Both lateral sides	233	11.12
		Distal side	286	13.66
		Proximal side	2	0.10
		Both sides	4	0.19
		All sides	30	1.43
		2 adjoining sides	189	9.02
		3 adjoining sides	74	3.53
		Absent	362	17.28
20.	Arrangement of marginal retouch	Obverse (dorsal)	189	9.02
		Obverse (ventral)	71	3.39
		Inverse	216	10.31
		Absent	1618	77.26
21.	Extent of marginal retouch	Sporadic	112	5.35
		Partial	733	35.00
		Continuous	883	42.16
		Absent	366	17.48
22.	Ridges on dorsal surface	Single	421	20.10
		Single cum double	398	19.00
		Double	279	13.32
		Multiple	821	39.20
		Absent	175	8.35
23.	Nature of ventral surface	Single flake scar	1570	74.97
		2-3 flake scars	345	16.47
		Multiple flake scars	152	7.26
		Contexted	27	1.29
24.	Direction of flake scars	Undirectional	195	9.31
		Bidirectional	747	35.67
		Multidirectional	1148	54.82
		Unidentified	4	0.19
25.	Shape of flake scar	Round	115	5.49
		Triangular	184	8.78
		Rectangular	660	31.51
		Irregular	1132	54.05
		Unidentified	3	0.14
26.	Size of flake scar	Small	165	7.88
		Medium	709	33.85
		Large	262	12.51
		Absent	958	45.74
27.	Size of flake scar	Small & medium	543	25.93

	(not uniform)	Small & large	80	3.82
		Medium & large	194	9.26
		Small medium & large	142	6.78
		Absent	1135	54.19
28.	Number of flake scar	Scanty	635	30.32
		Medium	1251	59.73
		Numerous	206	9.84
		Nil	2	0.10
29.	Trace of utilization	Present	1429	68.23
		Unidentified	516	24.64
		Absent	149	7.11
30.	Nature of utilization	Bruised	376	17.95
		Battered	463	22.11
		Ground	280	13.37
		Glazed	3	0.38
		Broken	300	14.32
		Absent	667	31.85
31.	Primary technique	Clactonian	437	20.86
		Levalloisian	984	46.99
		Mousterian	22	1.05
		Blade	368	17.57
		Unidentified	283	13.51
32.	Secondary technique	Free flaking	30	1.43
		Controlled flaking	1893	90.44
		Step flaking	15	7.35
		Unidentified	2	0.10

As all the fields and the categories of the attributes, mentioned above, are known-the detail descriptions of the same have been avoided here. But it may be noted that all the values are in accordance with the standard parameter.

ANALYSIS AND CLASSIFICATION

So far as the differnet attributes possessed by the specimens and their variable values are concerned, a list of the same has already been supplied earlier. Now it is necessary to find out which of the different attributes, under study, are important to discriminate between different groups or classes or types of tools. Unless it is stated with a system of classes or groups and with specimens belonging to such other groups or types, it is not possible to assess the extent to which the particular attributes distinguished between different types or groups. To this effect, the following 16 conventional types were recognised and the specimens were classified according to the conventional types and the categories of a particular attribute. The 16 conventional classes are as follows :

01. Scraper - side
02. Scraper - end
03. Scraper - Side-cum-end
04. Scraper - round
05. Scraper - nosed
06. Scraper - hollow
07. Scraper - side-cum-hollow
08. Point
09. Point-cum-scraper
10. Borer
11. Borer-cum-scraper
12. Burin
13. Knife
14. Awl
15. Blade
16. Others

Possible association between different categories of an attribute and the above mentioned 16 conventional classes were detected by carrying out the usual x^2 test of association between two classifications of specimens. The formula applied for this purpose applicable k x l contigency table, having k rows and l columns, is given below :

$$x^2 = \sum_{i=1}^{k} \sum_{f=1}^{l} \frac{fij^2}{fiofoj} - n$$

where fij is the frequency in the cell at the intersection of row number i and column number j, fio is the total frequency in row number i, foj is the total frequency in column number j and n is the grand total frequency. Here the number of conventional types is 16 appearing along the rows, hence the vlaue of k is always 16, while the value of l is the number of categories of an attribute and hence varies from one attribute to another.

The value of x^2 obtained from any such contigency table and the joint distribution can be tested by comparing its value with the value of the percentage point a 1% or 5% significance level of the x^2 distribution corresponding to (k-l) (l-l) degrees of freedom. It has been found by applying tests that all the attributes show significant associations between their categories and the 16 conventional types. In a sense, it indicates that all attributes studied are important for distinguishing different conventional classes or types.

From the total number of attributes, a number of them was selected on the basis of highest x^2 values, and they are : material types, general shape, location and shape of the cutting edge, profile of the cutting edge, primary technique and secondary techniques. These attributes are also expected to discriminate more effectively than other attributes between different tool types.

Studies on multivariate and proximity analyses with the specimens brought to a list of 28 classes. From the existing and conventional typological list again 16 main types with their salient features may be considered as follows. Although for a number of types, there are more than one unit type which may be labelled as sub-type. This division is primarily based on form of raw material, viz. core, flake, flake-blade and blade. For differentiation of a single type in the level of form of raw materials, additional differences are met with some characters, as of shape, size, thickness, cross-sections (logitudinal and transverse). At the same time, further distinctions are met with other features. These include arrangement of flake scars, form of lateral margin, details of proximal and distal parts, etc. The forementioned 16 major types are :

1. Side scraper : convex, single - on flake, blade, core and flake-blade.
2. Side scraper : straight, single - on flake, blade, core and flake-blade.
3. Side scraper : straight, double - on flake, blade, flake-blade.
4. Side scraper : straight, double - on flake, blade and flake-blade.
5. Concave scraper : Single - on flake
6. Side-cum-end scraper : on flake
7. End scraper : on flake and core
8. Side scraper : concavo-convex, double - on flake
9. Round scraper : on core
10. Point : on flake
11. Borer : on flake and core
12. Burin : on flake and core
13. Knife : double - on blade
14. Knife : double - on blade and flake-blade
15. Denticulate : single - on blade
16. Denticulate : double - on blade.

The above type list may be considered as a standard reference inventory for types of Flake-Blade elements from India. The same type list has also significant resemblance and affinity with the types and type list in other parts of the world (de Sonneville-Bordes and Perrot, 1954-1956; Bordes, 1961). It is interesting to note that a large number of types proposed here in this paper are found to be common with the European types. Examples of side scraper : straight, single; side scraper : straight, double; side scraper : convex, double; side scraper : concavo-convex, double; point; burin and denticulate are almost common in their features both in India and Europe. But types like side-cum-end scraper, round scrper, borer and knife which have emerged in this classification have seldom been mentioned in other works.

It requires to be indicated that in the list, already mentioned, with 16 major types, the sub-type level (based on form of material) give rise to a total of 30 units. In the type series there are units with varied assemblage of form of raw materials. These includes core; flake; blade; core and flake; flake flake lake-blade and blade; core, flake, flake-blade and blade. The authors feel that at the level of identification of type to form of raw material is an important character. At the same time it is to be found out the relevance and utility of "flake-blade" to be considered as a specific indicator with regard to form of raw material. At times it turns difficult to identify a "flake-blade" either as blank or as a tool type made on same, from a flake or a blade. If the category of "flake-blade" is eliminated, the problem emerges of its inclusion with flake or blade. The same problem may perhaps be solved to some extent on the basis of its higher affinity - with flake or blade. Despite this, the other issue on chrohology based on technology and associated form of raw material may turn conspicuous. It is high time to consider this as one of basic premises. Of course for this, larger samples, especially from transitional phases from different parts of India, are essential for working out. Further work with more data and greater amount of precision along this line will lead to more concrete and comprehensive type list and that will serve the urgent need of standardization and better communication.

References

AIYAPPAN, A. and F.P. MANLEY 1942. The Manley collection of stone age tools with topographical and other notes. *Memoir of the Archaeological Survey of India* 68 : 1-90.

ALLCHIN, B. 1959. The Indian middle stone age : some new sites in central and southern India and their implications. *Bulletin of Institute of Archaeology, University of London* 11 (2) : 1-36.

ALLCHIN, B., K.T.M. HEGDE and ANDREW GOUDIE. 1972. Prehistory and environmental change in western India : a note on the Budha Pushkar basin, Rajasthan. *Man* n.s. 7 (4) : 527-540.

ANSARI, Z.D. and R.S. PAPPU 1970-1972. Stone age in Kutch Gujarat. *Bulletin of the Deccan College Research Institute 32* : 150-167.

BORDES, FRANCOIS 1961. *Typologie du ancien on moyen*. Publication de l'Institut de prehistoire do l'Universite de Bordeaux, Memoir no. 1. Imprimeries Delmas, Bordeaux.

BURKITT, M.C. and L.A. CAMMIADE 1930. Fresh light on the stone age in southeast Asia. *Antiquity* 4 : 327-329.

DE SONNEVILIE-BORDES, D. and J. PERROT 1954-1956. Lexique typologique du palaeolithique superieur. *Bulletin de la Societe Prehistorique Francaise* 51 : 327-335, 52 : 76-79, 53 : 408-412, 547-559.

DE TERRA, H. and T.T. PATERSON 1939. *Studies on the ice age in India and associated human cultures*. Washington : Carnegie Institute.

FOOTE, ROBERT BRUCE 1866. On the occurrance of stone implements in laterite formations in various parts of Madras and north Arcot districts. *Madras Journal of Literature and Science* 3(2) : 1-35.

GHOSH, ASOK K. 1961. A new lithic site in Mandla district. *The Eastern Anthropologist* 14(3) : 209-215.

GHOSH, ASOK K. 1962. Discovery of prehistoric stone implements from northwest Midnapur, West Bengal. *Science and Culture* 28 : 338-339.

GHOSH, ASOK K. and A. BASU 1969. An appraisal on the palaeolithic industry of Mayurbhanj in the light of recent discovery. *Science and culture* 35(9) : 476-479.

JOSHI, R.V. 1955. *Pleistocene studies in the Malaphrabha basin.* Poona-Dharwar.

KHATRI, A.P. 1961. Stone age and Pleistocene chronology of the Narmada valley (central India). *Anthropos* 56 : 519-530.

KHATRI, A.P. 1962. Origin and development of series II cultures of India. *Proceedings of Prehistoric Society*. 28 : 191-208.

MALIK, S. C. 1959. *Stone age industries of Bombay and Satára Districts*. M.S. University Archaeology series, No. 4, Baroda.

MISRA, V.N. 1967. *Pre-and Protohistory of the Berach basin.*

Poona : Deccan College.

MOHAPATRA, G.C. 1962. *The stone age culture of Orissa*. Poona: Deccan College.

MOHAPATRA, G.C. 1966. Preliminary report of exploration and excavation of stone age sites in eastern Punjab. *Bulletin of the Deccan College Research Institute.* 25 : 1-17.

MOHAPATRA, G.C. 1973 "Lithic industry of Himachal pradesh", in *Perspecitives in Palaeoanthropology*. Edited by Asok K. Ghosh, pp. 192-212. Calcutta : Firma K.L. Mukhopadhaya.

MURTHY, M.L.K. 1968. Blade and burin industries near Renigunta on the south-east coast of India. *Proceedings of the Prehistoric Society*, 34 : 83-101.

MURTHY, M.L.K. 1970. Blade and burin and late stone age industries around Renigunta, Chittor district. Indian Antiquary. Third Series, 4 (1-4) : 106-128.

SANKALIA, H.D. 1952. *The Godavari palaeolithic industry*. Poona.

SANKALIA, H.D. 1956. Animal fossils and palaeolithic industries from the Pravara basin at Nevasa, district Ahmednagar. *Ancient India* 12: 3-52.

SANKALIA, H.D. 1962. *Prehistory and Protohistory of India and Pakistan*. Poona : Deccan College.

SHARMA, G.R. 1969. *Report on explorations conducted by the Institute of Archaeology*, University of Allahabad. Allahabad.

SEN, D. and ASOK K. GHOSH 1963. Lithic culture complex in the Pleistocene sequence of the Narmada valley, Central India. *Rivista di Scienze Preistoriche* 18 : 3-23.

SEN, D., ASOK K. GHOSH and MANJU CHATTERJEE 1963. Palaeolithic industry of Bankura, West Bengal. *Man in India* 43(2) : 110-113.

SUBBARAO, B.P. 1958. *The personality of India : pre-and Protohistoric foundations of India and Pakistan. Baroda* : Maharaja Sayajirao University.

TODD, K.R.U. 1939. Palaeolithic industries of Bombay. *Journal of Royal Anthropological Institute* 49 : 257-272.

THE DATE OF KING DHANADEVA OF KOSALA : A RE-EXAMINATION OF THE PALAEOGRAPHIC AND HISTORICAL EVIDENCE

B.B. Lal and K.K. Sharma*

An inscription from Ranopāl–i, a suburb of Ayodhyā in Faizabad District, Uttar Pradesh, refers to one Dhanadeva who was the Lord of Kosala *(Kosalādhipati)*. The inscription occurs on a stone-slab which is now fixed at the floor-leval of the door of a recent shrine in Ranopālī. That evidently is not its real location. It must have originally been affixed to a building/shrine *(Ketana)* constructed by Dhanadeva for (or in the memory of) his father Phalgudeva, as mentioned in the inscription itself, which reads as follows (pl. ID) :

L.1. Kosalāhipena dvira'svamedha-yājinah

senāpateh Pushyamitra-sya shashṭhena

Kai (u) 'sikī– putreṇa Dhana ———

L.2. ———*Dharmarājñā Pituḥ*

Phalgudevasya Ketanaṁ Kāritaṁ

On palaeographic grounds, many scholars, e.g. D.C. Sircar (1965 : 95-96), A.H. Dani (1963 : 57-59) and T.P. Verma (1971 : 84), have assigned this inscription to the early or first half of 1st century A.D.

We propose here to examine this dating, both on plaeographic as well as historical grounds.

In the script of the inscription the following major palaeographic features are to be noted (Pl.I.D.).

(i) the two vertical strokes *sa* are almost equal;

(ii) and so are the vertical strokes of *pa;*

(iii) The various limbs of *la* join one another at an angle (instead of through curves);

(iv) The lower part of *ma* is in the form of a triangle, instead of being round;

(v) likewise, the *va* is angular instead of being round;

(vi) the back of *ja* is not vertical but is bent in the middle of the latter;

(vii) likewise, the basal line of *na* is not straight but bends in the middle (except in one case);

(viii) in one case, the left arm of *ya* shows marked inward curve; and

(ix) in most cases the heads or upper parts of the letters are thickened

We will take up every one of these features and discuss the same in the light of evidence from coins, sealing and inscriptions of a comparable period. (Cf. Pls. I-IV ; Fig. 1 and Table I.)

(i) *Sa.* -Its characteristic feature, viz. the equalization of the two verticals, may also be seen on the seal and coin of Dhanadeva from 'Ṣriṅgaverapura (Pls. I A and I B). It occurs on the Mathurā coins of Rāmadatta, 'Sivadatta, Hagāmasha, Rājuvula and Soḍāsa (Allan 1936 : 179-191; here Fig. 1 and Table I). While Allan places all these kings in the first century B.C., Sircar (1965 : 114) puts the last two around the beginning of the Christian era.

This feature also occurs on the coins of Bṛihaspatimitra II of Kauśambi i (Fig. 1 and Table I) whom Allan (1936 : 151) assigns a date in the late second century B.C. According to Sharma (1969 : 23), however, he may be placed around the middle of the first century B.C.

Again, this very feature is noticeable on the Pañchāla coins of S–uryamitra, Phalgunimitra, Bhadraghosha and Bh–umimitra (Fig. 1 and Table I) who may be placed in the 1st century B.C. (Allan 1936 : 193-199 and cxx). Raychaudhury (1938 : 327) identifies Bhadraghosha 'with Ghosh, the seventh king of the Purāṇic list of 'Sunga Kings'. He further states that 'Bhūmimitra may be identified with the Kaṇva king of the same name'. Both these kings undoubtedly ruled before the beginning of the Christian era.

In the Pabhosa inscriptions (Pls IIA and IV), which refer to the maternal uncle of Bṛihaspatimitra and are ascribed to the 1st century B.C. by Sircar himself (1965 : 96), the same feature may be witnessed in respect of *sa*. Fúhrer (1894), however, is inclined to place these inscription a bit earlier, i.e. in 'the second or first century B.C.'

A sealing of Agnimitra from Vaiśali (Pl. IC) also shows the same feature. S.R. Roy, the co-excavator of the site, is inclined to identify Agnimitra with the homonym of the 'Sunga dynasty, and places the sealing in the second half of the second century B.C.

That the two verticals of *sa* had begun to equalize even by the second half of the second century B.C. is also attested to by the Reh inscription (Pl IIIA) which, according to G.R. Sharma, refers to the Indo-Greek king Menander and may be dated to *c*. 150 B.C. (Sharma 1980 : 10)

(ii) *pa*.- As in the case of *sa*, so also in the case of *pa*, the two verticals are of almost equal height (Pl. ID). This feature is also noticeable on the coins [illegible] -tta, Hagāmasha, Rājuvula and 'Soḍāsa (Allan 1936: 183-190; here Fig. 1 and Table I). As already stated, Allan places all these kings in the first century B.C., though Sircar (1965 : 114) would like the last two to go to the beginning of the first century A.D.

Amongst the inscriptions that show this equalization feature in respect of *pa*, mention may be made of one from

* C/o. Archaecological Survey of India, Janpath, New Delhi-110-001

TABLE SHOWING PALAEOGRAPHIC COMPARISON

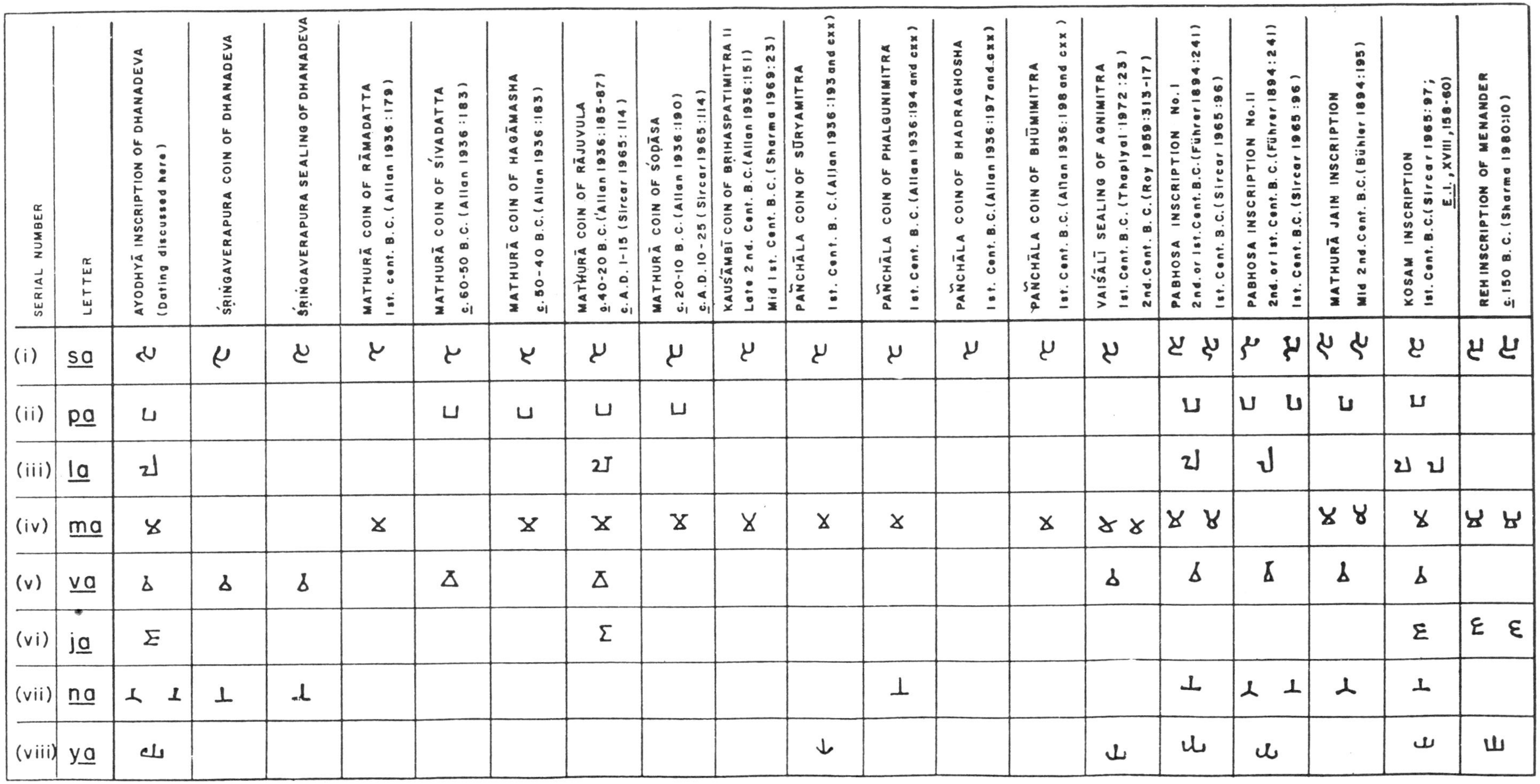

Kosam (Pl. III B) and two from Pabhosa (Pls.IIA and IV). All the three inscriptions are dated even by Sircar (1965 : 95-98) to the first century B.C. But Fuhrer (1894 : 241) thought that the Pabhosa ones may be earlier, ascribable to 'the second or first century B.C'.

(iii) *la*. -In the Ayodhyā inscription the various limbs of this letter join one another at an angle and not by means of curves. This feature is noticeable on the coins of Rājuvula (Allan 1936: 187; here Fig. 1). In this context, it may also be observed that whereas in the case of the Ayodhyā inscription the right-hand limb is longer and rises to a much greater height than does the left hand one (Pl. ID) in the case of the coin of Rājuvula, both the limbs have equal heights. Thus, if the equalization of the heights of the two vertical limbs is to be regarded as a sign of relative lateness, then the coins of Rājuvula will have to be treated as later than the inscription of Dhanadeva, and, as a result, the two rulers *inter se* too.

In so far as the other inscriptions are concerned, the angulation of *la* is clearly noticeable in those from Kosam (Pl IIIB) and Pabhosa (Pls IIA and IV). Thus, if we accept the dating of the Pabhosa inscriptions, as given by Fuhrer, to the second century B.C., this feature may be taken to have had its roots as early as that.

(iv) *ma*. -In the Ayodhyā inscription (Pl. ID), the lower part of this letter forms a triangle instead of circle. This feature may be noted on the Mathurā coins of Rāmadatta, Hagāmasha, Rājuvula and 'Sodāsa (Allan 1936 : 179-91), on the Kauśāmbi coin of Bṛihaspatimitra II (Allan 1936 :151) (here Fig. 1 and Table I), and on the Vaiśāli sealing of Agnimitra (Pl. IC), the dates of which, as already discussed above, go back to the first century B.C.

In so far the inscriptions are concerned, the triangulation of the lower part of *ma* appears to have commenced as early as the second century B.C., as indicated by the early Jain inscription from Mathurā (Bühler 1894 : 195 ff; here Pl. IIB) and by the Reh inscription of Menander (Sharma 1980 : Pl. VII; here Pl. III A). In the former case, both the rounded as well as the triangular varieties co-exist. The co-existence of both these features may also be noted in one of the Pabhosa inscriptions (Pl. IV) which are dated by Führer (1894 : 241) to the 'second or first century B.C.'. The Kosam inscription (Pl. III B), dated by Sircar (1965 : 97) to first century B.C., also has this feature.

(v) *va*. -In the case of *va* too, the lower part is triangular (Pl. ID). This is also to be observed in the case of the seal and coin of Dhanadeva from 'Sṛingaverapura (Pls. IA and IB).

The Mathurā coins of 'Sivadatta and Rājuvula show this feature (Allan 1936 : 183-91; here Fig. 1 and Table I C), and so does the sealing of Agnimitra from Vaiśāli (Pl. IC).

Of the inscriptions, those from Kosam (Pl. IIIB) and Pabhosa (Pls IIA and IV), which have been dated to the first century B.C. (Sircar 1965: 95-97) show this triangular formation of the lower part of *va*. That this feature may have originated still earlier is suggested by the evidence from the early Jain inscription from Mathurā (Pl. IIB), ascribed by Buhler (1894:195H) to 'the middle of the second century B.C.'

(vi) *ja*.-In the Ayodhyā inscription (Pl. ID), the vertical line of this letter show an inward bend in the middle. This feature has been taken as a sign of lateness Since it also occurs on the coins of Rājuvula. As stated earlier,, Allan dates this ruler, to the first century B.C., Whereas Sircar assigns him to the beginning of the Christian era. It may, however, be observed that this feature is noticeable in the Kosam inscription (Pl. IIIB), dated by Sircar (1965 : 97) to the first century B.C., as also in the Pabhosa Inscription No. I (Pl. IV), assigned by Führer (1894 : 241) to the 'Second or first century B.C.'

(vii) *na*. -In the case of this letter, the horizontal part has a bend (Pl. ID), which too has been taken as a sign of lateness. In fact, on this basis Dahejia (1972 :41) thinks that the Ayodhyā inscription of Dhanadeva may be later than even that of 'Soḍāsa from Mathurā.

It may, however, be noted that *this feature does not occur on the seal and coin of Dhanadeva* found at 'Sṛingaverapura (Pls. IA and IB).

But let that alone. There are at least two early inscriptions which show this very feature in respect of *na*, viz. (1) the early Jain inscription from Mathurā (Pl. IIB). and (ii) the Pabhosa Inscription No. II (Pl. IIA). Even according to Sircar (1965: 95-98), both these inscriptions are ascribable to the first century B.C., though Bühler (1894 : 195) would like to place the first one in 'the middle of the second century B.C.'

(viii) *ya*. -In the Ayodhyā inscription (Pl. ID), this letter shows an inward curvature of the left arm. The same has been taken to be a sign of comparative lateness of this inscription with reference to that of 'Soḍāsa from Mathurā (Dahejia 1972 :41). It may, however, be added that the letter *ya* occurs four times in the Ayodhyā inscription and the incurving is not so marked in all the cases.

(ix) *The thickening of the head or upper part of the letters* : This feature seems to have played a major role in assigning the Ayodhyā inscription to the first century A.D. For, it is held by palaeographists that this thickening of the head or the upper part was due to the use of reed pen and that the reed pen itself came into use at the beginning of the first century A.D. (Dani 1963 : 52; Verma 1971 : 82-83). To us this appears to be an argument in a circle. These scholars have taken for granted that all the inscribed material concerned belongs to the first century A.D. and, therefore, they think, the reed pen too must have come into use about that time.

But facts point in a different direction. On a personal examination of the Mathurā coins in the British Museum, Dahejia (1972 : 39) stated that 'these coins reveal a distinct thickening of the tops of the verticals in the legends of at least five of these kings - Purushadatta, Utamadatta, Rāmadatta, Kāmadatta and Balabh-uti'. Since most of these rulers had preceded the Kshatrapas of Mathurā, there is every reason to believe that the thickening of the head or the upper part of the

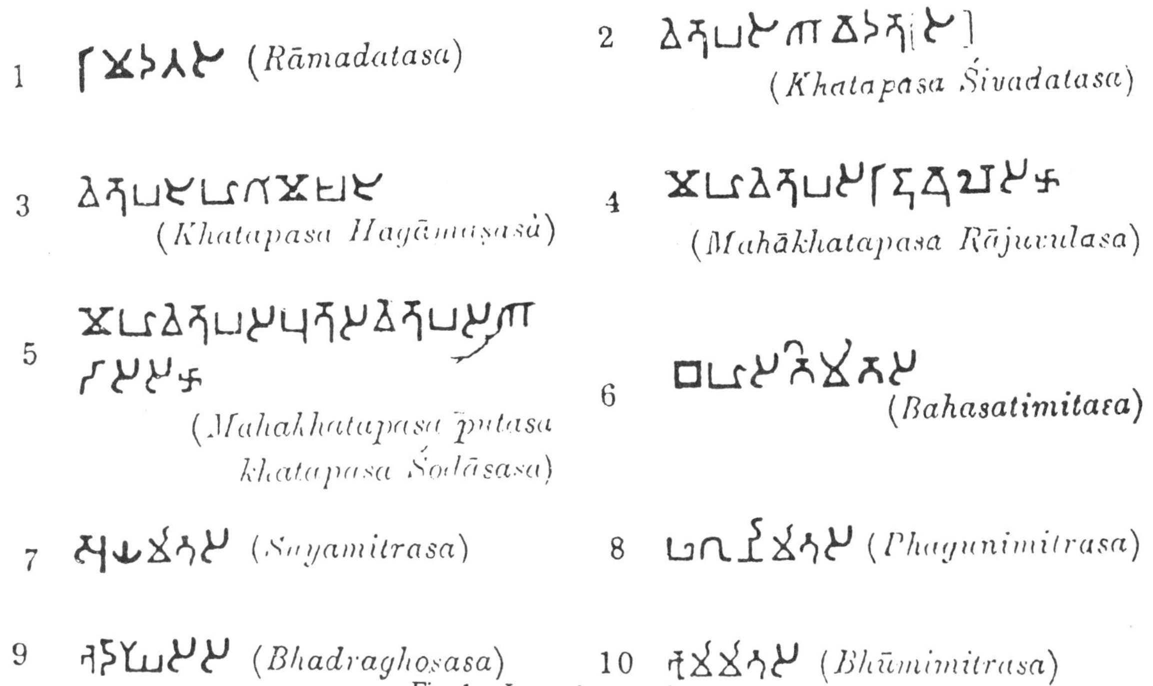

Fig. 1 Legends on various coins.

letters had come into vogue fairly early in the first century B.C. As to the introduction of this new style of writing with the reed pen, Dahejia (1972 :41) holds : 'The probable source for the new style of script evidenced in India on the Māthurā coins as early as *c*. 100 B.C. is likely to have been through contact with the Greek dynasties of the north-west.' In any case, the introduction of this feature cannot be attributed to the Kshatrapas in the first century A.D.

That this was the case is proved not merely by the evidence of coins, but also by that from certain lithic records. For example, one may notice very clearly the thickening of the upper parts of the letters in both the Pabhosa Inscriptions illustrated here (Pls. IIA and IV). While Fuhrer (1894 : 241) places them in the second or first century B.C.', even Sircar (1965 : 96) admits that they belong to the first century B.C. The Kosam stone inscription (Pl. IIIB) also shows this very feature and Sircar (1965 : 95-96), again, has no hesitation in assigning it to the first century B.C.

We may now pass on from the field of palaeography to that of history. The inscription says that Dhanadeva, king of Ayodhyā, was 'sixth from Pushyamitra'. The inscription also states that this Pushyamitra had been a Senāpati i.e. the Commander of an army, and had also performed two horse-sacrifices. Both these statements leave little doubt in identifying the Pushyamitra of our inscription with the Pushyamitra who was the Commander of the army of Brihadratha, the last Mauryan king, whom he (Pushyamitra) assasinated and became himself the king (cf. Raychaudhury 1938 : 306 ff.). While Pushyamitra himself ruled from Pātaliputra, his son Agnimitra governed from Vidisā. There appear to have been other centres too, of which Ayodhyā was one. Dhanadeva, the ruler of Ayodhyā, took pride in being connected with Pushyamitra and that is why he mentions the name of the latter.

Now comes the crucial question : viz. how far was Dhanadeva removed in time from Pushyamitra. Regarding this, the inscription only says ***'Pushyamitrasya Shashthena'*** i.e. Dhanadeva was sixth from Pushyamitra. it does not state the manner in which he was sixth : in ruling succession or in genealogical descent ? And this then becomes a matter of debate. Since Pushyamitra himself was ruling from Pātaliputra and his son, Agnimitra, from Vidisā, Dhanadeva, ruling from Ayodhyā, may not have belonged to this direct line of succession. There are perhaps greater chances of a genealogical relationship between the two. In this context, one point recorded in the inscription may be of interest. Dhanadeva mentions the name of his father (Phalgudeva) for whom he got a (memorial) structure ***(ketana)*** made. But he also mentions the name of his mother, Kauśikī.. It is thus not unlikely that Dhanadeva was related to Pushyamitra through the side of his mother, and was sixth in genealogical descent from him.

Scholars have raised eyebrows over the use of the term ***'Pushyamitrasya'*** which is in the sixth case. Normally it should have been ***'Pushyamitrāt'*** i.e. in the fifth case ***(Panchamī Vibhakhti)***. Some scholars have thus tried to say that, because of the sixth case, Dhanadeva may have been a brother of Pushyamitra (cf. *E.I.*, Vol XX, pp. 54-58). This seems quite improbable, both palaeographically as well historically. We have to accept this grammatical aberration as either a genuine mistake resulting from lack of adequate grammatical expertise on the part of the composer of the text, or as a permissiable usage of the time. That this may have been genuine mistake of the composer is suggested by another mistake in the second line of the text. Herein the term used is '*dharmarājña*',whereas according to the grammatical rule it should have been '*dharmarajena*'.

Leaving this grammatical debate aside, it would appear that Dhanadeva was sixth in genealogical descent from

Pushyamitra. But this relative position would not give us an absolute date for Dhanadeva. At the same time, from known cases a generation[1] may be computed around 20 years or, at the most, 25 years. (It could be less if the relationship is through females.) Since Pushyamitra ruled from 187-151 B.C. (Raychaudhury 1938 : 315), and there intervened four generations between Pushyamitra and Dhanadeva, the latter may be placed around the middle of the first century B.C.

All told, then, the palaeographic nuances as well as the historical perspective combine to suggest that Dhanadeva may have ruled around the middle of the first century B.C. and not at the beginning of the first century A.D. as suggested by some scholars.

Note : 1. In the case of direct succession on the same throne, the average is much less (cf. Lal 1976 : 56-57).

Bibliography

Allan, John. 1936. *Catalogue of the Coins of Ancient India*, British Museum, London.

Bühler, G 1894. Further Jain Inscriptions from Mathurā. *Epigraphia Indica*, Vol II, pp. 195 ff.

Dahejia, Vidya. 1972. *Early Buddhist Rock Temples : A Chronological Study*. Thames and Hudson, London.

Dani, A.H. 1963. *Indian Palaeography*. Clarendon Press, Oxford.

Führer, A. 1894. Pabhosa Inscriptions. *Epigraphia Indica*, Vol, II, pp. 240 ff.

Lal, B.B. 1976. Mahābhārata and Archaeology in S.P. Gupta and K.S. Ramachandran (eds.)

Mahābhārata : Myth and Reality, pp. 52-50. Agam Prakashan, Delhi.

Rayachaudhuri, Hemachandra. 1938. *Political History of Ancient India*. University of Calcutta.

Roy, S.R. 1959. A Terracotta Sealing of Agnimitra from vailśāli and its Bearing on Vai´sāligarh. *Journ. Bihar Res. Soc.*, Vol. XLV, pp. 313-17.

Shani, Daya Ram. 1925-26. *Three Brāhmī Inscriptions* from Kosam. *Epigraphia Indica*, Vol. XVIII, p.p. 158 ff. Sharma, G.R. 1969. *Excavations at Kauśāmbī 1949-50* Mem. Arch. Surv. of India, No. 74. Manager of Publications, Delhi.

Sharma, G.R. 1980, *Reh Inscription of Menander and the Indo-Greek Invasion of the Gaṅgā Valley*. Abinash Prakashan, Allahabad.

Sircar, D.C. 1965. *Select Inscriptions bearing on Indian History and Civilization*, Vol. I, University of Calcutta.

Thaplyal, KK. 1972. *Studies in Ancient Indian Seals*. Akhila Bharatiya Sanskrit Parishad, Lucknow.

Verma, T.P. 197. *The Palaeography of Brāhm-i Script in North India (From c. 236 B.C. to c. 200 A.D.* Siddharath Prakashan, Varanasi.

RAKTA-LOKE´SVARA IN INDIAN BUDDHIST ART

Shashi Asthana *

The National Museum, New Delhi acquired a miniature bronze image representing a Buddhist Deity in the year 1965. As the image was purchased from a dealer its exact find spot is unknown.

The image presents a two armed male figure seated in *Padmāsana* on the pericarp of a high double lotus pedestal mounted on a rectangular base. With his right hand he is shown engaged in opening the petals of a lotus which is held in the left hand. He is dressed in a *dhotī* and a scarf, whose ends are fluttering on either side, passing over the upper arms and back. Further, a piece of deer skin is shown flung on his left shoulder. He is adorned with a crown ornamented with three crests. The crest in the centre shows a tiny image of Dhyānī Buddha Amitābha seated in *dhyāna mudrā*. He is provided with eardisc & torque, bracelets and headed sacred thread. The face is serence and calm.

Its provenance may be Himalayan region-Kashmir as the form of his face and of the lotus petals of the pedestal would suggest. However, the form of the crest of the crown is of chamba lineage. On the basis of style this image could be dated to the 9th-10th century A.D. This is the only image of its own kind in the National Museum collection (Size 12.8 x 6.8 cm acc. No. 65.133, Fig. 1.

The presence of Dhyānī Buddha Amitābha on his crest clearly reveals his identity as one of his emnations. Besides Avalokite´svare, there are only two male emnations of this Dhyān–i Buddha : Mahābala and Saptasatika Hayagr–iva. As the iconography of both these deities is completely different from the iconography of the image in question, the latter may fall under the category of Avalokite´svara. Bodhisattva Avalokite´svara manifests himself in a number of forms for the sake of the ignorant people and to bring salvation to the mankind. Amongst his fifteen different forms, mentioned in the *Sādhanamālā*,[1] only two are relevant for this study : Rakta Lokesvara and Vajradharma, as both are similar to each other in form and posture. According to *Sādhanamālā*.[2] both are two armed, seated in *Padmāsana* holding the lotus stalk in left hand and blossoming the petals with the right hand.

The Vajradharma form of Avalokite´svara has been described vividly in *s–adhana* No. 10 of the *Sādhanamālā*,[3] mentioned below :

"Taṁ sitaṁ raktavarṇaṁ tu padmarāgasamadyutiṁ I

Pañcabuddhamukuṭadharaṁ harṣenotphullalocanaṁ II

Vāmato spardhayā nālaṁ dhṛtvā ṣoḍa´spatrakaṁ I

Padmani Vikā´sayantañca hṛdi dakṣiṇapāṇinā II

May–uropari madhyasthe niṣaṇṇaṁ Chandramandale I

Sattvaparyaṅkamābhujya sa´sṛngārarasotsavaṁ II

Caityāntaḥsthamahākarma-K–uṭāgāravihāriṇaṁ I

Bhāvayet Vajradharmāgryaṁ nityaṁ Bodhiṁ Avāpnuyat"
Sādhanamālā-p.33

"The worshipper should conceive himself as excellent Vajradharma, of reddish white complexion, bright as the Padmarāga gem, who bears the effigies of the Five Dhyāni Buddhas on the crown. His eyes beam with delight; and he holds with pride the stem of a lotus with sixteen petals in his left hand and with the right causes it to blossom against his chest, He sits on the moon over lotus on the back of a peacock,enjoys his seat of the animal and displays the delightful sentiment of amour. He moves in the sanctum of the caitya, the place for great performances. He (the worshipper) certainly receives the Bodhi who meditates (upon him) in this manner."[4]

In Sādhanamālā[5] only two *sādhanas* are prescribed for the worship of Rakta-Lokesvara. Sādhana no. 37 projects him as four armed holding the noose, the goad, the bow and arrow, while in Sādhana no. 38, given below, he is conceived as two armed which is relevant to the present study.

"...............Raktavarṇaṁ(_________) Amitābhagarbhajaṭāmukuṭadharaṁ vāmakaragṛh–itaraktapadmaṁ tacca dakṣiṇakareṇa vikā´sayantaṁ vividhālankaravastra vibhu–ṣitaṁ_________" Sādhanamālā p.84

"The worshipper should think himself as Rakta-Loke´svara of red colour having a jaṭāmukuṭa (crown of matted hair) bearing the effigy of Amitābha. He carries the red lotus in the left hand, and opend its petals with the right and is decked in various ornaments and dress ...."[6]

A study of both these sādhanas dealing with vajradharma and Rakta-Loke´svara reveals the fact that inspite of the identical *mudrā* there are some distinguishable marks of each of the two images. Thus, while vajradharma is provided with the peacock as a vehicle, Rakta-Loke´svara does not seem to have any association with this bird. Secondly, while the sādhana provides the effigies of all five Dhyān–i Buddhas to vajradharma, it recommends the effigy of Amitābha to Rakta-Loke´svara. However, where both these distinctive marks are absent for one reason or the other, the image is obviously difficult to be identified.

In the absence of peacock and with the presence of Dhyānī Buddha Amitābha on the crown of the deity in question, its identification with the Rakta-Loke´svara, therefore, appears to be beyond doubt also because the sādhana describes it as red in

* National Museum, Janpath, New Delhi

colour and we actually find traces of red paint on this image. As per the sādhana he is two armed and is seated crosslegged on a lotus pedestal. He carries the red lotus (traces of red paint on the petals of the lotus still visible) in the left hand and opens the petals to blossom it with the right hand. The face is benign.

The images of Rakta-Loke´svara and Vajradharma are very few in indian art. The only other identical image is presently housed in a private collection at zurich, published by P.Pal[7]. It belongs to Swat or some Western Himalayan region and dated to the 11th century A.D. Another bronze image of two armed Rakta-Loke´svara dated to 9th-10th century is found at Achyutrajpur[8] where he is draped in an *antariya* and *uttariya* covering the left shoulder only. He is bejewelled with ornaments. His hands are shown near the chest while his left palm holds a lotus, the right one is in attitude of opening the petals. As the bronze is considerably weathered the details are mostly lost.

Two stone sculptures from Nalanda and three from Ratnagiri are also to be considered in this context. There are two images carved on a stone votive stupa at Ratnagiri.[9] Both of them are in the posture of causing a lotus to blossom forth with the right hand poised near the chest. Both of them are devoid of Dhyān–i Buddha's images, However, as the pedestal of one of the image presents a peacock in faint lines, its identification with Vajradharmam is by and large definite. However, the other one, due to the absence of any distinctive mark defies exact identification. Still, the possibility of its being Rakta-Loke´savara can not completely be ruled out.

The third one is slightly complex.[10] A large stele from the same site, presents a two armed male diety seated crosslegged on a lotus pedestal and engaged in opening the petals of a lotus. Mount peacock is absent. However, five Dhyān–i Buddhas are present on the crest. The most important feature of this image is that the stele is carved with the four female deities, two on top and two on bottom. The upper ones have been identified as Ārya Saraswati who is marked with a lotus with a book on top. The lower ones are identified as Tārā and Bhrikuṭ–i. All of them are seated in *vajraparyankāsana* on double lotus pedestal with right hand in *varad mudrā*.

The identification of this image is difficult. The presence of the effigies of five Dhyān–i Buddhas on the crown makes him as Vajradharma while the presence of Ārya-Saraswati, Tārā and Bhrikuṭ–i crete some doubt in accepting this identification. There is no textual reference to this iconography in all its details. However, the four armed Rakta-Loke´svara has a provision of two female companions Tara and Bhṛikuti in Sādhana No. 37. But his attributes are completely different from these. Therefore only tentatively one can identify it as vajradharma. Here the mention of a few images from Ellora which have been identified by Gupta as Rakta-Lokasvara will not be out of context. Seven sculptures from Ellora present a Bodhisattva with his right hand in *varad mudrā* and left holding a full blown lotus. Out of seven three are standing straight and rests are seated in different possitions. He is flanked by Tārā and Bhrikut–i. As both these goddesses are described as the companions of four-armed Rakta-Loke´svara in *Sādhanamālā* Gupte has identified these images as of Rakta-Loke´svara. However, none of these carry the attributes of this particular deity. Therefore the identification based on the only presence of the companion deities is very unlikely.

Similary, two stone sculptures from Nalanda also pose the same problem, Both are dated to 10th century A.D. These have been identified as Vajradharma by Saraswati.[12] Both of them are portrayed in cross-legged posture seated on lotus pedestal with hands causing a lotus to blossom forth. While one of them clearly reveals its identity as Vajradharma though its pedestal mounted on peacock, the other headless stone sculpture creates some doubt in accepting it as Vajradharma since its pedestal is mounted on the back of two lions. The textual reference associating lion with Vajradharma or Rakta-Loke´svara is not known so far, therefore, it is difficult to identify with any two of these.

There is another very interesting image from Swat Valley, presently housed in the Metropolitan Museum, New York. This has been identified as Vajradharma Loke´svara By P.Pal.[13] It is dated to the 9th century A.D. However, its inconographic features are very complex and therefore worth reviewing here. The bronze image presents a four armed male deity seated in *Vajraparyakāsana* on a double lotus pedestal mounted on curious looking birds. The major pair of hands is engaged in opening the lotus bud. Bow and arrow are held in the rear hands. He is dressed in *Dhoti* and scarf and adorned with jewelled ornaments. A tiny image of Dhyani Buddha Amitabha is shown on the crown. Pal has indentified these birds as peacocks and therefore, he takes this deity as Vajradharma. However, while distinguishing this bronze from Rakta-Loke´svara he mentions that the gesture of the principal hands is common to both Rakta-Loke´svara and Vajradharma but the former is further distinguished by the effigy of Amitābha in his crown, while the latter is to be given peacock as his mount. Surprisingly both are present in this bronze. In addition to this the image varies from the text. The Sādhanmālā prescribes only two arm for Vajradharma Loke´svara while he is shown here four armed, two carrying bow and arrow which are neither the attributes of Vajradharma nor of two armed Rakta-Loke´svara.

In order to justify the bow and arrow in the hands of Vajradharma, Pal[15] has shown the far fluing relationship between the Vajradharma and Mañju´sr–i who sometimes takes these attributes too. These two attributes are very popular with the godds and goddesses in Buddhist pantheon. However, it is significant to note that *Sādhanmālā*[16] allots these two attributes in addition to noose and sword to the form of four armed Rakta-Loke~svara, which is more relevant here than Mañju´sr–i.

The presence of Dhyān–i Buddha Amitābha, which is the distinctive mark of two armed Rakta-Loke´svara, the bow and arrows, connected with four-armed Rakta-Lokeśvara create doubt in accepting this image as Vajradharma Loke´svara.

Iconographic elements of all the three deitises (Vajradharma and two forms of Rakta Loke´svara) are fused in making this icon.

This survey or images representing vajradharma and Rakta-Loke´svara shows that these two forms of Avalokite´svara are rare in Indian art and thus this bronze image is a valuable addition to our knowledge.

REFERENCES

1. Bhattacharya, B. *Indian Buddhist Iconography*, Calcutta 1858, pp. 125-143.
2. *Sādhanmālā*, ed. by B. Bhattacharya, Baroda, Second ed. 1968
3. *Ibid*, p.33
4. Bhattacharya, B. *op. cit*, p.143
5. *Sādhanmālā*, pp. 83-85
6. Bhattacharya, B. *op. cit* pp 138-139
7. Pal, P. *Bronzes of Kashmir*, New York, 1975, Cat. No. 80.
8. Mitra, D. *Bronzes from Achyutrajpur* Delhi, 1978, p.72 (1958-61) Vol. I
9. Mitra, D. *Ratnagiri, Memoirs of the Arch. Survey of India*, New Delhi, 1981, pp. 121-122
10. *Ibid*,Vol II, p 291
11. Gupte, R.S. *Iconography of the Buddhist caves of Ellora* Aurangabad. 1964, pp. 77-80, pls 5c, 5d, 6a, 6b, 6c, 6d, 79
12. Saraswati, S.K. *Tantrayāna Art An Album*,Calcutta, 1977 Cat. No.s 81-82.
13. Pal. P. *Bronzes of Kashmir*, New York, 1975, Cat. No. 79.
14. *Ibid* p. 206
15. *Ibid*, p. 206
16. *Sādhanamālā*, pp 83

URBAN AND PALACE WATER-WORKS DURING THE MUGHAL PERIOD

Mohd. Afzal Khan*

The Mughals, from the beginning, realized the necessity of laying out elaborate water-works in India. Babur had expressed dissatisfaction with the absence of artificial water channels or aqueducts in India : "Except for the rivers and here and there standing waters, there is little 'running-water'. So much so is this that towns and countries subsist on the water of wells or on such as collects in tanks during the rains."[1] By the scarcity of 'running water', what he actually meant is explained by the author of the *Ma'asir-i Rahimi* who writes : "Unlike Iran the inhabitants of India do not have running water and clear water springs in their houses and gardens; they just depend on the water of wells, ponds and rivers and never think of bringing this water into their dwellings and gardens".[2] In 1623-24 Pietro Della Valle also makes somewhat similar observations.[3]

The hydraulic enterprises of the early Mughals, besides the construction of bath, *baolis* and laying-out of gardens, included the renovation of old water-works in Delhi and other parts of the empire. Abul-Fazl mentions that Firoz Shah's Jamuna Canal was repaired by Shihabuddin Ahmed Khan as it had silted during the early years of Akbar's reign.[4] Shah Jahan also re-excavated and re-aligned the same canal and brought its water upto Delhi and renamed it as *Nahr-i Bihisht*.[5] *The Shah Nahr* canal was also excavated during his reign in order to provide sufficient water to the inhabitants of Lahore.[6] Lachhmi Narain Shafiq refers to the construction of a canal in 1614 in Khirki after its conquest by Jahangir. Later in the reign of Aurangzeb, Khan-i Jahan Kokaltash excavated another canal to which one more big canal *(Nahr-i azim)* was added in 1747[7].

Lakes, natural as well as artificial, also sought attention of the Mughals. Near Fatehpur Sikri a dam was constructed under Akbar's direction, and a large lake created by this means, writes Monserrate, 'not only was a copious supply of water assured, but the discomfort of the climate was mitigated.[8] During his stay in Ajmer Jahangir is said to have reconstructed the dam on the Nil Tal in 1616 which had broken long back.[9] The artificial lakes were built of stone, with stairs at several angles and sometimes an island and a garden in the middle of which access was provided by a causeway.[10]

A large number of ornamental tanks and reservoirs of diverse nature and dimensions have also been reported by contemporary and later sources. *Hauz* is the common term but sometimes, especially in the case of garden tanks, *tal*, *talab* and *talao* are also used all signifying a masonry tank. Thus, Cunningham refers to Guru Ka Tal near Sikandra,[11] and most of the 17th century travellers to Gopi *talao* in Surat.[12] Jahangir describes a great square tank *(talab)* in the middle of the Nur Manzil garden at Agra which was filled with rain water. Whenever, due to the excess of heat, the tank dried up it was supplied by the well water.[13] Some of the big tanks were centrally provided with beautiful buildings and gardens and causeways leading to them. Bhimsen mentions two big tanks *(talab-i Kalan)* in the courtyards of the two gardens in the fort of Ahmadnagar. Of these the *Bagh-i Farah* garden had a three storyed building which was known as *Manzar-i Saba* to the Deccanis.[14] In 1632, Peter Mundy saw a square tank called *'I' timad katalao* at Firozabad near Agra. It had a fair octagonal building in the centre with a causeway leading to it.[15]

Baolis[16] or stepwells, an old Indian invention, were an important part of the Mughal water-works. They are multi-chambered and sometimes multi-storied structures[17] with flights of steps leading down to the water. While the steps provided direct access to the water level at the bottom, the side chambers served as summer retreats. What the Mughals added to these was an elaborate Persian wheel apparatus for raising water. Babur's *wain* (baoli), a chambered-well 10 x 10 yards in the Agra Fort, was a three storyed building, the lowest-storey containing three rooms each of which opened on the descending steps. In dry seasons the water was one step below the bottom chamber, while during monsoons it sometimes touched the top storey. In the middle storey an inner chamber was made which connected with the domed building in which the bullock turned the well-wheel. The top storey was a single room, reached from two sides of the enclosure above the well head by 5 or 6 steps. At the side of this well was another, the bottom of which was at half the depth of the first and into which water came from the first one when the bullock turned the wheel in the domed building. This second well, which practically served as a storage tank was also fitted with a wheel by means of which water was lifted above and carried along the ramparts to the high garden.[18] In Fatehpur Sikri Akbar built several *baolis* of which the two most important and largest ones - the northern water-works and the southern water-works have been surveyed and described by many scholars, with figures and illustrations. Water was raised several stages up to the top level by means of Persian Wheels, installed in the side chambers of the well, drawn by bullocks. The water was stored into overhead storage tanks whence it was finally lifted up by manual effort to be drained into channels which carried the water into different parts of the complex.[19] The interseting point, on which all the authorities are silent, is as to how actually the Persian Wheel functioned in such a deep well surrounded by a huge super structure ?

In a couple of paintings from Nizami's *khamsa* which was illustrated in Akbar's ateliar at Fatehpur sikri a Persian wheel is shown drawing water into the palace garden. The

* Department of History, Aligarh Muslim University, Aligarh - 202001

gearing is shown atop of a long vertically fixed shaft or axle which rotates the wheel with chain of pots above while the oxen are moving below. The water can be seen flowing from a high channel attached to the trough and from this higher channel the water shown falling into a storage tank from where it is being drained into another tank.[20] (Pls. I and 2). It may therefore, be presumed that a similar system was used in the water-works of Fatehpur Sikri. The bullocks could be on the ground, while the wheel moved by vertical shaft and gearing poured water into channels at a considerable height above. This is however corroborated by the two paintings from *Akbarnama* preserved in the victoria and Albert (V & A) Museum London, showing the northern waterworks near the elephant gate. The first painting[21] depicts construction of the gate and water works in progress. The persian wheel with chain of pots is vertically fixed above the well with a horizontal exle (not visible). On the roof of a nearby pavilion of equal height (i.e. parralel to the wheel axle) a water channel is being made to join the trough (yet to be made) near the wheel (Pl.3). The second,[22] a later illustration of post construction period, taken at the time of Akbar's return to fatehpur sikri after his victory in Gujarat (1573), shows two persian wheels fixed on two wells built at different levels (one over the other). The arched openings of the side rooms in the adjoining wall suggest the whole structure being a multi-storyed building and that the bullocks probably moved in the side chambers. (Pl. 4).

The *Mirat-i Ahmadi*, mentions that the people of Gujarat constructed *baolis* and such other buildings for the public benefit and also as works of charity. One of these public buildings was the *Dahiri Baoli*, a three storeyed structure supported by stone pillars. It was constructed in scuh a way that whatever amount of water was needed, one had to open the mouth of the well, clean (or dig) out before water could be taken. A passage from the top led through the flight of steps down to the water in such a way that the traveller, without any difficulty, could reach the bottom and drink water by his own hands.[23]

In Bijapur we notice several big and small *baolis* and tanks which supplied the city with water the year round. The Taj Baori, the Chand Baori, Mubarak Khan's Baori and the Jama Masjid Baori are some of the important *baoris* there.[24]

Birka or the underground rainwater cistern or well also occupied an important place in the Mughal urban and palace water-works. It appears that these underground wells served as emergency tanks. Thus, Jahangir writes about Ahmadabad that water here is scarce and sandy, and the tank situated out side the city always remains dry except for the monsoon days; the wells were generally saline *(shor)* and brackish *(talkh)* and the lakes situated in the vicinity of the city have become brackish as a result of the use of soap by the bleachers there. Therefore, great men and nobles of the city constructed *birkas* and fill them during monsoon period with rain water and then use their water throughout the next year which he believed turns unhygienic because to air entered into the tanks for the long time.[25] In 1603 (1013 A.H.) the author of *Ma' asir-i Rahimi*, along with his master Khwaja Abul Hasan Turbati, Just for the sake of pleasure and amusement visited the fort of Asir and climbed its roof. It was a very high hill on which there was level land over half a *kuroh* in which some springs of water *(Chashma-i Ab)* were situated, some *birkas* had also been constructed out of precaution so that if there happened a drought and the springs stopped flowing these *birkas* could still supply water.[26] In the courtyard of the *Jama Masjid* of Fatehpur Sikri a *birka* was constructed for the same purpose it can still be seen and now collects rain water through underground channels. Jahangir says that it was built to conserve rain water, as the water was scanty and bad in Fatehpur Sikri, so that the Shaikh's descendants and other saints who acted as caretakers *(mujawir)* of this mosque could be supplied with water the whole year round.[27]

Like Ahmadabad, in Cambay also we find that in big houses, such as those of merchants, rain water reservoirs were established. The term *pansal* repeatedly occur in the documents sometimes comprising one *abdar Khana* and two *khum-i ab*, all signifying the water amenities in the households.[28]

In Burhanpur the Tapti water was not consumed by the inhabitants. Abdur Rahim Khan-i Khanan introduced *kariz* or subterranean strings of wells to catch the water percolating from the hills and bring it to the centre of the valley; through conduits it was drawn into masonry reservoirs. From these reservoirs water was distributed to the town by means of clay or stone pipes. These pipes were furnished, at short intervals, with tall hollow columns of masonry which served the purpose of stand pipes from which the water could be drawn off.[29] The author of *Ma' asir-i Rahimi* tells us that it was Abdur Rahim Khan-i Khanan who during his governorship in Jahangir's reign, constructed the *Kariz* allowing the water of a spring to flow into the city of Burhanpur, for a distance four *kurohs* or two *farsang* from the Lal Bagh. The spring was one kuroh on the other side of the garden. He named it *Sabil Kafa-i Anam* *i.e.* 'for the service of humanity', so that everyone could be benefitted from it.[30] Subsequently, From Lal Bagh upto the Jama Mosque which lies in the centre of the city a water canal was excavated. He also constructed a stone tank in the mosque for ablution in which water was supplied from this canal. The inhabitants of the city also carried water from this canal to their houses. The canal passed through the residence of the governor and also ran by or through several houses *(manazil)* of the citizens of Burhanpur.[31]

It may be pointed out that Abdur Rahim Khan-i khanan made the experiment of *Kariz* i.e. subterranean water channels for catching water from the hills for the first time in Burhanpur and thus introduced the Persian technique of *Qanat* in Indian water works. This underground waterconveyance was achieved by means of a series of wells sunk at a certain distance from one another and linked by a gallery *(Qanat)*. The water tapped by this method flows gently through the *Qanat* towards the centre of habitation it supplies or irrigates.[32]

The author of *Haft Iqlim*, (C.1600) however, claims that Ahmadnagar had already free flowing Qanat *(Qanat-i Jariya)* which was still not practised in India.[33] This means that the Ahmadnagar water-works should be given precedence in time over those of Burhanpur laid out by Abdur Rahim khan-i Khanan.

We have seen that rain-water was generally supplemented by lakes, tanks, subterranean aqueducts, reservoirs and canals. Water was drawn from these sources by means of Persian wheel (also called *rahat*, and *charkh*), *charas* (also known as *pur and mot*), and *dhenkli* or the lever contrivance. The last, Needham suggests, was the oldest and simplest mechanism known to the Islamic west by its Arabic name of *Shaduf*.[34] Babur looked down upon *charas* as a laborious and filthy method, while the *rahat* interested him very greatly.[35]

It appears that whereas Persian wheel was the more prevalent device in North India,[36] in the Deccan *charas* and *dhenkli* were the common methods of lifting water. Thus in Hyderabad state the ordinary *mot* or leather bucket was the common water-lift and was worked by a pair of Oxen. On the banks of rivers and streams the *yatam or bhudki* (a lever like contrivance) was used by one or two men.[37] In the royal palaces of Bijapur the reservoirs were filled from nearby wells, the water being drawn up by a *mot*.[38] In Jahanara's garden at Surat water was lifted out of the well by Oxen to supply the main channel running in the middle of the garden.[39]

The water so drawn was brought into the cities by means of underground pipes. There was always a small tank (catchment) at the entry point which, Peter Mundy has rightly conceived, was made so that dirt in the water might settle there before it ran into distributive channels.[40] From the second tank the water was allowed to run slowly into the open channels or underground pipes.

Clay or earthenware pipes were commonly used but sometimes stone pipes and later leaden pipes are also mentioned. The clay pipes were glazed from inside. The pipes were also built into the thickness of the walls traces of which can still be seen in *Hammams* (baths) at Fatehpur Sikri and other places.[41] The workmanship of piping is also interesting. It appears that pipes were smaller in length and were made with a shoulder on one end into which the next pipe fitted, the whole being then embedded in concrete;[42] at corners they were curved so as to enable one to lap over the other.[43] The pipes varied in dimension. Smith mentions glazed pipes 4½" diameter and ½" thick in Hakim's bath at Fatehpur Sikri. Fuhrer gives 20" in diameter and 4" in depth at Mohan Tehsil District Unnao, and R. Nath in Taj Mahal finds pipes measuring 6 to 9 inches in diameter.[44]

It seems that leaden and copper pipes were used for fountains and showers etc. In Cordova, under Abdur Rahman III (912-960) however, the leaden pipes were used in bringing water from the mountain springs and then conducted to numerous basins, tanks and fountains.[45] In the 17th century Iran use of leaden pipes seems to have been common.[46] In Taj Mahal copper pipes are said to have been used.[47] Over head tanks were constructed to ensure adequate pressure in the fountains and jets in the palaces and gardens.[48]

We know little about the purification of water, if turned impure, during the Mughal period. However, the Mughal emperors were quite hygeine-conscious as Jahangir criticises the people of Ahamadabad for storing water in the underground *birkas* without exposing it to air for the whole year which, says he, obviously caused diseases.[49] In 1626 Pelsaert found people of Achbal in Kashmir using water of Śaluara lake after boiling because the water was not sweet and healthy. The king and nobles had their water carried from a distant place where the water was clear and snow white.[50]

That the Mughal emperors were conscious of good water is further corroborated by the establishment of a separate department for drinking water, *Abdar Khana*, by Akbar, which forms the subject of separate chapter in *Ain-i Akbari*.[51] Akbar called water 'the source of the life *(Ab-i Hayat)*. He Always used Ganges water whether at home or on travel, which was supplied in sealed jars from Soron.[52] Bernier comments that water in Delhi is full of impurities, and feels satisfied when Danishmand Khan assured him a *surahi* (clay pot) of Ganges water every morning.[53]

Thus we find that indignance of the Mughals from Babar onwards, for the crude water devices before their coming appears to be justified. Soon after their conquest of India, a serious attempt was made to refurbish the water resources which were not only aesthetically constructed but technologically superior as well. The real impetus was given to this industry when Akbar established a separate department of water in his court. It was under the Mughals that a wide use of running water came into its own in India, Canals were dug, underground channels constructed and sophisticated *hammams* with the facility of mixing cold and hot water, established. The surviving monuments and gardens of the Mughals bear testimony to the fervour with which the water devices were shaped and introduced in the country during the 16th and 17th century India.

Refernces

1. *Baburnama*, (Eng. tr.) A.S. Beveridge, Vol. II, p. 487
2. Mulla Abdul Baqi Nihavandi, *Ma'asir-i Rahimi*, ed. M. Hidayat Hussain, Calcutta 1925, Vol II, p.601
3. *The Travels of Pietro Della Valle In India*, ed. Edward Grey, London, 1892, Vol. I p.p. 32-33.
4. Akbarnama (tr) H. Beveridge (Reprint), New Delhi, 1979, Vol. III p. 885, n.
5. Muhammad Waris, Badshahnama (Transcript, Deptt. of History, Aligarh), Vol. I, pp. 39-40
6. Abdul Hamid Lahori, *Badshahnama*, Bib. Ind. Calcutta 1867, Vol. II pp. 168-69.

7. *Khulasat-ul Hind* (Transcript, Deptt. of History, Aligarh), 1210 A.H., p. 125.
8. *Commentary of Father Monserrate*, (Tr.) J.S. Hoyland, London, 1922, p. 31.
9. *Tuzuk-i Jahangiri*, ed. Syed Ahmad, Aligarh, 1864, p. 168.
10. *The Travels of Pietro Della Valle, op.cit.*, p. 102.
11. *Delhi and Agra*, A.S.I, Report for the year 1871-72, Vol.IV, Varanasi, 1966, pp. 184-85
12. *Pietro Della Valle, op.cit.*, pp.33-34; Peter Mundy, *The Travels of Peter Mundy*, ed. R.C. Temple, London, 1914, Vol. II, pp. 31-32; Thevento, *Indian Travels of Thevenot and Careri*, ed. S.N. Sen, New Delhi, 1949, p. 35.
13. *Tuzuk*, p. 264.
14. *Nuskha-i-Dilkusha*, B.M. Or. M.S. 23 (Rotograph), f, 45 (b).
15. *Travels of Peter Mundy, op. cit.*, p. 84
16. They were also known as baori, bain, wain, and in Gujarat as *vaw*. For detailed description of *baoils* see Petter Mundy, *op. cit.*, Yule and Burnell, *Hobsón Jobson* (S.V. Bowly).
17. For instance Bai Hariri's*Baoli* in Gujarat consisted of six storeys in all. See Thevenot, *op.cit.*, p. 16.
18. *Baburnama*, II p. 533.
19. For details see E.W. Smith's *Fatehpur Sikri*, being the A.S.I. Report, N.W. Provinces part III, S.A.A. Rizvi and V.J.A. Flyn's *Fatehpur Sikri*, Bombay, 1975, pp. 111-12, 120-21; and R. Nath's *History of Mughal Architecture*, New Delhi, 1985, Vol, II. pp. 173-77.
20. *Khamsa*, B. M. Or M.S 12208, ff. 65R and 99V. I owe my indebteness to Prof. Irfan Habib for letting me use these paintings from his personal collection. Dr. S.P. Verma has also studied these paintings and arrived at the same conclusion suggesting that this type best suited to the palaces and buildings etc. See "Technology in Mughal India-Evidence of Mughal Painting", in *Technology in Ancient & Medieval India*, ed. Aniruddha Ray and S.K. Bagchi, Delhi, 1986, pp. 17-18.
22. 'Akbar being welcomed at Fathepur Sikri after his victory in Gujrat', *Akbarnama*, V&A, IS No. 117, pl. III (Two persian wheels at two different levels shown on left hand margin).
23. Ali Muhammad Khan, *Mirat-i-Ahmadi*, (Supplement), ed. Syed Nawab Ali, Baroda, 1930, p. 23.
24. Henry Cousens, *Bijapur and Its Architectural Remains*, New Delhi, 1977, p. 9.
25. *Tuzuk*, p. 213.
26. *Ma'asir-i Rahimi*, II, pp. 473-74.
27. *Tuzuk*, p. 262.
28. See M. Javed Akhtar, "Merchants and Urban Property" A study of cambay Documents of 17th-18th centuries" paper presented at the 49th session of I.H.C. at Dharwar, 1988,
29. Modern description in *Imperial Gazetters of India*, (Reprint) Vol. IX, p. 105.
30. *Ma'asir-i Rahimi*, II, pp. 601-602.
31. *Ibid.*, p. 602.
32. A.K.S. Lambton in *The Encyclopaedia of Islam*, (New edition) Vol., (Q.V. *Kanat*).
33. Amin Ahmad Razi, *Haft Iqlim*, Bib. Ind., Calcutta, 1939, Vol. I, PP. 80-81.
34. Joseph Needham, *Science and Civilization In China*, (Reprint), Cambridge, 1974, Vol. IV, Pt. II, pp. 331-33. Needham calls it 'the counter balanced bailing bucket'.
35. *Baburnama*, Vol. I, p. 388, Vol. II, pp. 486-87.
36. As late as in 1837 Donald Butter, however, categorically says that Persian wheel was not in Oudh. See *Topography and Statistics of Southern Districts of Awadh*, ed. Safi Ahmad (Reprint) Delhi, 1982, p.67.
37. *Imperial Gazetteer of India (Provincial Series), Hydrabad State*, Calcutta, 1909, pp. 32, 34.
38. Henry Cousens, *op. cit.*, p. 9
39. Thevenot, *op. cit.*, pp. 35-36.
40. Peter Mundy, *op. cit.*, p. 32.

    In Burhanpur the water was delivered into a large square reservoir, known as *Jali Karanj*, "and from here was distributed to the town by earthen tile pipes surrounded with masonry". See S.N. Sen's note in Travels of Thevenot, *op. cit.*, p. 101, fn. 1.
41. Smith, *Fatehpur Sikri*, pp. 48, 50; Henry Cousens, *op.cit.*, p.9. In the subterranean *Hammam* of the Old Fort Delhi, clay pipes can still be seen.
42. Henry Cousens, *op.cit.*, p.11.
43. A. Fuher, *The Moumental Antiquities and Inscriptions*, A.S.I, Varanasi, 1969, p. 272.
44. Simth, *Fatehpur Sikri*, Part III, p. 50; Fuhrer, *op.cit.*, p. 272; R. Nath, *The Immortal Taj Mahal*, Taraporevala, Bombay, 1972, pp. 42, 60.
45. Stanley Lane-Poole, *The Moors in Spain* (9th edition) London, 1912, p. 132.
46. A.U. Pope and P. Ackerman (ed.) *A Survey of Persian Art*, (Reprint), Tehran, 1964, Vol. III, p. 1401, 1433.
47. R. Nath, *The Immortal Taj Mahal*, p. 59.
48. *Ibid.*, pp. 59-60, gives a detailed description of the ingenious method that was devised to ensure uniform and undiminished water pressure in fountains, irrespective of the distance and the outflow of water.
49. *Tuzuk*, p. 231.
50 Francisco Pelsaert, *Jahangir's India* (tr.) W.H. Moreland and P. Geyl, Delhi, 1972 p. 33.
51. Abul Fazl, *Ain-i Akbari*, ed. Blochmann, Bid. Ind. Calcutta, 1867, Vol. I, pp. 51-52. See also S.M. Latif, *Agra : Historical and Descriptive, Lahore, 1981*
52. Ibid, ., Soron is the well known place on the Ganges south-west from Badaun.
53. Francois Bernier, *Travels in the Mughal Empire, 1656-68* ed. A. Constable, Delhi, 1968, pp. 355-56.

KNAPPING TECHNIQUE AND CRAFT SPECIALIZATION : AN ETHNOARCHAEOLOGICAL INVESTIGATION IN GUJARAT

Valentine Roux and Jacques Pelegrin*

The concept of craft specialization is one of the main criteria used in archaeology to describe both the complexity of societies as well as the process of urbanization (Brumfiel and Earle. 1987, Dow 1985, Evans 1978, Rice 1981, Tosi 1984). According to the authors, the term specialization refers to full-time or part-time, independent or affiliated specialists, with several or a single source of income. As for us, we will distinguish in the framework of this study :

technical specialization : the exclusive production by a sub-group of individuals, of goods consumed by the community (village or regional community); these goods may or may not be a source of income;

techno-economic specialization : the production of goods by a sub-group of individuals who draw an economic income from them (through exchange or sale on the village or regional scale).

On the basis of these definnitions, we turned our attention to the material evidence significant of technical and/or economic specialization, independently of the question concerning the reasons for specialization which, predictably, vary depending on the socio-economic milieu. The objectives of our study are defined as research into regularities between material facts and specialization (Gallay 1986, 1989), and into conditions of their utilization for archaeological interpretation.

To company with this objective, two techniques of northwest India were studied :

the wheel-throwing technique of ceramic pots in Haryana and Rajasthan.

the knapping technique of agate and carnelian beads in Gujarat.

Wheel-thrown pots and hard stone beads are part of the Indus archaeological assemblages. Wheel-throwing is mentioned right from the 5th millenium BC (Samzun 1988). It follows the coiling technique. Beads are also knapped out of hard stones right from the 5th millenium BC. Their techno-morphological evolution is marked by a peak attained during the Harappan period (first half of the 3rd millenium) characterized by the long, tubular carnelian beads (see particularly kenoyer 1986, Mackay 1943, Rao 1973, 1979 Vidale 1985).

In the framework of this article, our results on the wheel-throwing technique will be very briefly presented (for details, see Roux, 1989). Our aim is to discuss in comparison with another case, the value of our conclusions and the application of the "craft specialization" hypothesis to objects other than wheel-thrown ceramics or carnelian beads.

C/o French Embarry, 2 Aurangzab Road New Delhi.

India appeared to be a privileged place for investigating into material facts relating to the Indus civilization : such as the wheel-throwing technique, as knapping of carnelian beads etc.

KNAPPING OF BEADS AT KHAMBAT

Research hypothesis

Our reasearch objective was defined in relation to the results of an earlier study on the wheel-throwing technique (Roux, 1989). This study is based on observational and experimental data which demonstrate on the one hand that the throwing technique is a complex one, on account of the numerous parameters which intervene (physical and motor parameters), and on the other hand that it involves a long apprenticeship.

For the purpose of archaeological interpretation, we proposed the following hypothesis : the wheel-throwing technique is significant of technical specialization on account of the investment in time and skill which all the groups in the community are not able to put in. The terms of the hypothesis are dependent on a strictly functional relationship. We do not want to say that a technique, by itself, is the determining factor of certain socio-economic milieu or socio-economic structures (ex. Balfet, 1973). But it is possible to think that only certain socio-economic milieu enable long and difficult learning techniques to appear and to persist, at the cost of specialization by a sub-group. Our hypothesis is applicable to every human group, taking into account of the relationship on which it is based : "wheel-throwing technique - long and difficult apprenticeship" and the context in which at is valid. In other words, it must be applicable to every archaeological site where wheel-thrown ceramics are present.

One of the ways to support this hypothesis is to study for other crafts the relationship between the apprenticeship variable and the phenomenon of craft specialization. In this perspective, we made a study on the manufacture of agate and carnelian beads at khambat (Cambay) (ethnoarchaeological investigation, V. Roux, technological study, J. Pelegrin, archaeological study, M.L. Inizan).

Study at Khambat

More precisely, we approached the problem of specialization through an analysis of the knapping technique and of the relationships between the socio-economic status of the craftsmen and the types of bead manufactured. The Study of these relationships will involve the successive analyses of a) the levels of performance displayed in the knapping of the different types of beads, b) the competence required for the different performances, c) the duration of apprenticeship associated with the acquisition of this competence. The performance includes the knowledge and the know-how *involved* in the manufacture of the finished products. The competence relates to the knowledge and the know-how *actually* possessed by the craftsman. Regularities will be brought out between beads manufacturing and techno-economic specialization; their fields of application will be discussed.

The knapping activity takes place in an ethnographic framework - the manufacturing process and organization of the production - which we present hereafter. The presentation will be restricted to the information required for an understanding of the study.

1. ETHNOGRAPHIC CONTEXT

1.1 Manufacturing process

The different beads manufactured at Khambat are all in various coloured and/zoned chalcedonies. In the rough state, they are pebbles extracted from the Narmada terraces 200 Km southeast of Khambat (Ratanpur, Bharuch district). These pebbles are sorted out on the spot, then carried by truck.

A primary heat treatment is carried out to give the rough material, originally "dry" and fibrous, a finer grain suited to knapping. Repeated heat treatment is applied to carnelians, yellow chalcedonies in the rough state which become red when heated; the latter are the most prized.

Once the stones have cooled they are knapped by indirectreverse percussion which we will describe further on in detail. The beads are then ground either on carborundum wheels (artificial vitrified carbosilicium), or in dry rotating wooden drums; the rubbing of the beads against each other abrade them while grinding down their shape. It can reduce their size by half.

The bead is then drilled with the help of a bow-drill. The bead is held in a wooden frame while the craftsman holds the drill with the left hand, and with the right hand he makes the bow execute a front to back movement which makes the drill turn in an alternating circular rotation. The drilling is done in two stages, each of the halves of the length of the bead being drilled from the distal and proximal ends respectively[1].

The polishing and glossing is generally done in rotating wooden drums which turn slowly with water mixed with emery dust (for the polishing operation) and with detergent and chalcedony dust (for the glossing operation). Faceted beads and large fragile objects are polished by hand on wheels made of lacquer and of carborundum dust. They are glossed on wheels made of lacquer and of chalcedony dust.

1.2. Organization of the production

The knapping of the beads is done, traditionally, in workshops located in the city. These workshops employ 2 to 15 workers. A total of a dozen workshops employ 10 to 15 workers while about fifty of them employ between 2 to 5 workers. Within the workshops, the operations of heating, knapping and sometimes grinding are executed. The drilling and polishing operations (generally including grinding) are done outside by some specific enterprises. These operations are financed by the workshops which, at the end, get back the finished products and sell them. Seven to ten workshops export directly abroad. The others market their production through traders. The orders are distributed among the workshops according to the quality of the products : one must distinguish the workshops which produce superior quality objects (their number is very limited, on account of the small demand for these products), from workshops whose production is of an inferior quality (75% of cases) . The number of the latter has increased during the last ten years with the very repid development of an international market for "costume jewellery. In these workshops, the workers are paid on a piece basis (depending on the shape of the beads; or by kilo. In some workshops whose bead production is of superior quality, the craftsmen receive a daily salary.

The beads are also knapped outside the workshop, in the streets, by a population made up, in the majority, of women and children who knap during their free time. This is a recent situation which developed 10 years back with the introduction of manufacture of small beads of very inferior quality (as regards the chipping). The production is sold per piece or by the kilo, either directly to the workshops, or through middlemen who resell them to the workshops or to traders, while the beads are not yet either ground or drilled. It is difficult to specify the number of craftsmen who are working in this manner. According to our informant, their number is approximately one hundred.

2. THE KNAPPING TECHNIQUE AND THE PRODUCTS

2.1. The technique

The knapping technique is that of indirect-reverse percussion. The knapper uses two tools in conjuction (description in the general case of a right-handed knapper) : - a bar of iron pointed on both sides (*shik*) about fifty centimeters long and having a diameter of two centimeters, driven obliquely into the ground in front and slightly to the left of the knapper ; a buffalo horn hammer mounted on a thin bamboo stick (*Shingadi*) or, for the smaller pieces, a sort of iron nail with a flat head (*madiya*) mounted also on a thin bamboo stick.

To detach a flake (*car*), the knapper holds the piece to be knapped between the fingers of his left hand and applies the edge of the piece against the extremity of the iron bar. The hammer held in the other hand strikes the piece to detach a flake from the point of contact with the iron bar.

1. The drill itself is made up of a wooden handle into which an iron rod is inserted, generally an umbrella rib. The rod has at its end one or two cavities in which either one or two diamonds are inlaid. The utilization of the type of rod depends on the stage of drilling. The first stage consists in shaping a hollow on the bead. The drill required (tankni) has a rod with one dimond. The second stage consists in deep drilling. The drill (Shardi) used has two diamonds whose extreme dimater is larger than that of the rod. The rods of the shardi may be of a variable length and diameter depending on the size of the bead.

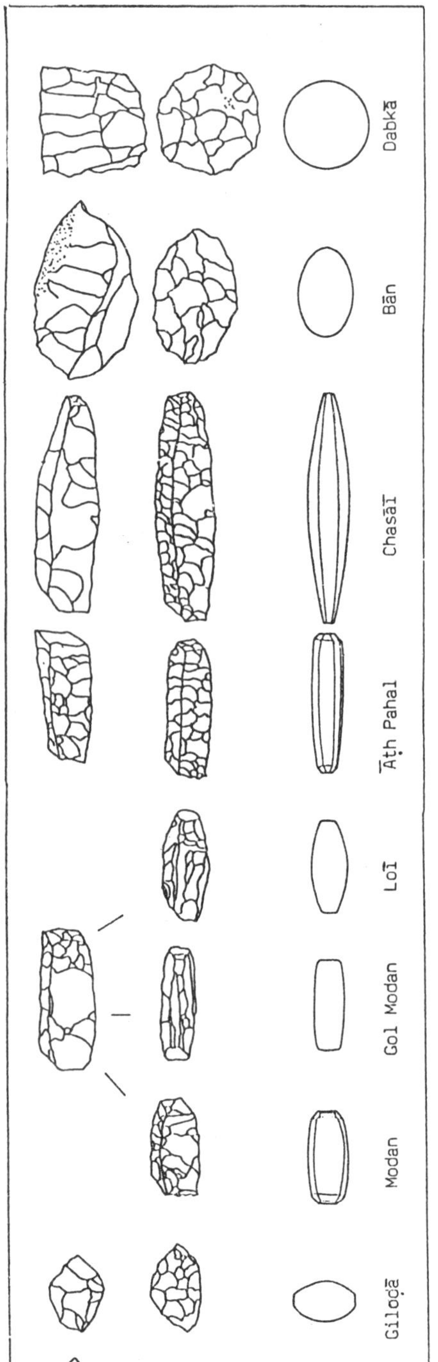

1 = Rough-out 2 = Preforms 3 = Finished products

Fig. 1. Rough-outs, preforms, and finished products of the main types of beads knapped at present in Khambat.

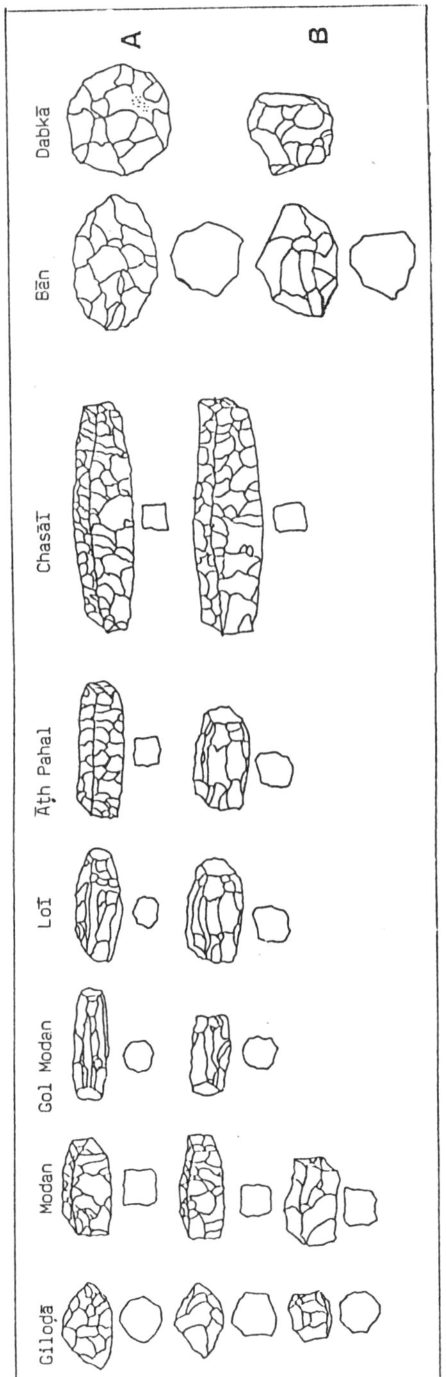

A = superior quality B = inferior quality C = disco quality

Fig. 3. Different knapping qualities of preforms - ready for grinding - of beads knapped in Khambat.

Apart from the knapping of "disco" beads (see hereafter the definition) done in one stage, the knapping of a bead - or rather of a series of beads of a single type - is done in two stages. An initial preliminary roughing out (*parvana*) leads to a rough-out (*cirita*, rough piece which displays its main geometrical characteristics). The finishing of the knapping (*khandvana*) leads to a preform (knapped piece ready for ginding) which will then be ground, drilled, polished and glossed. The knapper changes the iron bar (more pointed for (*khandvana*) and the hammer (lighter) between these two stages.

2.2. **The products (shapes and qualities)**

The main shapes of beads are the following (figure 1) :

Mani : small spherical bead of 5 mm to 10 mm in diameter.

Nagina : small cabochon having a circular base whose diameter is between 5 mm and 10 mm.

Pasiys : three sided bead whose length is between 1.5 cm and 2.5 cm and sides are between 0.9 cm and 1.1 cm.

Giloda : small ovoid bead available in two sizes. The beads of standard size are 1.5 cm to 2 cm long and 1.2 to 1.4 cm in diameter. The large sized beads are 2.5 cm to 3 cm long and 1.8 cm to 2 cm in diameter.

Modan : elongated square section bead in two sizes. The standard size beads are from 2 cm to 2.5 cm long and the width of the sides is from 0.9 cm to 1.1 cm. The large sized beads are from 2.5 cm to 3 cm long and the width of their sides is from 1.3 cm to 1.5 cm.

Loi : bead in the form of a bitrucated spindle whose length is between 2 cm and 2.5 cm and mesial diameter between 1.1 cm and 1.4 cm. The *loi* destined for the Tibetan market have a length of 6 cm to 10 cm and a mesial diameter of 2 cm to 3 cm.

Gol Modan (also called "pipe") : tubular bead whose mesial diameter is identical to the distal and proximal diameters. The dimensions of the length are similar to those of *loi*.

Ath pahal : bead in the shape of a truncated, elongated pyramid with 8 faces, whose length varies between 4 to 6 cm, its basal diameter between 0.8 cm and 1.3 and the apical diameter between 0.6 cm and 1 cm.

Ban : large ovoid bead whose length is between 3 cm and 4 cm and diameter between 2.4 and 3 cm. The *ban* destined for the Tibetan market are from 7.5 cm to 10 cm long and have a diameter of 4 to 5 cm.

Dabka : large spherical bead ordinarily of a diameter of 10 to 30 mm. The *dabka* destined for the Tibetan market may have a diameter upto 6 cm.

Chasai : bead in the shape of a bitruncated spindle with an octogonal section, destined mainly for the Naga market. The length varies mainly between 6 cm and 11 cm and the diameter between 1 and 1.5 cm.

Chasali, ath pahal, ban, dabka, loi and *gol modan* may be of what is called superior or inferior quality. The other types of beads on the list may display three qualities : superior, inferior and "disco" (see figure 2 and 3). The latter term was introduced locally ten years ago to designate beads of irregular shape whose grinding is done by riotation in drums.

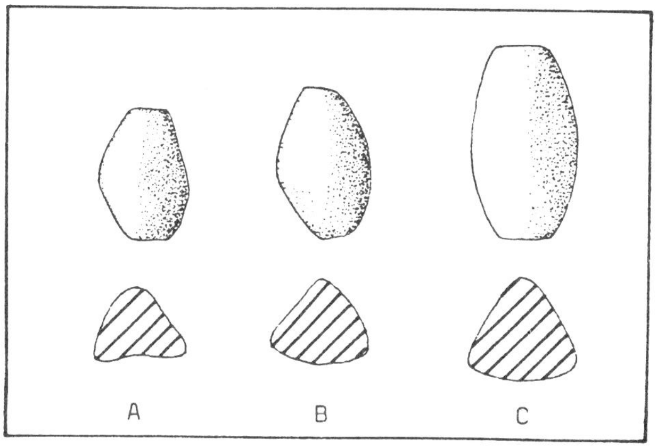

Fig. 2. different qualities for a same type of bead (pasiya)
a) superior quality, b) inferior quality, c) disco quality.

The beads of so-called superior quality are distinguished by the regularity and the symmetry of their shapes. More precisely, ovoid, curved; their faces are equal and their ridges are rectilinear. On the contrary, the beads of so-called inferior quality are not perfectly regular and symmetrical. What are called disco beads are characterized by shapes of a very mediocre quality. The retouch is short and irregular and the ridges are not rectilinear. These beads are made in a single phase on the same *shik*.

Not only different qualities of raw material, but also different grinding processes are used for the different qualities of knapping. The superior quality beads are ground by hand on carborundum wheels while the inferior quality and disco beads are first ground in bulk in rotating wooden drums. The disco beads of standard size are put in a dry processing drum for 6 hours, while the inferior quality beads are similarly treated for 2 hours. For the latter, the grinding in the drum is followed by a slight regularisation on the carborudum wheel. In addition, except for the spheroid and large ovoid beads, disco and inferior quality beads undergo a preparatory grinding for drilling.

The appearance of these three qualities of beads is a relatively recent phenomenon. During the 20th century and up to the end of the 60s, the production was homogeneous in quality (superior quality in terms of knapping) meant basically for the internal markets (Assam, Nagaland) and the African markets (Nigeria and Ghana). These latter were given up in 1969, due to changes in the banking rules. Following this, an international market (Saudi Arabia, South-East Asia and the West) developed, which become a buyer not only of superior and inferior quality beads but also of disco beads. The latter quality appeared during the late 70s, at the time when the grinding process by drum started.

3. DIFFERENTIATED PRODUCTION AND LEVELS OF KNOW-HOW

According to the shape, the size or the quality of the beads, three levels of difficulty in knapping (performance) are distinguished : They correspond to the respective production of three groups of craftsmen, their difference with relation to each other being expressed in terms of the know-how required for the manufacture of each bead production.

FIRST LEVEL : manufacture of disco beads of the *mani, nagina, paisya* and *giloda* types. They are all made repidly (in some tens of seconds) from rejected raw material and from knapping wastes from the workshops. The small round beads (*mani*) are obtained through the simple, repeated ablation of the asperities of small fragments of raw material. The cabochons (*nagina*) are manufactured by simple direct retouch of a flake on its dorsal surface. There first two beads do not involve any veritable strategy (operational know-how), but the simple repetition of an elementary act : the knocking off of an asperity or outgrowth of the volume or the contour. The small ovoid beads (*giloda*) and the three-sided beads (*pasiya*) of disco quality are made in accordance with a still rudimentary strategy which consists is setting some series of small flakes starting from each extermity in such a way as to make the piece regular. On this level of disco quality, the motor know-how is, in all cases, elementary. Only small flakes are detached, without any great adaptation of the detachment.

SECOND LEVEL : manufacturing disco *modan* and standard sized beads of inferior quality. They include the different types of beads enumerated earlier, except *chasai* and *ath pahal*.

THIRD LEVEL : manufacturing beads of superior quality, of shapes and all dimensions.

These last two levels are distinguished on the basis of the quality, the dimensions and the shapes of the finished products. For each of these parameters there is a corresponding degree of difficulty in knapping.

1. *The knapping quality*. The superior quality is more difficult to obtain than the inferior quality because it involves a better operational and motor control for removing thin and covering flakes required for shaping perfectly symmetrical and regular pieces.

2. *The dimensions*. Whatever the type, the large beads are always more difficult to make. There are several reasons:

-the detaching of controlled elongated flakes, necessary for obtaining big beads, clearly requires greater skill than the detachment of short flakes, more "natural" for the technique at issue.

-the removal, for the big pieces, of large flakes controlled in varied series requires the arranging of series in a larger number of organised sequences than for the small pieces. Their arrangment then corresponds to the deployment of a more elaborate operational know-how, which is more critical in the evaluation of the situation and more strict in decision-making. This is all the more so since every combination of sequences inaccurately estimated endangers the success of the following sequences and/or the success of particularly delicate, critical removals when they are of large dimensions.

Thus, the bigger the piece, the less it is possible to be satisfied with approximations or with taking recourse to a simplified variation of a complex sequence.

3. *The shapes*. The different shapes of beads also present different degrees of difficulty. They are classified by the craftsmen in growing order of difficulty as follows : *mani, nagina, pasiya, giloda, modan, loi, gol modan, ath pahal, ban, babka, chasai.* This order corresponds to the growing technical difficulties, perceived as such by the craftsmen who learn to progressively master them in this order. The given order is the only one prevalent among the craftsmen of the higher level. It varies among craftsmen of the lower level. It is therefore only once the technique of percussion has been mastered that the craftsmen perceive in an identical manner the knapping difficulties. These are then explainable according to the general physical constraints of hard stones knapping, which enables us to consider as insignificant the eventual local variations in the perception of the given order. These constraints are the following :

-it is easier to knap 60° dihedrals than 90° dihedrals, this latter angle representing the classic limit of detachment by chonchoidal fracture. The pieces of triangular section, such as *pasiya* and *giloda* (whose outline is of triangular section) are thus easier to knap than the pieces whose outlines are of quadrangular section as *modan, loi* and *gol modan* ath pahal and chasi.

- on the other hand, *ban* and *dabka* are more difficult to make than *modan*, loi and *gol modan* as the shaping of their wide section requires thin, oblique, angle removals, in which the success of each removal conditions that of the next one. In addition, the removal of the crests of these pieces must be done not only from the ends but also from a mesial nagative which requires a much more delicate preparation. This negative removal of the crest from this negative it particularly necessary for the knapping of the *ban* whose difficulty lies in the passage from the rough-out to the preform. The difficulty of these removals is greater than that of removing the crests from the extremities in the quadrangular section pieces. Lastly, the very big *dabka* can be considered as the most difficult piece of the series for two reasons that are specific to them :

- the knapping of the rough-out brings out several patterns (6 or 7 have been observed), presenting the problem of choosing the best strategy according to the raw material ;

- a perfectly spherical piece depends on a balance that is difficult to obtain taking into account the difficulty in perceiving a sight asymmetry and in controlling the covering oblique flakes specific to the final chipping of this shape.

-the *chasai* adds to its own difficulty through the risk of breaking a preform which ends up thin and long and whose homogeneous, translucid raw material has been made very fragile by successive heat treatments.

4. PERFORMANCE AND COMPETENCE

4.1 Performance and groups of craftsmen

At Khambat, the three levels of performance brought to light through technological analysis of the different types of beads correspond to three distinct groups of craftsmen from the point of view of technical performance as well as of economic resources and of working time.

Level 1 (the weakest) corresponds to a population made up in the majority of women and children who knap in the street, during their free time, the simples of disco beads (*mani, nagina, pasiya* and sometimes *giloda*) finding in this activity a supplementary source of income.

Levels 2 and 3 correspond to craftsmen operating in workshops. These workshops are specialized in terms of the quality of their production :

-the craftsmen of level 2 work in workshops specialized exclusively in a production of inferior and disco quality (pieces of the same quality as the pieces manufactured by level 1, but having slightly larger dimensions; knapping also of disco modan).

-the level 3 craftsmen work in workshops specialized exclusively in a high quality production.

In the last two cases, knapping constitutes the main source of income of the craftsmen.

4.2. Relationship between performance and competence

Keeping in mind the specialization of the workshops according to their production, the question arose about the relationship between performance and competence, that is to say the relationship between the knowledge and the know-how deployed in the bead manufacturing and the knowledge and know-how actually possessed by the craftsman. The study of the performance-competence relationship represents one of the essential points of the investigation, the observation of the performance not enabling us to define a level of competence.

Experimentation

The problem was to evaluate, in particular, the actual competence possessed by the level 2 and 3 groups. The level 1 group was put aside as the know-how deployed is so rudimentary that there is not even a combination of knowledge and therefore possible criteria of comparison with the 2 and 3 levels. We asked 16 craftsmen of these two latter (8 per level) to manufacture beads of different shapes and dimensions : *loi. gol modan, giloda, ban, dabka*. Each craftsman produced three specimen of each of these shapes in standard dimensions, and one specimen of 7 cm in length for *loi* and *gol modan* and of 5 cm in diameter for *ban* and *dabka*. The instruction was to make beads of superior quality. The experiment was filmed on video and the finished products were kept.

Method of analysis

We set out a descriptive grid which enables : the study of the finished products from the point of view of the defects that a grinder would face : the knapping quality is evaluated in terms of the time that the grinder has to spend for grinding a bead of regular and symmetrical shape.

The descriptive grid of the *finished products* consists in noting the following defects : hollows, asperities, asymmetry of the extremities and of the volume, bad finish of the extremities. The severest defects in terms of grinding time are doubly panalised : these are the hollows and the asymmetrical volume. The analysis of the finished products in terms of this grid enables the evaluation of :

the motor know-how of the craftsmen. A restricted know-how is evaluated with regard to the hollows and the bad finish of the extremities, determined through rough or unsuccessful removals,

-the operational know-how of the craftsmen. A restricted know-how is seen in the presence of asperities and in the asymmetry of the extremities and/or of the volume that the artisans has not been capable of controllong.

The descriptive grid of the *knapping sequences* relates to the passage from rough-out to preform, as the variety of the raw material does not allow the definition, for the knapping of the rough-out, of stereotyped sequences. On the contrary, the knapping of the preforms displays such sequences, known here as remarkable sequences. Two types of remarkable sequences are distinguished depending on whether it is the knapping of tubular beads or of ovoid beads that is described (only these two shapes of beads have been analysed). The analysis of the films in terms of remarkable sequences consists in noting their organization and the time devoted to each step. It enables us to evaluate the operational know-how of the craftsmen.

Results

We are giving here the first results that come out of an analysis of the experimental production of 6 craftsmen of level 2, and of 5 artisans of level 3 (three results are given in a summary manner as we are awaiting the completion of the entire analysis of the experiments for a detailed publication).

The analysis of the performs craftsmen make twice as many defects as the level 3 artisans. These defects consist essentially in hollows, which are the result of a bad control either over "flutings"* (removals of the crests from the extremities) and/or axis removals, or transversal removals. The asperities or asymetries which are also more numerious on the pieces of the level 2 group are evidence of a succinct operational know-how which compromises the obtaining of a regular piece.

The analysis of the knapping sequences done on the basis of the video films also shows this inferior degree of operational know how of the level 2 craftsmen. It is seen:

-either in an incorrect evaluation of the constraints; thus the regularization of the crests of the large, elongated beads which conditions the success of a fluting is an operation that is near-absent among the level 2 craftsmen (the latter spend, on an average, 7 seconds on this, out of a manufacturing time equal to 5 mn, while the level 3 craftsmen spend on an average, 1.35 mn on this, out of an indentical manufacturing time). Similarly, the importance of the removals of crests from crests or of crests from the ends, is radically underestimated by the level 2 craftsmen. The result is that the latter have to reduce the crests of the *ban* basically by means of transversal removals, which promote hollows and irregular and/or asymmetrical shapes.

-or in bad decisions; the sequences are combined in an inadequate manner. We thus observe some reductions of crests through transversal removals before the completion of the fluting series, or then flutings which are not preceded by any preparation of the extremities, which results in bad fluting and the presence of residual crests. In fact, the young level 2 artisans seem to apply some stereotyped sequences without really pondering over their adaptation to the concrete problems encountered during the course of knapping.

To sum up, the first results of our analysis clearly show that to the three levels of performance observable at Khambat, defined by the quality, the shape and the dimensions of the products, there are three corresponding levels of competence, capable of being analysed in terms of knowledge, operational and motor know-how (for a definition of these terms in relation to knapping activities, see Pelegrin, in press). We will now see that these levels of competence correspond to different durations of apprenticeship.

5. LEVELS OF COMPETENCE AND DURATION OF APPRENTICESHIP

In the level 1 group, for disco production, children start to knap right from the time they are 6 years old. They learn first of all to knap *mani* and *nagina*,then *pasiya* and, in rare cases, *giloda* of disco quality. The apprenticeship is done through trial and error. It is very rapid (a few days). The advice, or rather the opinions generally expressed by a member of the family always relate only to the shape of the finished product to be obtained. A beginner is distinguished from an experienced knapper by his rate of production and not by the quality of the finished products.

In the level 2 and 3 groups, the apprenticeship follows the same growing order of difficulty related to the manufacturing of different types of beads. However, if differs from one group to the next in its nature, its duration and its priorities.

The workshops of superior quality

Data about the learning in superior quality workshops refer to a time before the development of the inferior quality or disco production. At present, this form of learning is not practiced any more as all the children learn in the low quality or disco workshops, for lack of employment in the workshops making superior quality beads.

In these workshops, the children started at around 10-12 years old. The transmission of the knowledge and of the know-how was systematic and total, done by a master who gave them oral instructions and/or showed them the gestures for progressively tackling the knapping difficulties. The oral instructions related to the way in which to hold the stone, the angles from which to make the first strikes, the preparation of the striking platforms so as to remove the desired flakes, the strength with which to make the removals and lastly the final shape to be obtained. The blocks of raw material never being of the same type and each displaying peculiar problems, the child learnt the know-how through successive adjustments, but in accordance with rules transmitted directly by the master. The duration of training required for the mastery of the knapping was estimated at around 7 years. By mastery was than understood the knapping of the different types of beads of all dimensions. The passage from one stage of apprenticeship to the other, market out by the different types of beads, was all the slower since an apprentice had to prove to be profitable to the production, which necessitated, in order to respect the quality sought after, a prolonged training (refining the know-how) once the knowledge and the basic gestures were acquired.

Inferior quality workshops

In the inferior quality workshops, the children also start at around 10-12 years old. The handing down of the knowledge is minimal as those in charge of the workshops feel that it is no longer necessary to teach the details of the method, considering the quality of the products asked for. They merely make a few observations about the way to hold the stone and make the strikes and some comments about the quality of the production. The child learns by trial and error and develops operational abilities without thinking over the rules : the latter remain succinct as the priority is no longer quality but productivity. The learning duration, which includes not only the acquisition of the knowledge but also the daily output, is between 2 and 3 years. The competence to be acquired is limited here to the knapping of inferior quality beads of standard dimensions.

Whether it be in the workshops producing inferior or superior quality, the succession of the learning stages follows the growing scale of the manufacturing difficulty of the different types of beads. Its study enables us to better explain the difference in competence and in respective duration of apprenticeship between the 2 and 3 levels.

First the apprentice practices, on wastes, the knapping of very small *fara*, rough rough-outs of *tasbi*, then the knapping of *tasbi* (name given to the preform of *mani*). This consists in removing the ridges of the cube from the apex and in reducing the asperities through small, short removals, in a more or less fine manner depending on the quality of bead desired. The learning then consists in knapping some preforms of standard size on the basis of rough-outs made by experienced craftsmen. The latter are indeed more difficult to make than the former as the variety of the raw material does not enable the application of stereotyped sequences. The apprentice practices first of all on the preforms of *pasiys* and *giloda*. The knapping of *pasiya* is easy in the sense that it simply involves regularizing the three crests and the three sides through small transversal removals in accordance with a motor know-how already acquired during the knapping of *tasbi*. The knapping of the preforms of *giloda* of inferior quality that is followed is a simplified one, being restricted to axe removals from the extremities. For the superior quality *giloda* the faces of the rough-out are first made convex on the basis of transversal removals, then the crests are removed from the ends or from mesial negatives. The ends are regularized by means of small axial removals. The knapping of the preforms of *modan, loi* and *gol modan* whose rough-outs in all three cases are seen in the form of a quadrangular section stick, is then learnt. It is simple for *modan* : it is only a matter of calibrating and of regularizing the faces and the crests of the stick through transversal removals whose thinness and regularity will be more or less carefully done depending on the quality desired. In the case of *loi* and *gol modan* of superior quality, the craftsman has to learn to calibrate the faces and to regularize the crests as a first operation, then to remove the crests from the extremities (fluting) prepared for this purpose. The residual portions of the crests are reduced through tiny transversal flakes which should not lead to hollows on the piece. The knapping of the same beads of inferior quality does not require such an elaborate strategy and the craftsman, in this case, learns essentially to master the fluting operation.

The learning of the preforms is followed by that of the rough-outs of the beads mentioned earlier. The order is similar when keeping in mind the difficulties which also increase progressively (ex. the greater difficulties are presented by the quadrangular section pieces as compared to the triangular ones). In all cases, there is no absolutely stereotyped approach. It is only the final result that counts, that is to say,a calibrated piece with symmetrical sections and regular lines.

After the learning of these forms comes that of knapping the rough-outs and preforms of *dabka* and *ban* of standard size, beads which are particularly difficult to produce. The making of the large dimension beads is then learnt. The last stage is the apprenticeship in knapping (for the workshops specialized in these productions) either large spherical pieces, or large *chasai* whose special difficulties we have already mentioned.

6. REGULARITIES BETWEEN MATERIAL FACTS AND CRAFT SPECIALIZATION

At Khambat, the three groups of craftsmen corresponding to the three levels of competence show different degrees of specialization which is spread over two distinct axis.

On the socio-economic axis of specialization, the craftsmen of levels 2 and 3 and distinguished from the level 1 craftsmen in terms of time and income which the knapping work involves : full time work and main source of income in the first two cases, part time work and supplementary source of income in the last case.

On the technical axis of specialization, the three levels are distinguished from each other on the basis of their production which correspond not only to different levels of knowledge and of know-how but also to different durations of learning.

Regularities

In the framework of research on regularities between material facts and craft specialization, it is on the technical and economic axis that two regularities are seen:

1. a regularity which brings out a relationship between "product of high technicality" and "technical specialization" : a group of craftsmen is distinguished from other craftsmen in terms of competence.

2. a regularity which brings out a relationship between "products of high technicality", "large quantity" and "techno-economic specialization" : the craftsmen are differentiated from the rest of the population in terms of technical competence and economic resources.

Explanation

These regularities can be explained in terms of :

1. duration of apprenticeship which varies according to the levels of competence related to the different degrees of technicality of the products. At Khambat, the differenciation of the groups of craftsmen in terms of competence is a recent phenomenon linked with the following factors :

-the use of grinding techniques which enable, at the same time, the grinding of badly knapped beads (of inferior or disco quality) and a considerable reduction of the grinding cost;

-the development of a market for beads of inferior or disco quality;

-the maintenance of a traditional market for large dimension beads and of superior quality beads;

-the specialization of workshops according to the types of products.

2. manufacturing time for pieces of high technicality. When the production of these pieces exceeds a limited number of specimen (as is the case with prestigious objects), it is possible to associate technical specialization with economic specialization, on account of an investment in time which is done necessarily to the detriment of other economic activities.

Generalization

The regularities distinguished above are akin to what we have observed for the wheel-throwing technique. In both cases, the relationship between degree of technicality and technical specialization depends on the duration of apprenticeship.

We will now ask the following question : is it possible to consider every object of high technicality, which is defined by the duration of apprenticeship, as having been made by a specialist ? To answer this question, we will return to our definition of technical specialization. This is made up of the following two terms :

-an exclusive production by a sub-group of individuals,

-a consumption of this production by some domestic groups other than the manufacturers.

This definition excludes from specialization the productions differentiated on the scale of the domestic group. Now, the single criterion of high technicality will not enable us to distinguish between the assemblages whose differentiation can be the result either of a sexual distribution of the tasks (a case that has been considered for the Paleolithic), or of the distribution of tasks within the community. It is therefore a matter of specifying the context in which our criterion is significant for technical specialization. We will state it as follows :

-presence of a small number of pieces of high technicality with respect to the assemblage considered. The combination of the criteria "small number and high technicality" imply that only some individuals, having a specific competence, have made these objects.

-presence of pieces of high technicality in a technical system which includes numerous craft activities (the case for example of the chalcolithic periods as compared to the palaeolthic periods). The duration of learning required for the achievement of a craft activity, among others, then becomes relevant as, in this context, an activity that takes long to learn cannot be practised by all the domestic groups of a community.

It should be specified that technical specialization could be seen through other criteria, such as, for instance, spatial distribution : from the moment that it is recognized that some objects are utilized by domestic group other than manufacturers, it is possible, by definition, to infer a technical specialization.

We are in fact in search of criteria that point out to technical and/or economic specialization. The criterion of high technicality, defined by the duration of apprenticeship, must be considered as a possible criterion, among others.

From archeological assemblages, the learning durations may be inferred with reference to ethnoarcheological or experimental studies (e.g. wheel-thrown ceramics, carnelian beads, "debitage" by pressure (Pelegrin, 1988)). The duration thus inferred will be admissible with regard to the following postulate : the difficulties of acquisition of knowledge are identical among all Homo sapiens sapiens. This postulate could be justified by research conducted at present in intercultural psychology on the existence of cultural constants concerning operational development (level of competence), the cultural differences acting on the modalities of operational development and the utilization of competence (level of performance; Dasen, 1983).

CONCLUSIONS

In prospective, the two regularities stated in the course of this study can be considered as the first of a series which will enable us *not* to define the motors of development of differentiated societies (from a techno-economic or socio-economic point of view, whichever the angle of analysis adopted), *but* rather to recognize, on a site, or an assembly of sites, a form of specialization. The diversity of cultures will be perceived through the description of the modalities according to which the societies will integrate the different degrees of specialization, established with reference to regularities. These are then not a reduction of the social phenomenon (the specialization of a group) to an individual fact (apprenticeship on the scale of an individual) but the bringing to light of a functional link between two elements, presented here in terms of learning problems of individuals and the solution required to these problems on the scale of the community.

Let us specify also that the statement of these two regularities does not exclude the fact that some objects of a low technicality can be made by specialists (example of handmade ceramics). If it is possible to characterize craft specialization on the basis of assemblages of low technicality, it will then be possible to also describe the conditions is which, according to each site, craft specialization characterized by high technicality has developed (development on the basis, or not, of an already present specialization).

In an ethnoarchaeological perspective, the technological analysis, in terms of knowledge and of know-how, promises to be a particularly fruitful area of research. The ethnorachaeology considered here aims at studying the relationships between material facts and anthropological propositions applicable to archaeological sites. This last clause implies the formulation of relationships of a transcular order. We have seen that such relationships are valid within restricted contexts whose definitions always need to be respecified during the course of research. Thereafter, it is not illusory to think that numerous regularities can thus be established. The study of the cultural peculiarities will be done during the reconstitution of the prehistoric events, made on the basis of regularities (Gallay, 1989).

References

H. BALFET, 1973 : A propos du tour du potier : l outil et le geste technique, in *L'homme, hier et aujourd' hui. Recueil d' etudes en hommage a A. Leroi-Gourhan*, Cujas, Paris, p. 109-122.

E.M. BRUMFIEL & T.K. EARLE (ed), 1987 : *Specialization, exchange and complex societies*, Cambridge University Press, Cambridge, 145 p.

P. DASEN, 1983 : Aspects fonctionnels du developpement operatorie : les recherches inter-culturelles, in *Archives de psychologie*, 51, p.57-60.

M.M. DOW, 1985 : Agricultural intensification and craft specialization. A non recursive model. In *Ethnology*, vol. 24, n02, p.137-152.

R.K. EVANS, 1978 : Early craft specialization : an example from the Balkan Chalcolithic, in *Social archeology : beyond subsistence and dating*, ed. byC. Redman and al., Academic Press, New Yourk, p. 113-129.

A. GALLAY, 1986 : *L'archeologie demain*, ed. Balfond/sciences, Pariis, 319 p.

1989 : Logicism : a french view of archaeological theory founded in computational perspective. in *Antiquity*, vol. 63, n 238, p.27-39.

J.M. KENOYER, 1986 : The Indus bead industry. Contributions to bead technology. in *Oranment*. Vol. 10, N1, p. 18-21.

E.J. MACKAY, 1943 : *Chanhudaro Excavations* : 1935-36, American Oriental Series 20, New Haven, 338 p.

J. PELEGRIN, 1988 : Debitage experimental par pression "du plus petit au plus grand", in Technologie prehistorique, Notes et petit au plus grand". in *Technologie prehistorique*, Notes et Monographies Techniques n 25, Editions du CNRS, Paris, p. 37-53.

sous presse : A framework for analysing prehistoric stone tools manufacture and a tentative application to some early lithic industries, Communication au colloque de la fondation Fyssen, Versailles 25-29 novembre 1988.

S.R. RAO, 1973 : *Lothal and the Indus civilization*, Asia Publishing House, Bombay, 215 p.

1979 : *Lothal : 1955-62*, Memoirs of the Archaeological Survey of India 78, Delhi, vol. 1.

P.M. RICE, 1981 : Evolution of specialized pottery production : a trial model, in *Current Anthropology*, 22, p. 219-240.

V. ROUX, and D. CORBETTA, 1989 : *The Potter's Wheel : craft specialization and technical competence*, Oxford & IBH Publishing, New Delhi, 145 p.

A. SAMZUN, 1988 : La ceramique chalcolithique de Mehrgarh III et ses relations avec celle de l'Asie centrale (Namazga I-II), in *L' Asie centrale et ses rapports avec les civilisations orientales des origines a l'age due fer, Actes du colloque franco-sovietique*, Paris, 19-26 novembre, 1985. Diffusion De Boccard, Paris, 1988, p. 125-133.

J. TIXIER, M.L. INIZAN et H. ROCHE, 1980 : *Prehistorie de la pierre taillee 1*, terminologie et technologie, Cercle de Recherches et d'Etudes Prehistoriques, Antibes, 120 p.

M. TOSI, 1984 : The notion of craft specialization and its representation in the archaeological record of early states in the Turanian basin, in *Marxist Perspectives in Archaeology*, ed. by M. Spriggs, Cambridge, p. 125-133.

M. VIDALE, 1985 : Some aspects of lapidary craft at Mohenjodaro in light of recent surface record of the Moneer southeast area, in *Interim Reports : ISMEO-Achen University Mission*, vol. 2, M. Jansen and G. Urban eds., Aachen, p. 113-150.

ETHNO-ARCHAEOLOGY OF THE TRADITIONAL CEREMONIAL POTTERY OF GUJARAT

Syed Anis Hashim*

Pottery is one of the most and wide spread crafts which still continues more or less in the traditional form and pettern in our country, provide an important link between the present and the past. Therefore, it is one of the most important tools for interpretation and understanding of the ancient civilzations.

In our country evidence for the use of pottery is found right from the pre-Harappan period which goes back to circa 6000 B.C. Our literary records also give descriptive evidence for the use of pottery at many ceremonial occasions in the past. For instance, the Maller inscription of king Jayalladeva II, present a description of a 'mangala kumbh' auspicious pot, for the worship of god Siva.[1] The Tirumakkudal inscription of veera Rajendra Subrahmanya, dated to 11th century A.D., gives evidence for the display of one hundered and eight pots of clay, drapped with clothes before a goddess on the occasion of the king's birthday.[2]

Beside the vessels and pots, terracottas in the form of mother goodess and human and animal figurines are also found from the very ancient period. The preparation and use of terracottas is described by Bana in the context of the marriage of princess Rajyasri in the Harscharita.[3] Description of terrocattas figurines, prepared and coloured, is also supported by a passage from the sakuntala.[4]

In this paper attempt has been made to throw light on the clay pots which are speicially produced, by the traditional potters, of Gujarat, to be used in different social and religious ceremonies, and to trace their origin and spread through the archaeological evidence.

A number of clay objects used for ceremonial purposes in this region are made by the potters. They can be classified into three man categories :-

1. Objects used on the occasion of marriage ceremonies.
2. Objects used on the occasion of festivals or worship.
3. Objects used for worship by the tribes, Bhils and Rathawas.

1. Object Used on the Occasion of Marriage Ceremonies :-

Gujra : It is a ceremonial object which is used at the time of marriage (Fig.1). Five 'gujras' are kept on a raised platform, known as 'chori'. The following varieties of 'gujras' are found in these districts :

(i) It is about six to nine cms long conical object having four or five grooves. Its head is roundish and the base is flat. The longer ones are more conical than the shorter ones. The longer ones are generally found in Baroda district and the shorter ones are used in Broach district. (Fig. la).

(ii) This type of 'gujra' is similar to the first one, but it has a hole inside. this type of 'gujra' is used in Dediapada taluka of Baroda district. (Fig.1b).

(iii) This 'gujra' is very different from other 'gujras'. It has a globular body, thin small neck and a disc type of base. This type of 'gujra' is mostly used in Panchmahals district (Fig. 1c).

Tradition of keeping 'gujras' at the time of marriagte is found in various communities of this state. But it is not a common custom in all the villages and districts. For example, in the district of Kaira it is not used in all the talukas, while in Surat district it is used almost everywhere. Therefore it seems that it is a local and adopted custom.

Gotraj :It is a pot like 'ghada' or 'Matla'. It has a globular shape with short neck, beaded curved rim and saggar base (Fig.1d). Main features of this pot is that it is highly decorated with floral designs. At present, in most of the districts potters paint it with floral motifs in oil paints.

This pot has a great ceremonial value. It is used at the time of marriage, as the first step in which the 'Gotra devi' goddess of gotra, is represented by these pots.

Bujaro :It is a bell-shape lid having a small round knob and a flaring mouth. It is kept on the 'gotraj' as a lid and thus it is also used at the time of marriage. One coconut is placed in 'bujaro' at the time of the marriage ceremony and this 'bujaro' is placed at the top of the 'gotraj'. It is also painted with various floral designs. Oil painted 'bujaro' is also available at some of the places (Fig. 1 e).

Kumkavati : It is a very small pot having very small shallow bowl type shape with short them and a flat base. It is used for keeping 'kum kum' or 'Sindur' (lead oxide) at the time of marriage or after that. It is also used by the tribal people while offering the sacrifices to their deities, as they also offer 'kum kum' or sindur along with other things (Fig.1f).

At present it is not much in use as many substitutes made of metal or glass and more beautiful in appearance are available in the market.

2) Objects used on the Occasion of Festivals or Worship

Garbi :It is a perforated small pot like a 'ghada' in shape (Fig. 1g). It is also a globular pot with short curved beaded rim and

* C/o Dr. Shashi Asthana, National Museum, New Delhi.

Fig 1. CEREMONIAL CLAY OBJECTS FROM GUJARAT.

having saggar base. It is used during 'Navratri' festival at the place of 'garba' (a ceremonial dance infront of Amba devi) for keeping a lamp inside it. This pot is used in almost all over Gujarat. After 'Navaratri', this pot is kept somewhere near a temple or a tank.

Agardani: It is a small solid bulbous object with short stem and flat base. It has many small holes in the body which are used for inserting 'incense sticks' 'agarbatti'. It is available in various sizes. It is also not much in use now, as there are many substitutes to it (Fig. 1h).

Dhupiya (Incence burner) : It is a shallow bowl type of object with a handle for holding it. It is used for burning incense. There are variety of shapes found in these districts.

(i) One is a shallow bowl type with broad mouth and beaked rim. It has a deep groove in the lower part of the body, where the body and bottom join together. It has a flat base and a handle which is attached with the rim portion only and it is bent towards the base. Just opposite the handle it has a preforated small ledge on the rim. Inside the bowl there is a deep hollow. This type of 'dhupiya' is found in Devagadh baria taluka of Panchmahals district (Fig. 1i).

(ii) Another type is a small deep bowl without curved beaded rim having two small ledges on the outer side of the body with a short stem and disc base. It has a handle which is attached with the body on the upper side and with the base on the lower side. It is given a red mica slip. This type of 'dhupiya' is also found in Panchmahals district (Fig. 1j).

(iii) Yet another type is a deep bowl with one carination on the lower side of the body with a short stem and disc base. It bears perforation on the upper part of the body. This 'dhupiya' has no handle. It is mostly found in Karjan taluka of Baroda district (Fig. 1k).

(iv) The fourth type is a small bowl with beaded excurved rim and a short stem with disc type of base. It has double handles, one on either side. These handles are attached with the upper side of the body and with the base. This type of

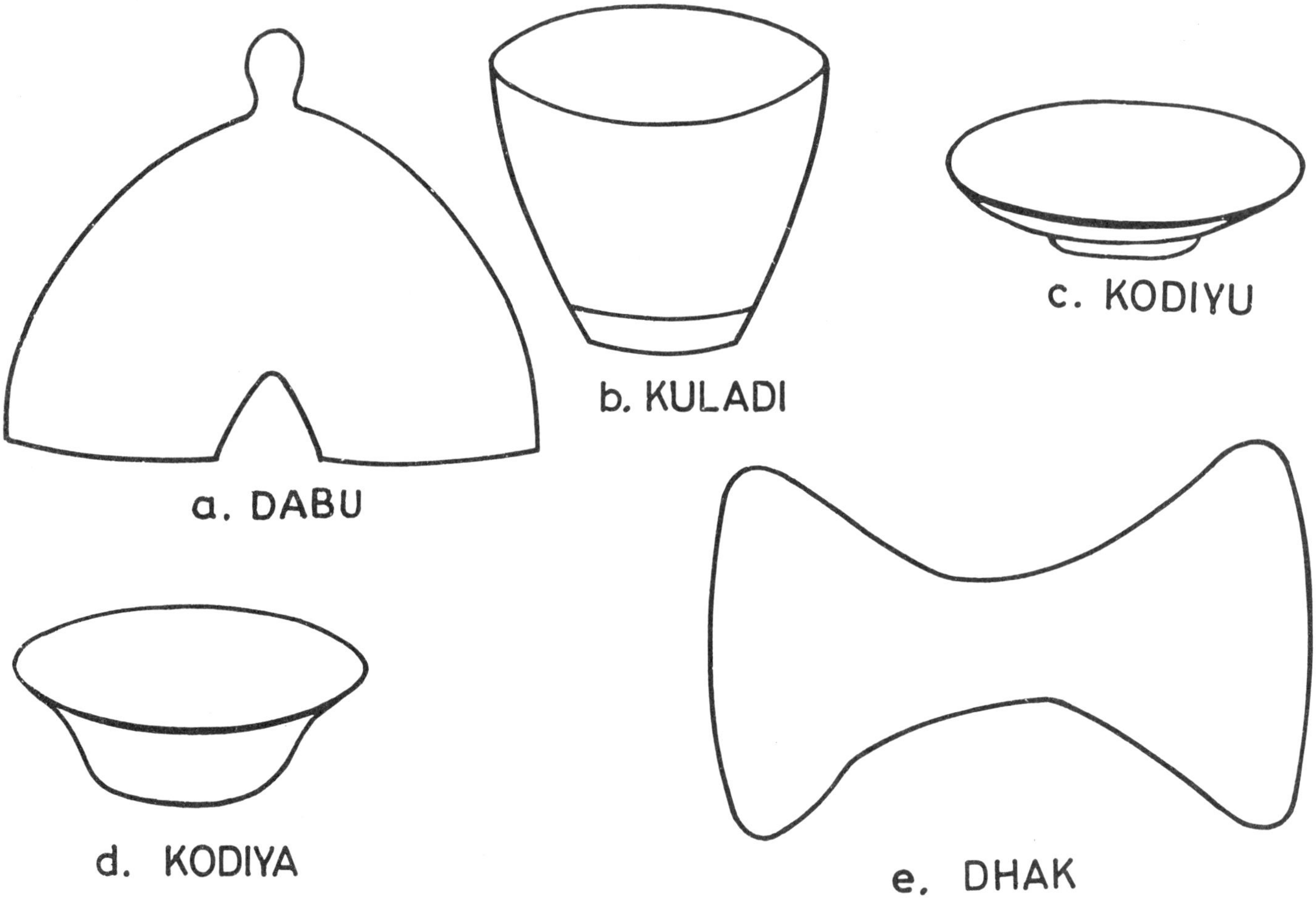

Fig 2. CEREMONIAL CLAY OBJECTS FROM GUJARAT.

'dhupiya' is generally made in Baroda district (Fig. 11).

3. Objects used for Worship by Tribal People

There are a number of clay objects which are used as ceremonial objects by Bhils, Rathwas and other tribal people at the time of offering worship or sacrifices to their godds and goddesses. These are described below :

Dabu : It is a hollow object of a dome shaped having a knob on the top. It has one opening on the lower-side which is generally angular or round shape. It is available in various sizes. It is considered to be an abode of gods and goddesses and also known as 'mandir' i.e., temple. People in the tribal areas of these districts offer it to their respective gods and goddesses (Fig. 2a).

Kuladi : It is a small deep bowl or pot like vessel with broad mouth, featureless rim, the body tapering towards the lower side and a flat base. It is also available in various sizes. It is used as a container for sweets at the time of offering sacrifices to the deities by Bhils and other tribal people. It is also some times used by other people (Fig. 2b).

Kodiyu : It is a very small shallow type of bowl with broad mouth, flaring rim and a flat base. It is also available in various sizes. It is used as a 'diya' or 'dipa' i.e. an oil lamp at the place of worship or sacrifice. It is also used at other occasions like 'Dipawali' festival and other ceremonies. It is made almost everywhere in the villages (Fig. 2c)

Kotvo : It is a variant of a bowl. It is used by the tribal people of Chhota Udaipur in Baroda district and in Panchmahals district, as a container of eatables to be offered as a sacrifices at the 'Devasthan' i.e. the place of worship. This name is used only by the tribal people. It is a shallow bowl with flaring rim and a flat base. It is mostly made in black colour (Fig. 2d).

Dhak : It has a shape like 'damaru' and has two broad and open ends, both ends tapering towards the middle. Open ends are covered with goat-skin. It is used by Bhils and Rathwas as

Conclusion

In Gujarat many types of ceremonial objects of clay are produced by the traditional potters, and used by the most of the people of the region, on different occasions. Among these ceremonial objects 'gujra' is one of the most important one.

The antiquity of 'gujra' is difficult to trace as we do not get any literary or archaeological evidence for this. The significance of 'gujra' at the time of a marriage is not clear through literary sources. According to a oral tradition, it is kept as a symbol of the five natural elements 'Panch tatva' i.e. Earth 'Prithvi' Fire 'Agni' Water 'Jal' space 'Akash' and air 'Vayu'. According to another tradition it is kept as a symbol of a 'Mangal Kalasa' i.e. the pitcher of auspiciousness. In support of this view it is said that it has various groves and it tapers towards the upper side which represent various 'Mangal Kalasas' kept on each other to form a tower. But 'gujras' are found to be without grooves also. Another interesting thing is that they keep five 'gujras' as well as a 'mangal kalasa.' Thus, this theory does not account for this repeatation in performance According to the potters in Panchmahals and Broach districts, it is a symbol of god and the name of the god they do not know. This being so, they do not bake the 'gujra' in fire. Therefore in these districts unbaked 'gujras' are used in the marriages. But in some parts where different tradition prevails they bake, it.

In kasnmir a similar type of object known as 'sani-patul' is used in marriages and worship by the people as 'siva-linga'. It is possible that in our area of study also, it might have been introduced as ling of siva, to be worshipped at the time of marriage, but in course of time actual meaning was forgotten and it became only a ceremonial object.

It is also possible that this tradition might have been introduced in this region during the flourishing period of Lakulisa sect in circa 10th cent A.D. when Gujarat was much influenced with this sect and due to this, worship of 'Sivalinga' became more popular, and so 'Gujras' as symbol of 'siva linga' in miniform would have been introduced to bless the occasion. This idea might have been borrowed from the immigrants of Kashmir.

The more common vericties among these ceremonial object i.e. 'Kodiyu' oil lamp 'Kuladi' small cups and 'dhupiyu' incense burner etc. which have house-hold uses, have been found from almost all the excavated sites of Gujarat and their antiquities go back to circa 2500 B.C. Their patterns and shapes seem to have been changed very little through the ages.

As for the other ceremonial objects are concerned, they have not been idntified separately and it is very difficult to trace their antiquities in archaeological or historical context. Probably, they were introduced from time to time in age long Indian ceramics tradition.

Notes And References

1. *Epigraphia Indica* (E) Vol. xxi, p. 60ff.
2. Ibid.
3. Harscharita IV, p. 142, Quoted from *Memoirs of the Archaeo logical survey of India* no. 73, p. 96.
4. Ibid. Please also refer *Potters and Potteries in Ancient Indian Inscription* by Sushil Malti Devi.
5. For more details on this topic please refer, Hashim, S.A. "Potters and Ceramics Traditions in Panchmahals. Baroda and Broach Districts of Gujarat" Unpublished Ph. D. Thesis from M.S.U. Baroda - 1978.

EXPOSING AND CONSERVING A WORLD HERITAGE MONUMENT

A.K. Sharma*

Centuries old Churches and Convents at Old Goa (15°33' N, Lat; 73°15'E Long) have been declared as world heritage monuments.

This reclaimed land from sea by Prasurama to settle the Aryans, was subsequently ruled by Mauryans, Satavahanas, Bhoja Kings, Chalukyas, Silaharas, Kadambas, Yadavas, Vijayanagar Kings, Bahmani Sultans and Adilshahi Kings of Bijapur.

With the conquest of Goa by Portuguese in 1510 AD. and uninterrupted rule of nearly 450 years by them, Old Goa witnessed hectic activities of establishment of Churches and Convents by different Orders as for Portuguese, politics and religion went hand in hand.

All the Churches and Convents in Old Goa are built either wholly or largely of locally available lateritic blocks of reddish shade. Basalt, brought from outside Goa, was used in making of pilasters and columns to decorate the facades. The laterite, being not so strong and durable, was protected by a coating of lime plaster.

The style of art and architecture prevalent in Europe at that time influenced the artistic and architectural creations in Goa. Though, they were modelled on the European ones they are marked by certain limitations due to climate, availability of material, labour and artisans. The lime plaster needed to protect the laterite structure had to be repeated frequently keeping the building in a state of constant repair. Failure to do so lead to their early collapse of which the Church complex of St. Augustine is the finest example.

The Church which was built on the 'Holy Hill' in 1602 A.D. by the Augustinians friars was one of the biggest complex of its kind in India. After the Augustinians deserted the complex in 1835, due to religious supression, the building fell into neglect resulting in the collapse of the vault on 8th September, 1842. The entire property was appropriated by the Portugues and materials were sold. The facade and half of the north-eastern tower fell in 1931. Another collapse was in 1938. The remaining part of this imposing tower now stands as a land mark which could be seen from distance, forcing one's mind to think of its glorious past. Till February 1989 the whole complex was covered with vegetation and debris and hardly attracted peoples attention except the massive tower.

With the begining of world heritage celebrations in Old Goa by the Archaeological Survey of India, it was decided to scientifically dig, expose and simultaneously conserve the exposed members of the structure. The climatic conditions of the area and expected exposure of plasters and paintings demanded simultaneous conservation using mostly the recovered laterite blocks and basalt slabs. It was also noted that the exposure would attract not only the internal and external tourists but would also evince keen interest in Georgions, as, as per literary evidence the mortal remains of Queen Ketevan, lie buried in a black stone tomb in this complex.

Queen Ketevan, a 17th Century queen of the Soviet Socialist Republic of Georgia was captured in hosilities with the Persians and forcibly abducted by the Shah of Persia. After conversion to Islam she was installed as Queen in 1624. She was greately influenced by Rev. Fr. Ambrosio Das Anjos, a missionary priest sent by the Augustinians from Old Goa to Persia in order to establish a convent at Shiraz and revive Catholicism in the region. It was after the personal interest of the queen that the Shah permitted the Augustinians to set up their convent. But when the monarch found his queen getting more attached to the Augustinian order and shunning the state religion of Islam, he had her beheaded on September, 22, 1624. After her death some of her mortal remains were brought to Goa by Augustinian priests and buried in a black stone tomb in the Augustinian church complex.

Coupled with the adventure to search out the mortal remains of this legendary Queen, begain in February, 1989 one of the biggest exposure, search and simultaneous conservartion operation by Mini Circle office of Archaeological Survey of India in Goa.

Before starting the colossal task, a team of dedicated workers was formed so that every thing exposed could be immediately conserved and well documented, as very little authentic exists in the available records about the architectural details, paintings and inscriptions.

It is decided to take up the area of the church first as this was the most important member of the complex. One season's dig has exposed major portion of the Church. The excavations have brought out a clear picture of plan of the church (Fig.1). On the east three doorways enclosed in a square each and flanked by basalt corianthian colums have been exposed. There are five chapels each on the north and south with their ceilings having ribbed vaults. The main altar in the west had three windows on northern and southern wings. The alter was approached by slowly ascending flight of steps. Evidence show that the vault in the nave and the choir were supported by massive pillars. The hall is oblong on plan but has a cruciform layout in the interior.

The main hall is 67.50 m. long and 16.50m. wide. Two huge basalt slabs bearing inscriptions in Latin with quotations

* Archaralogical Survey of India, Iampath New Delhi-110 011

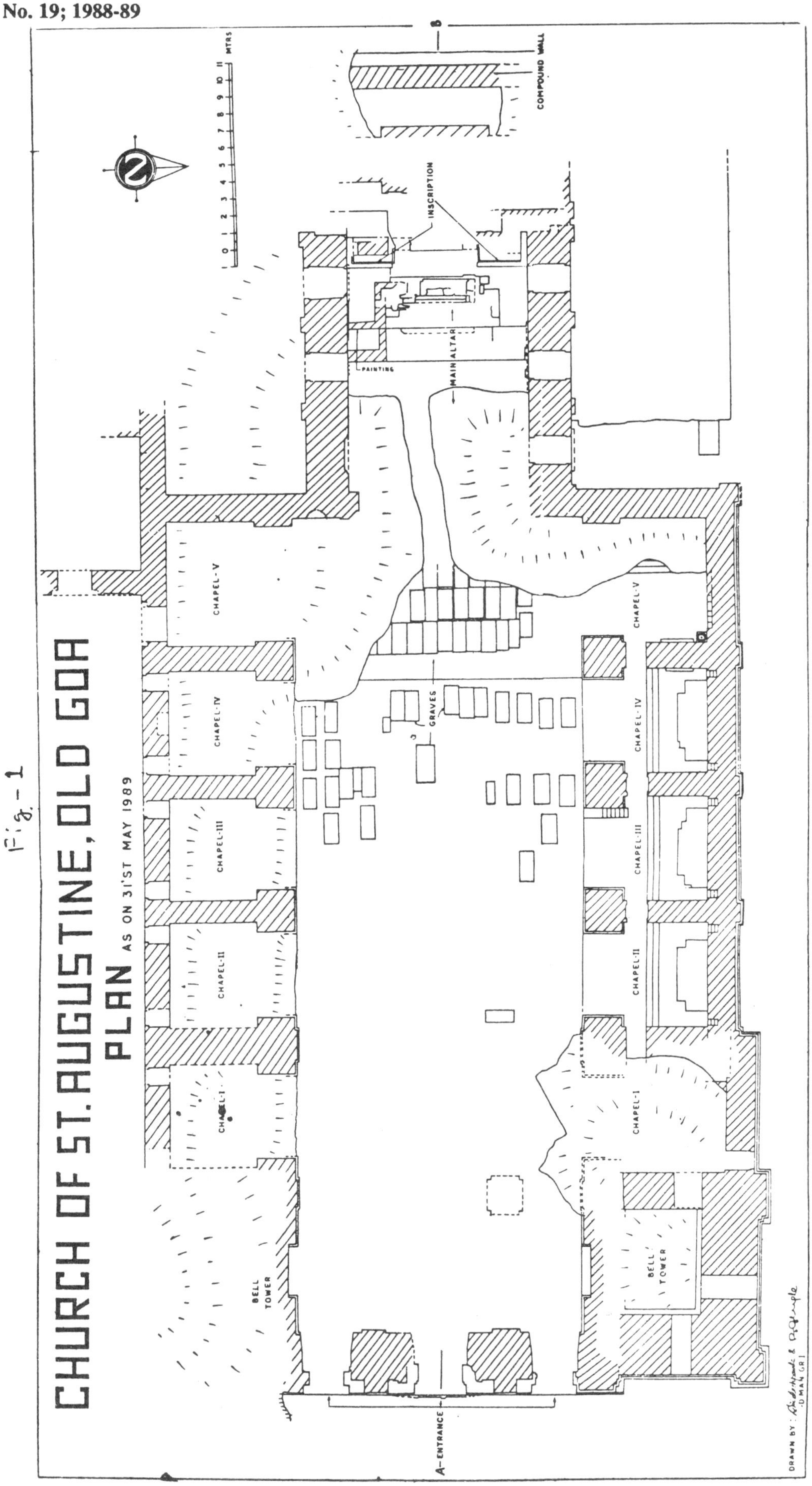
Fig. - 1
CHURCH OF ST. AUGUSTINE, OLD GOA
PLAN AS ON 31'ST MAY 1989
MTRS
COMPOUND WALL
B
INSCRIPTION
MAIN ALTAR
PAINTING
CHAPEL-V
CHAPEL-IV
CHAPEL-III
CHAPEL-II
CHAPEL-I
GRAVES
BELL TOWER
A-ENTRANCE
DRAWN BY :

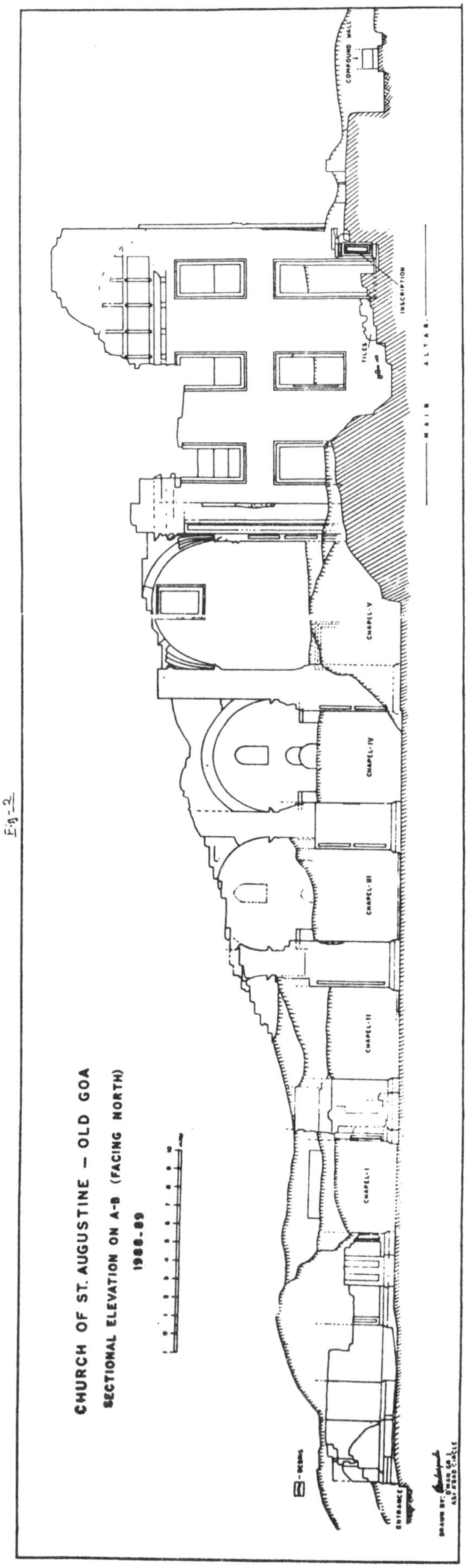
CHURCH OF ST. AUGUSTINE – OLD GOA
SECTIONAL ELEVATION ON A-B (FACING NORTH)
1988-89
COMPOUND WALL
INSCRIPTION
TILES
MAIN ALTAR
CHAPEL-V
CHAPEL-IV
CHAPEL-III
CHAPEL-II
CHAPEL-I
ENTRANCE

Fig-2

from the 'Holy Bible' have been unearthed below the main alter on two sides. Evidence show that the whole hall was plastered and painted with floral designs. Four to Five successive layers of paintings could be recorded. The pigments used were mainly red-ochre. yellow and green with red dominating.

At a later stage some additions and alterations were made in the main altar, During this phase the entire inner walls around the main alter were embellished with coloured Italian tiles which could be surmised on the presence of impressions on the plaster of the walls and also few surviving tiles in intact condition. The subject of the tiles are intricate floral designs using yellow and blue pigments. In order to check these remaining tiles from falling they have been preserved by using filleting technique. During addition phase some cubicles on north and south were created infront of main altar. In one of the northern cubicles a beautiful painting depicts lower portion of the legs of a priest in flowing robbes and bare feet. The window near the main altar were blocked in later years for unknown reasons.

Major portion of the floor of the main hall is occupied by graves of important personalities who were buried at different times in 17th Century. The grave stones are embellished with interesting and variegated emblems. Different types of emblems will itself make an interesting study. The earliest grave stone noticed so far dates back to 1612 A.D. Mention may be made of an unusual grave stone kept in north-south orientation and bearing the date as 1566 A.D. It appears that the person to whom this grave stone was dedicated died earlier elsewhere and his remains were shifted to this church later on.

Evidence also establishes that apart from laterite blocks, terracotta tiles were profusely used in between the blocks for erecting pillars.

Due to advancing Monsoon the work had to be stopped. But before doing so all the exposed members were properly plastered and water tightened with lime cement mortar to save them from further damage. While conserving the exposed portions, whereever necessary, from the point of structural stability, parts of fallen portions have been reconstructed with the material recovered from excavations. This includes the reconstruction of walls and pillars. The broken and fallen slabs in front of the main altar, bearing quotations from the 'Holy Bible' have also been collected, Peaced together and re-erected.

The inscription on the left side of the main altar reads as:

A DORATESCA
BELLVM PEDVAM
EIVS QVONIAM
SANCTVMEST
P.S. 98

"Worship at his footstool, Holy is He-P.S. 98."

A niche in one of the altars on the northern side contains a basalt slab bearing an impressive emblem and an inscription which reads that the chapel belongs to a nobleman Castelo Branco whose coat of arms declares him to be a man of peace.

Whereever necessary fallen parts of the platforms of chapels and altars have also been reconstructed. After the clearance of the entire hall of the church it is proposed to reconstruct the main altar and relay the grave stone after concreting the floor. The remaining portion of the north - easter bell tower is in most precarious condition and needs immediate care. In order to save it for the posterity it is necessary to reconstruct various parts and replace the badly weathered and worn out laterite blocks with seasoned ones.

The portions of the arched ceilings whereever left intact also need immediate conservation. At some places the plasters on the ceilings and walls contain intricate embossed floral designs. Paintings whereever exposed have been initially chemically treated but in order to preserve them they should be treated more thoroughly and periodically by the experts.

The work is enormous. But after the entire Augustine church and convent is exposed, reconstructed partly and conserved, it will be one of the biggest monument of its kind to be preserved which will be a place of great tourist attraction. We do hope the coming seasons work may also be rewarded with discovery of mortal remains of the legendary Queen.

Acknowledgements

I am grateful to the Director General and Additional Director General, Archaeological Survey of India who gave all the encouragements and facilities to under take the job. I am also beholden to Dr. S.K.Joshi, Shri Chandrakanta Rama, S.L. Jadhav, Ajit Kumar, Sirdeshpande, R.D.Ingle, D.T. Asar and Satbhai for their untiring efforts to undertake the job under tiring circumstances and to Shri R.G. Londhe for the final type script.

Excavations of A Vedic Brick Altar At Purola, District Uttarkashi, Central Himalaya.

K.P. Nautiyal*
B.M. Khanduri*

Purola (31°70'N, 78°40'E) an ancient site in Uttarkashi District, is situated on the left bank of river Kamal, a tributary of the Yamuna, in the inner region of Garhwal Himalaya. The entire Yamuna Valley covering a stretch of about 150 Km from the source to the region when it passes in the plains near Kalsi is culturally very rich from the most ancient times. Already a few known remains such as the temple at Lakhamandal, Syenachiti at Jagatgram[2] and Kalsi Rock Edict of Asoka[3] speak for its greater significance.

Archaeological Data

After an initial exploration in the valley of Kamal we encountered a round-shaped mole on the plain surface of the river terrace. We, therefore, intended to excavate the same. The excavations at Purola for a continuous two seasons (1986-87 and 87-88) bring forth for the first time a massive structural complex of burnt brick. This mound at PRL-1, locally known as Intakot, about 20 m. aside from the left bank of the present bed of river Kamal was nothing but a structure which has been identified as a Syenachiti, measuring 24x18 m. laid in the east-west direction in the shape of a flying Garuda, the head being exactly towards the east and the tail towards the west (Pl.1) .

The Garuda (eagle or hawk) has two outstrectched wings in the directions of north and south showing an indication of the bird more or less in flying position. A square central chamber exactly in the middle of the altar measuring 60x60 cm. goes down to a depth of 2.60 m. from the top (Pl.2). Excavation of this pit yielded Sunga-Kushana pottery like the incurved bowl, minature vase, cup, lamp etc. The five intact miniature red ware bowls resembling closely the Sunga-Kushana miniature bowls from Ahichchatra contain ash, charcoal mixed with bone pieces, sandy clay and copper coins of the Kuninda dynasty. These coins closely resemble those of Amoghabhuti having symbols like tree-in-railing, Swastika, Triratna, stag etc. (1st Century B.C. to C. 2nd century A.D.) and finally covered by tiny river pebbles. The discovery of such coins from this region indicates that the Kunindas must have occupied this inner-zone of the Himalayan region. Besides several earlier evidences[4], this is very recently testified by the discovery of a Kuninda silver coin-hoard from Athoor in Tehri Garhwal closely juxtaposed to Uttarkashi district.

The miniature bowls inside the chamber were purposely placed in a straight line in north-south direction. In the middle of the pit was found a large sized thick grey ware pot covered by a shaftlid in a highly broken condition. But the most remarkable discovery of this chamber was a thin impressed-gold leaf showing a human figure standing in frontal position with a flowing apparel. Along with this was found a circular gold pendent and a small piece of a chain. The human figure can tentatively be identified representing Agni as has been enjoined in the Vedic texts that before conducting a sacrifice propitiation of Agni was a first pre-requisite[5]. It therefore, appears that gold as an auspicious and valuable metal was placed inside the chamber as a mark of respect to Agnideva and his effigy impressed on the gold leaf.

The bricks used in the Garuda structure are of various sizes. The largest size of 80x50x11 cms. is invariably found all along the corners of the structure. Two other sizes i.e. 50x50x11 cms and 55x40x11 cms. are generally used in the inner side of the altar.

The most significant discovery of the excavation was an iron-axe (21.5 cm.long) below 1.30 m. just near the right wing, suggesting that the same was used for the performance of sacrificial rite connected with the Chiti (altar), (Pl.3). The animals so sacrificed by this hatchet during the ritual await identification.

The excavation also revealed that in ancient time the recurring floods in the river Kamal had damaged this structure particularly its left wing and the tail portion. On account of such a serious damage to the altar in the remote past attempts were made to protect it by a stone rubble wall all around its periphery. Even some of the bricks in the foundation having been under-cut by gushing flood-water were filled up by such rubble.

Literary Data

The discovery of a Syenachiti or Garudachiti is interesting in view of the religious history of the Vedic pantheon. The literary records regarding the sacrifices go back to the Rigvedic period where we have evidences of domestic as well as community sacrifices. In the community sacrifices there were more than one sacred fires and, therefore, altars or Chitis for these were erected on a large sacrifical place set up according to the rules of the rituals. The nature of the Vedic sacrifice has been interpreted by various scholars as ancestor worship, gift-offering, a fertility rite, a communion with the deity.[6] Wheeler pointed out that Agni or fire is depicted in the Vedas in a variety of forms as a priest, a divine messenger, a devouring element, and a deity who is the source and diffuser of light throughout the Universe.

The religious texts also point out that the Vedic ritual fundamentally symbolized the act of creation and in the later Vedic period this symbolism of creation was elaborately worked out in the constructions of special fire altars or agnichayana. The importance was given to the fire god and in a sacrificial rituals he is treated as a priest and like an officiating priest he is supposed to have brought prosperity to

* Department of AIHC and Archaeology, Garhwal University, Srinagar, Garhwal - 246174

the worshiper. The famous Rajasuya, Asvamedha and Vajapeya sacrifices were special elaboration of the Soma sacrifice intended for securing special gains for their patrons.[8]

So far as the Garuda altar is concerned the bird has been auspiciously mentioned in the Rigveda. The Garuda or Garutman known as Suparna also, was a mythical feathered bird. The words Suparna and Garutman have been prolifically mentioned in the Rigvedic hyms[9]. Monier-Williams has identified Suparna with Garutman[10]. By all indications Suparna thus stands for one with beautiful wings representing a huge bird-like vulture, eagle etc. The Taittriya Samhita also mentioned a formula in which the bird like altar is praised as Suparna[11]. The text further says that he who wants to go to the heaven should perform the Syena-kit sacrifice. He (the sacrificer who performs this sacrifice) becomes a hawk and flies to the Svarga world.[12].

On the basis of the above it seems that the altar has been taken in ancient literary texts as a most sacred structure serving as a communion between the performer of the sacrifices and the gods. Its very structure and the material in the form of Garuda symbolised Agni Surya and all other supernatural powers. Gold and brick are the sacrificial substances of the Vedic altar.[13].

Architecturally, Chiti (Vedika) or altar is taken as a forerunner of the Hindu temple. The lower most part of a temple is also called a Vedika. The Vedika embodied the memory of the sacred ground (Vedi) with its piled altar (Chiti) by which the sacrificial offerings were carried up by the flaming fire[14].

Thus massive excavated structure at Purola now designated as a Syenachiti is an ancient Vedic altar of its own kind ever excavated so far in India in such an intact and well-preserved condition. This discovery by all its archaeological evidences appears to have been an eventful episode in the history of Himalayan region particularly connected to its religion, when great sacrifices such as the Asvamedha, Agnishtom etc. were being perfomed here between the second century B.C. to C. 1st century A.D. by some ruling kings of the region; may be a king of the Kuninda lineage.

Acknowledgement

The authors acknowledge the help rendered by Dr. Vinod Nautiyal, Dr. Atul Saklani, Dr. (Mrs) Rekha Thapliyal, Dr. D.L. Rajput, Dr. S.S. Negi, Sarvashri Rakesh Bhatt, V.P. Hatwal, Pradeep Saklani, R.S. Rawat, Govind Nautiyal, J.S. Rawat, J.S. Negi and Kishori Lal Nautiyal in the excavation and later the preparation of this paper. The excavation at Purola was carried out by the Garhwal University under an excavation grant jointly shared by the U.P. Hill Development Department and the UGC under the DRS Programme.

References

1. Nautiyal. K.P. *The Archaeology of Kumaon*, Varanasi, 1969 pp. 102-103
2. Ramachandran. T.N. *Indian Archaeology (1953-54)-A Review, pp.* 10-11 and also "Asvamedha site near Kalsi", *Journal of Oriental Research*, Madras, Vol.xxx.pp.1-31.
3. Hultzsch.E. *Inscriptions of Asoka*, C.I.I.vol, 1, 1925, p.XI.
4. Kala S.C. "Further Light on the Terrtory of the Kunindas "*J.U.P.H.S.* vol.viii,pt,. 1, pp.36-37.
5. Pande. G.C. *Foundations of Indian Culture*, vol.1, 1984, p. 119
6. Ibid. p. 76.
7. Wheeler J.T. *India of the Vedic Age*, 1973, p. 18
8. Pande. G.C. Op cit. p. 38
9. Rigveda (1/64 and 1/149)
10. Williams, Monier *Sanskrit -English Dictionary*, 1958, pp. 348-49
11. Narayan, Aiyangar *Ancient Hindu Mythology*, 1983, p.240
12. Ibid p,253
13. Kramrisch, Stella. *The Hindu Temple* vol, 1, 1976, p. 153
14 Ibid p, 146.

SOME MORE COPPER OBJECTS FROM SHEORAJPUR

Suryakant Shrivastava*

Since the discovery of the first copper hoard in 1822 more than ninety sites have been reported from different parts of Indian sub-continent to have yeilded this category of objects. of these as many as thirty five fall in Uttar Pradesh (Lal 1984)

In 1951 Professor B.B. Lal brought to light some more (nearly thiryt five) copper implements from various sites. Sheorajpur, District Kanpur, was also one of them. There are only three anthropomorphic figures from Sheorajpur, housed in the State Museum Lucknow.

Recently the present author had a chance of having a look at the collection of Acharya Ram Charana Sharma, Vyakula, placed now in the S.R.C. Museum of Indology, Jaipur. The Museum has a collection of eight copper implements from Sheorajpur, District Kanpur. Beside the already know three anthromorphic figures (Lal. 1951) this group included celts, both flat and shoulderd, spear heads and pick-like obejcts However, this is not a full fledged research paper but for all practical purposes a sort of note on objects which are not known so far.

The entire collection of the Museum is aquired through purchase. Therefore the exact location of these objects at Sheorajpur and the other antiquities or pottery that may have been associated with them are not known. It appears that the group under discussion was a chance discovery.

The Sheorajpur collection in the State Museum Lucknow, includes only three anthropomorphic figures, where as the collection of S.R. C. Museum Jaipur, represents so many other types.

The details of the object are as under :-

Celts :

Celts account for the largest number in the hoard. They are five in numbers, of which four are illustrated here.

Celt No. 4

This is broken at the butt end. However, it is the largest specimen. Its available length is 8.6 cm. and width is 10.00 cm. The section is thin being 0.5 cm only. The unillustrated celt, also broken, is 7.9 cm long, 9.6 cm wide, and 0.5 cm thin.

Celt No. 3

This celt is unusually small having a length of 6.0 cm and maximum width of 3.9 cm at the working edge. The butt is only 3.0 cm wide. Its section is very thin being 0.35 cm only. It has almost straight sides and splayed out cutting edge. It has also three shallow circular marks on one side.

Celt No. 2

This is a shouldered celt. It has an almost squarish butt measuring 7.4 cm. in width. Its full length is 13.2 cm. out of which the blade portion accounts for 5.8 cm. The maximum available width of the splayed out portion is 12.0 cm. (the ends are borken). It has maximum thickness of 0.7 cm.

Celt No. 6

This specimen though not exactly like other barcelts may perhaps be regarded as performing a similar function. It has a length of 11.5 cm, whereas the maximum width at working edge is 4.3 cm. The butt is 3.6 wide and partially damaged. Its section is thin being 0.4 cm only. A notable feature of the celt is that it has a number of shallow lines on both sides. What exactly these indicate it is difficult to say.

Spear Heads : No. 1

It has a leaf shaped blade with prominent mid rib which produced a fine lozenge shaped section. There is a small flat tang. The upper portion of blade is broken. The maximum width is 5. cm. Both the edges are partly damaged. The tang is roughly 4.4 cm long and circular in section.

The sepcimen, no. 7, is broken at the blade end, also its sides are partially damaged. It has a maximum length of 18.2 cm. It has slightly longish flat tang, of which power end is more or less like an antennae. The blade has a lozange shaped section.

A Pick-Like Object No. 5

It is perhaps the borken part of pick - like object. It measures 7.8 cm in maximum available length. The working edge is 0.9 cm wide. It is similar to a complete specimen from the Nasirpur hoard, housed in Archaeological Muesum, Gurukula Kangri Vishwavidyalaya, Hardware.

Sheorajpur was known only for the anthropomorphic figures so far. This collection of S.R.C. Museum of Indology, Jaipur, adds quite a few new types to our knowledge. The mini celt (no 3) perhaps the smallest so far found in the Ganga basin.

Acknowledgements :

The author's grateful thanks are due to Shri Ram Charana Sharma, Chairman and Shri Sharad Kumar Sharma Director of

* Archaeological Museum, Gurukula Kangri Vishawavidyalaya, Hardwar.

S.R.C. Museum of Indology, Jaipur for the permission and facilities to study the objects. Author is also thankful to Prof. B.B.Lal who has always encouraged me.

References :

Lal, B.B. 1951. Further Copper Hoards from the Gangetic Basin. *Ancient India. No. 7*

Lal, M. 1984. The Distribution of Copper Hoards : A Reassessment. *Puratattva* No. 14

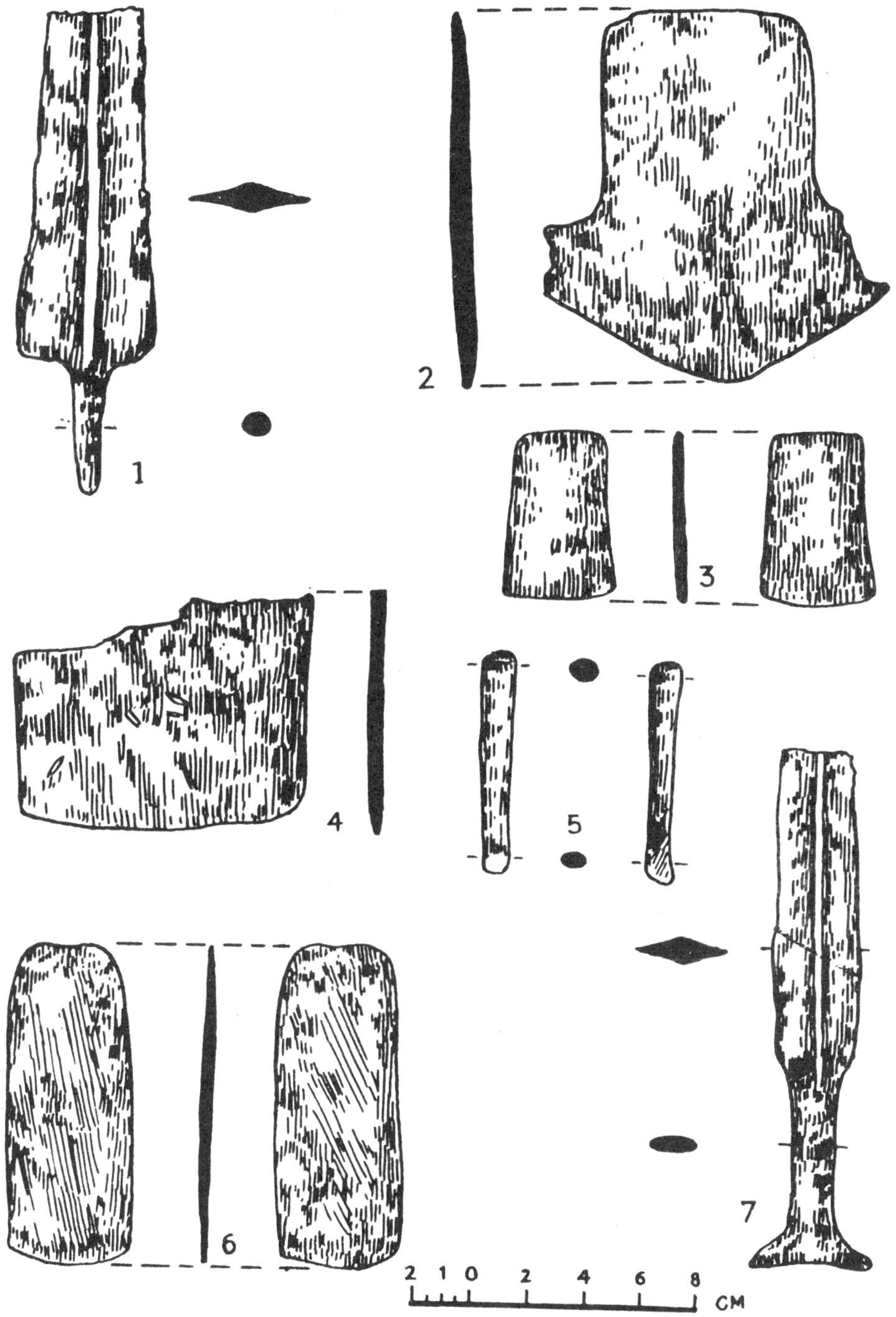

Fig. 1. Copper Hoard from Bithur

CASING SLAB FROM NAGARJUNKONDA - A REAPPRAISAL

Anamika Pathak*

Excavations at Nagarjunkonda have yielded a large number of casing slabs which once adorned the dome of the stupas at this site, during 3rd cent. A.D. One such casing slab (Pl. No.1) in the National Museum collection is divided into three board horizontal panels bordered with the floral bands. The panels depicts Buddha's life scenes such as casting of Horoscope.[1] Nativity scene, asist's visit to king Shudhodhana and child Siddhartha taken to the tutelary deity. While the last three scenes are clearly identified and fully corroborated by literary texts, the first is still controversial.

The lower most panel (Pl. No. 2) presents a court scene in which a royal figure adorned with jewelled ornaments is seated on a throne looked after by female attendants in vitark mudra on the right side. On the left side four noblemen are shown seated on higher seat with wicker stools before themselves containing plates full of eatables. It appears that there was some sort of celebration. One royal personage wearing a crown and holding a spouted vessel, stands in the centre, everyone is looking at the royal figure. An old man is seated on the ground in the left corner and busy in writing something. In front of him two dwarfish figures are standing holding some indistinct objects on their back. The scene is very lovely and details are minutely carved.

So far there are two major views on this representation. First represent the casting of Horoscope of child Siddhartha and the second represents the interpretation of Maya's dream.

In early Buddhist narrative art the scenes were always depicted in chronological order. Therefore, this is definite that this scene represents the scene before the birth of Buddha. Before we discuss further, the identification of the central male figure with a spouted vessel is essential, as he is depicted very prominently and on the basis of this identification depends the identification of the whole scene.

In the early Buddhist art Indra is shown wearing such type of Kiritmukuta and holding a spouted vessel.[2] Sculptural reliefs of Sanchi,[3] Amaravati,[4] and Nagarjunakonda,[5] are full of such type of representations where Indra is wearing such type of crown and holding a spouted vessel. His identification with Indra is beyond doubt. Now, if we accept this scene as the scene presenting the casting of horoscope the following objections come in:-

(i) the casting of horoscope before the birth of Buddha appears to be an abnormal phenomenon and the textual reference for this episode is not available.

(ii) Secondly, the priest or scribe who is casting the horoscope has not been treated honourably. The least importance has been given to him though he is attending such an important job. He is seated directly on the ground in the court without even a cushion, which appears absolutely impossible in the court of king Shuddhodhana.

(iii) His back is facing the kind which is very unusual in the court and sort of dishonouring the king.

(iv) The king is in vitarka mudra or discoursing which is unusual at the time of casting the horoscope.

(v) Lastly, what Indra is doing in the court of Suddhodhana at this time ? It is not mentioned in any text.

In view of the above mentioned object, the scene does not appear to represent the scene of casting of horoscope.

Second, the identification of this scene is the interpretation of Maya's dream. As the scene before the Nativity scene it appears logical at the first instance, but then the cause of celebration and presence of Indra in court of Shuddhodhana creates the problem in accepting the identification for this representation. Then the noble men do not appear to the priests, who were called by Shuddhodhana to interpret the dream.

A close look at the scene and presence of Indra calls for an altogether different identification for this scene.

As already mentioned the middle panel of this slab represents the nativity scene, therefore, this scene in the lower panel must belong to the event that took place, before the birth of Buddha, i.e., when Buddha was residing in Tushit heaven and he was supposed to descend on the earth. The Lalitvistara,[6] Nidankatha,[7] Abhinishkramana Sutra,[8] Majjhima-Nikaya,[9] and Anguttara Nikaya,[10] refer to this event. The Buddha in the form of Boddhisattva was residing in Tushit heaven before his birth as child Siddharth. he was known as Prabhapala.[11] After a certain period of time he proclaimed to descend the earth to remove the miseries of the world.[12] After hearing this all the devas, Yakshas, Nagas, Kinnares, visited him before his descent to the earth.[13]

According to Nidan Katha four devas called Suyama, Santusita, Paranimitta - Vasaviatti and Maha-Brahma, along with Sakka (Indra) came to see him.[14] At this time, they all assembled at one place and discussed the time, continents, country and family where Bodhisattva was going to descend on the earth.[15] When everything was finalised and Bodhisattva was about to leave the heaven. All the Devas assembled at one place in the Tushit heaven, celebrated the occasion and listened the discourse given by Bodhisattva.[16] After this he descended into the womb of Maha-Maya.[17]

The above description tallies with the representation of

* National Museum, New Delhi

this panel. Here Bodhisattva Prabha-pala is shown seated on a throne in the Tushit heaven surrounded by Devas. Four Devas known as Suyama, Santusita, Paranimitta - Vasaviatti and Maha-Brahma are present there and participating in the celebration. Sakka (Indra) is shown standing in the centre with a spouted vessel. All of them were honoured at that time. At this moment prabhapala preached them the precepts of law which everybody listened patiently. After this he descended to the womb of queen Maya. After this the second panel presents the Birth of Buddha is in continuation. Like this there is one more panel from Amaravati housed in British Museum.[18] In this panel the birth story of prince Siddhartha had been carved in four compartments divided by railings. From the upright, beginning with the Tushita heaven scene. Bodhisattva is sitting on a throne, near him, two ladies are sitting. Around them four guardians are seated on a high seat and all are in vitark mudra. This part of a pannel is also identified as the dream interpretation of queen Mayadevi. This again does not make the sequence that before the dream how was it possible to interpret the dream. Thus if one looks at this panel clockwise it becomes clear that first it is the scene of the Tushit heaven, the next is the Maya's dream and below it the nativity scene and in the last prince Siddhartha is shown taken to the tutelary deity.

Still there are a few things which could not be clearly identified such as the old man or scribe. He may be tentatively identified with the 'Gold Mass' who is mentioned in Abhinishkramana sutra as the person who visited Jambudvipa repeatedly and was consulted at the time of deciding the town and family to which Bodhisattva Prabhapala was going to descend.[19] However, the identification is tentative.

Similarly, there are two figures carrying something on back.[20] These are shown in front of the old man or scribe. One can see similar representation in the Gandharan art. Where, this had been depicted on a pillar and known as a sherpard-boy.

About the two ladies who are sitting, near the Bodhisattva, it is difficult to say anything because reference for them has not come to the notice of the authors.

References.

1. Sivaramamurti, C *The Art of India*, Harry N. Abrams, New York 1977, pp. 60, pl.-74
2. Coomaraswamy A.K.: *Early Indian Iconography:* Eastern Art,1928, pp. 33-41
3. (a) Ibid : pp-37, pl. 2;

   (b) Ibid : pp-37, pl-6;

   (c) Ibid : pp-37, pl-5.
4. Sivaramamurti, C: (a) *Amaravati; sculptures from Madras Museum*, Thomson & Co., 1956, pp.86; pl. LIV;

   (b) Ibid : *Early Andhra Art and Iconography* Govt. of Andhra Pradesh, 1979, pp.4.
5. Gupta S.K.: (a) *Elephant in Indian Art and Mythology*, New Delhi-1983, pl. 17.

   (b) *Marg publication, X VIII*, No. 2, 1965, March Nagarjunkonda sculptures pp.23, pl. 28.

   (c) Ibid, pp.25, pl. 34.
6. Vaidya P.L. ed: *Lalita - Vistara*, Mithila Institute Darabhanga, 1958, ch-2 & 3, pp. 7-11.
7. Davids R :Tr: *'Nidana Ka tha'*, Indological book house, 1973, pp-144-149.
8. Beral. S, (Tr:) *'Chinese version of Abhinishkaramanasutra as the Romantic legend of Sakya Buddha*, New Delhi - 1985, pp.24.
9. Sariskrityayan, R.: *Majjima Nikaya*, Sarnath 1964,
10. Morris ed: *Aniguttara - Nikaya*, II, p-130.
11. Beal. S. (Tr:) Chinese Version of the Abhinish karamarisutra as, "*the Romantic legend of Sakya Buddha*, New Delhi - 1985 pp. 24.
12. Davids R.(Tr:) *Buddhist Birth Stories* pp-144.
13. Beal S. (Tr:) Chinese version of Abhinish karamarisutra as "*Romantic legend of Sakya Buddha* Delhi, 1985, pp-25.
14. Davids, R. (Tr:) *Buddhist Birth Stories*. p.p. 146
15. Beal. S.(Tr:) Chinese Version of Abhinish karamasutra *as "Romantic legend of Sakya Buddha"* pp.25.
16. Ibid. pp-34-35.
17. Kern. H., *Manual of Indian Buddhism*, pp.13.
18. Parimoo Ratan : *Life of Buddha in Indian Sculpture*, New Delhi, 1982, pp. 7-8, pl. No. 5
19. Beal.S.(Tr:) Chinese Version of AbinishKarmansutra as *"Romantic legend of Sakya Buddha"* pp.26-30
20. Hand gesture of two dwarfish figures shows that they are holding something; may be some dead animal or clothing still it is not very clear.

ARCHAEOLOGICAL TESTIMONY OF SURUNGA AND THE MAURYANISM OF THE ARTHASASTRA OF KAUTILYA

Suresh Chandra Mishra*

Frequent references to the term *Surunga* in the sence of underground passage or tunnel in the *Arthasastra* of Kautilya [1] (here after KA) is taken as one of the major grounds against considering this text as a work of the 4th century B.C. On the contrary, it has been taken as an additional argument supporting the view of the later date for this work. The proporent of this view is M.Winternitz, who, following Otto Stein, does not think, it possible to derive Greek *Syrinx* from the sanskrit *Surunga*, whereas he finds that syrinx in Greek has an etymology.[2] According to him subterranean passage called *Surunga* occurs in connection with siege operations or burglaries, or love intrigues in poetical and technical works from about the 3rd to the 12th Centuries.[3] In his opinion those scholars who see in the Kautiliya a work of the 4th Century B.C. will have to reject the derivation of *Surunga* from Greek *syrinx* and to find an etymology of the word in Sanskrit.[4] Another point which is made in favour of the late date of the *Arthasastra* is that Greek *syrinx* in the sense of subterranean passage, does not occur before the 2nd century B.C. in Greek literature and that in Indian literature the word *Surunga* can not be proved for certain to occur before the 3rd Century A.D.[5] On the question of how *syrinx* came to India Winternitz quots the view of Stein who attributes its knowledge to India through Indians serving in Hellenistic armies.[6] This has become another ground for Winternitz's upholding the 3rd century A.D. as the date of the *KA*.[7]

A non-Sanscritic Indian origin for *Surunga* is suggested by F.B.J. Kuiper, who thinks it possible that khmer *run* in the sense of 'a hole' and santali. *Surun* also meaning 'a hole' are at the basis of the sanskrit *Surunga*. He very rightly cautions that one must be on one's gurard when postulating a linguistic influence from Greece on India.[8] A Greek orgin for the word *Surunga* can by no means be taken for granted.

The scepticism of Winternitz regarding the possibility of any etymological derivation of the term *Surunga* in Sanskrit, does not hold good at all, for there are many etymological derivations for the same in ancient Indian lexicons.[9] Hemachandracharya very rightly defines *Surunga* as a fissure or Secret underground passage and derives it as : *saratyanaya surunga, "Sartteh surca" (una - 108) ityunga.*[10]

It is very surprising that otto Stein and Winternitz, and following him a very large number of other scholars on the basis of *Surunga's* derivation from Greek *syrinx*, should have assigned the *KA* a date of third century A.D. Etymological derivation apart, at least archaeological evidences from two places go to prove the antiquity of *Surunga* much anterior to and coeval with the Greek *syrinx*. The subterranean passage as alluded to in the *KA* has been found by Waddel in the Asokan Strata near Dargah leading to Pancapahari in the exavation at Pataliputra. Relying on a village tradition which spoke of the existence of a substerranean masonary passage leading for several hundered yards in a north-westerly direction, Waddel undertook the excavation at Kumarahar where by lateral mining he was able to reveal a structure of large bricks twelve feet below the surface with a cavity partly faced which looked as if it might be a passage. But owing to objections against further undermining of the houses over it, the task was abandoned mid-way and the interesting question of this subterranean passage remains unsolved. [11] The excavator thought it to have been a building once upon a time above ground, while the village legend says the passage leads to the Dargah about a mile to the north-west, there is also at the latter place a subterranean passage twenty feet below the surface and also running north-west, in the direction of Bhikna Pahari.[12]

Waddel has drawn our attention to a stone passage 25 feet below the large ancient well on the borders of the Gunsagar. According to the then current tradition it led to Bhikna Pahari on the one side and to the subterranean passage at Kumrahar on the other, each of the points being nearly a mile distant. He saw its orifice on the north-west border of the well having regularly built lintelled doorway of stone. It was explored for a few yards.[13]

Much more pronounced evidence comes from kausambi where excavations have thrown valuable light on early fortification and its modification in successive periods necessiated by changing ideas of defence. Structural exitstence of a curved entrance, enclosing an underground passage built on corbelled arch is revealed in structural periods III. 11 and III. 12, that is, during c. 465 B.C. to c. 395 B.C. and c. 395 B.C. to c.325 B.C., respectively.[14] The *Marmavabodhini tika* on the *Harsacarita* of Bana defines *surunga* to be a curved underground trench,[15] a definition well corresponding to this structure.

To the structural period III. 11 belongs this curved wall measuring 63 feet 4 inches and 67 feet 10 inches respectively on the inner and outer (city) sides of the curve. It was 6 feet 10 inches wide and encased a stone-paved passage 6 feet 10 inches deep. The wall available to a height of 7 feet 9 inches and comprising 32 courses was built in the packing against subsidiary rampart 2. At its northern junction with revetment 2 there were traces of guard rooms.[16] According to the description of the excavator, the passage had a corbelled arch finally capped with bricks laid width-wise. At either end of this passage was a pair of slits, 3 feet 5 inches wide and 3 feet 5 inches set inside the walls into which the planks may have been inserted. In the curved wall two manholes (2 feet x 2 feet) divide the extant length in

* Satyavati College, Delhi.

three nearly equal parts. G.R. Sharma, on the basis of the above descriptions, has rightly taken this passage to be underground tunnel instead of a drain.[17] During the life span of structural period III.12, the curved wall was rebuilt and the second manhole closed.[18]

In order to test the Mauryanism of the textual references to the term *surunga*, a tally between the archaeological exhibits of the structural remains of *surunga* and its description in the text becomes imperative. Our text[19] prescribes the construction of a living chamber in the centre in accordance with the procedure laid down for the treasury, or a maze-house, with concealed passages in walls *(gudhabhitti)* and its centre, a living chamber, or an underground room with many subterranean passage *(surunga-samcaram)* having its outlets covered by the post, or the wooden image of a deity and above it a place with a staircase concealed in a wall or having an entrance and an exit through a hollow pillar as a living chamber with the floor fixed to a mechanism and thus capable of sinking below in order to counteract a calamity. In another reference we have suggestions of making underground passage with many openings up to the enemy camp.[20] There is also a suggestion of an escape by an underground passage or its opening *(kuksipradarena)* or by breaking the rampart.[21] The agents are shown entering the hollow images of deities *(daivata pratimachidra)* in fire sanctuaries by an underground passage.[22]

Apart from making references to *surunga* in the *Arthasastra*, these citations are important in that they refer to the existence of holow posts or images on the outlets of the *surunga* and *gudhabhitti*, that is, concealed walls in the scheme of fortification and strategy.

The high antiquity of the existence of *surunga* is very well demonstrated by the two excavations referred to above. Although the underground passage at Kausambi, with two manholes almost at an equal intervals at the roof of it does not give any evidence for existence either of a hollow pillar or perforated images over these manholes, one can think of the presence of such a contrivance which might have been employed to hoodwink the enemy. Waddel refers to the image of Bhikna Kunwar over six feet high found at Bhikna Pahari, having the shape of elongated hillock deeply scooped out on its southern face to form into masses with a deeper recess between them near the centre from which latter point to a track runs obliquely down to the bottom.[23] He has compared this with the abode of prince Mahendra.[24] But the description gives us an impression as if the image found could be compared with the hollow images of the *Arthasastra* which were used for some strategic purposes.

Although G.R. Sharma terms the passages with the flank walls leading from the top to the toe of the rampart found in the structural period III.13 [25] and also in structural period III. 15[26] as a tunnel, but in view of the similarity of its description with the concealed wall of the *Arthasastra* it should be considered a distinct class in itself and may be taken to be a *gudhabhitti and gudhabhitti-sopana*, that is, concealed wall and the flights of steps with concealed walls. The life span of the structural period III.13 would fall between century 325 B.C. and 255 B.C., a period very much falling in the range of Mauryan period.

A graphic description of the building of two subterranean tunnels in Kampilya by sixty thousand warriors and seven hundred men under the supervision of the royal counsellor Mahosadha is preserved in the *Jataka*. The mouth of the great tunnel *(mahaummagga dvaram)* was upon the bank of the Ganges whereas the entrance to the small tunnel *(jamghumaggassa dvaram)* was in the city. It began under the staircase of Culani's palace and came out with the city. The great tunnel was built up with bricks and worked with stucco; it was roofed over with planks and smeared with plaster and whitened. Most remarkable of all was the fact that all its 80 great doors and 64 smaller ones were fitted with machinery so that one peg being pressed closed them all or again opened them. The building of the great tunnel, little tunnel and all the city was finished in a record time of four months with a view to trapping the retinue of the hostile king Culani of north Pancala.[27]

In a comparative study of Mahosadha and Daedelus, the two great tunnel and labyrinth builders of their ages, Merlin Peris has compared the tunnel-building of the *Jataka's* story with the palace complex of Egypt and Crete. He has tried to prove that the familiarity of such intricate structures to the Knossians goes back to the Bronze Age. In any case by 500 B.C. it appears as a popular type on their coins [28].

Like *surunga, ummagga* also conveys the sense of an underground tunnel or watercourse. The etymology (ud + magga = off tracks) gives the meaning of a side track or a wrong way. [29] Peris has compared the above account of the *Jataka* with a labyrinth or mazehouse of the Greeks.[30] Surprisingly Winternitz, the protagonist of the late date for the origin of *surunga* in India, held elsewhere that in any case this description of tunnel-building by the master builder Mahosadha, presupposes the knowledge of magnificant subterranean buildings to the narrator. [31] The results of the digging operations at Kampil under K.K. Sinha do not corroborate the descriptions of the *Jataka* story. The only interesting feature of the ancient settlement found at the site was a mud-embankment rising to a height of 1.70 meter, which by no stretch of imagination can be thought of as a tunnel or a segment of a tunnel, big or small. However the candid expression on the part of the excavator that the sequence obtained from the limited area may not be universal in all trenches, and in view of that this suggestion for further spadework, [32] has not finally clinched the issue.

General Alexender Cunningham, himself noticed a subterranean passage near Garibnath temple in Pehova or Prithudaka which was said to have extended for 2 kos or nearly 3 miles. But in his view it could not be traced beyond 50 feet. Some people, however held that it was 24, Kos in length and that it was actually explored for 2 Kos' but the more general opinion is that the 2 Kos' refer to the actual length of the passage.[33] But since this structure has not been assigned to any particular period, it can not be of much use to us for ascertaining the antiquity of the *surunga* or establishing its existence during the Mauryan period to which our text is generally believed to belong.

Another very fascinating literary account of how the 5 Pandavas along with their mother Kunti escaped through the *Surunga* from the jaws of the fire, set in the palace made of inflammatory materials at Varnavata is available in the *adiparva* of the *Mahabharata*.[34] Although the ancient city of Varnavata has not been identified so far; situated on the bank of the Ganges with some high mounds the village Lacchagir in the Handia subdivision of Allahabad District answers some of the *Mahabharata* descriptions. It preserves the tradition of the episode & it is even now a centre for the annual fair which is held here. The oral tradition about the existence of the *Surunga* and the transmission of the accounts of the *Mahabharata* coming from sire to the son persist among the natives.[35] But since, no archaeological spade-work has taken place on the site, we are not in a position to examine the accuracy of the *Mahabharata* account and the tradition connected with it. However, the description of the *Surunga* in the backdrop of a backward social setting gives a picture of its being dug out in olden times-prior to the Mauryas.

On the whole, even if we set aside other doubtful evidences the excavations at Pataliputra and Kausambi prove the knowledge and existence of *surunga* at least by the Mauryan times. Therefore, the contention of some scholars to place the *KA* to a later date on the basis of the occurence of this term in the text is untenable. On the contrary, it proves, that the portions of the text employing this contrivances in adverse times belong to the Mauryan age.

References

1. R.P. KANGLE, *The Kautiliya Arthasastra* Part I Bombay 1969. 1.20.2, 5.2.42, 7.17.33; 12.5.18-20, 13.1.3, 13.2.16, 44, 13.4.9.
2. M. Winternitz, "*Surunga* and the Kautiliya *Arthasastra*", *Indian Historical Quarterly*, 1925 p. 420.
3. Ibid. p. 431
4. Ibid.
5. Ibid.
6. Ibid. p. 432
7. Ibid.
8. *Acta Orientalia, XVII*, (Leiden, 1939), pp. 30-34.
9. The etymology suggested by *Halayudhakosa* is : *Su+rujo bhange, ghana, Kutvam numi prsodaradih*, *J.S.* Joshi (ed.) p. 715; *Vacaspatyam*, i,v, p. 4318.
10. *Surunga tu sandhila syad gudha margo bhuvontare, bhumikanda* 51 Hargobind (ed.), *Abhidhanacintamanih* (2.51) p. 393.
11. L.A. Waddel, *Report on the Excavation at Pataliputra*, Patna.1903, p.30.
12. Ibid.
13. Ibid. p. 43
14. G.R. Sharma, *The Excavations at Kausambi (1951-59)* Allahabad, 1960 p. 41
15. Suranad Kunjan Pillai (ed.) *Harsacarita of Banabhatta with the Commentary Marmavabodhini of Renganatha* (Trivendrum) 1958. VI p. 302.
16. G.R. Sharma, op.cit., p. 32
17. G.R. Sharma, *The Excavations at Kausambi (1957-59)*, Allahabad, 1960, p. 33.
18. Ibid.
19. *KA*, 1.20.2.
20. Ibid.12.5.16.
21. Ibid.12.5.36.
22. Ibid.13.1.3.
23. L.A. Waddel, *Reports on the Excavations at Pataliputra* 1903, p.13.
24. Ibid.
25. Ibid. p.34
26. Ibid. p.35
27. *Jataka*, VI.546, V.Fausboll (ed.) *The Jataka Together with Its Commentary*, London 1964, p.p.431-3, and E.B. Cowell (trans.) *The Jataka or Stories of the Buddha's Former Births*, Cambridge 1907, pp.222-36.
28. Merlin Peris, "The Tunnel-Maker and the Labyrinth-Builder", in Senart Paranavitan Commemoration Volume, *Studied in South Asian Culture*, Volume VII (ed.) J.E. Vanlouhuizen De Leeuw, Leiden 1978 pp.145-61.
29. T.W. Rhys Davids and William Steel (ed) The Pali Text Society's *Pali English Dictionary* Surrey, 1925 p.154
30. Merlin Peris, op.cit., pp. 145-61.
31. M. Winternitz, *A History of Indian Literature*, ii (trans.) S.Ketkar, Second Edn. New Delhi 1972. fn 2, p. 139. Winternitz gives 3rd century B.C. and 5th or 6th century A.D. as the uppermost and lowest date limits for the composition of the *Jataka* stories ibid. p. 156
32. *Indian Archaeology, 1975-76 - A Review* pp.51-2.
33. Alexender Cunningham, "Pehova or Prithudaka", *Archaeological Survey of India Report II*, XXVIII. p.225.
34. *Jnatva tu tadgrham sarvvamadiptam Pandunandanah. Surunga vivisusturnam matra sardhamarindamah* 1/149/11 *Mahabharata adiparva*, critical edition, Poona.
35. On the basis of my personal survey of the area.

Prehistoric Research in India.: As Viewed by Two Senior American Archaeologists

K. Paddayya*

While it is the European scholars, particularly the British, who must be given credit for initiating and nurturing antiquarian studies in India over a period of two centuries, there are other countries too which have contributed in a significant way towards our understanding of the archaeological heritage of the country. Among these the U.S.A. holds a prominent place. To put it in the words of Jerome Jacobson, at the moment the American involvement is "the most pervasive single foreign presence in South Asian archaeology."

From what was just a trickle some 20 years ago the American interest in Indian archaeology has now developed into a steady stream of workers. The late Helmut de Terra, Walter Fairservis Jr., George Dales, Kanneth Kennedy, Gregory Possehl, Jerome Jacobson, John Lukacs, Jim Schaffer and John Fritz are of the workers who have conducted detailed field investigations in different parts of the country. The topics of research range from primatological studies and the remote Stone Age to the Indus civilization to Vijayanagara ruins at Hampi.

As against the culture-historical format provided by the European workers, the American scholars have imparted an anthropological orientation to the Indian archaeological materials. The wide scope and depth of this contribution could be gauged from two anthologies of essays entitled *Archaeology and Palaeoanthropology of South Asia* (1984) edited by Kenneth Kennedy and Gregory possehl and *Studies in the Archaeology of India and Pakistan* (1986) edited by Jerome Jecobson, both published by the American Institute of Indian studies, New Delhi.

More recently, two other American archaeologists have been associated with prehistoric research in India. They are J. Desmond Clark, now Emeritus Professor of Anthropology, University of California at Berkeley and Lewis R. Binford, Leslie Spier Professor of Anthropology, University of New Mexico at Albuquerque.

Professor Clark is the doyen of African prehistory and ranks with the late L.S.B. Leakey for his contributions to Early Man studies. He has first-hand knowledge of prehistoric research in India. In collaboration with the University of Allahabad he and his team have carried out (from 1980 to 1982) very detailed archaeological and geomorphological investigations in the Belan and son valleys forming part of the Ganges drainage system. *Palaeoenvironments and Prehistory in the Middle Son Valley* (jointly edited by G.R. Sharma and J.D. Clark and Published in 1983) is a major publication devoted to the results of this joint work. Moreover, Professor clark has served on the expert committee of Ford Foundation for awarding and supervising grants-in-aid to select institutions in India engaged in archaeological research.

Professor Binford is known the world over as the father of what is rightly or wrongly called the New Archaeology, which regards understanding of culture process rather than reconstruction of culture history as the ultimate goal of archaeological research. He has conducted ethnoarchaeological research among the Nunamiut Eskimos of Alaska, and this piece of work has served as a model for other workers in different parts of the world. His recent researches challenge the prevailing idealistic views about Early Man: that he had home bases, that he was a mighty hunter and that he was bringing home excess food for sharing with Kith and Kin. In 1986 Professor Binford spent one full month in India. He gave a series of Lectures at the summer institute in the New Archaeology organized by Deccan College, Poona and then visited several important archaeological sites in the country.

The author had an opportunity to visit the U.S. as a Fulbright fellow from November 1986 to February 1987 and work with Professors Clark and Binford and their associates on the topic of recent theoretical and methodological trends in stone age research and their relevance to Indian prehistory. As part of this work he held interviews with Professors clark and Binford (on 9th January and 21st February 1987 respectively) for eliciting their views about the state of prehistoric research in India. Excerpts from these interviews are reproduced below :

Paddayya : Professor Clark, Stone Age research started in India with Robert Bruce Foote's discovery of stone implements near Madras in 1863 and we now have a fairly good picture of the cultural materials belonging to this remote phase of its past. All the same, it is surprising that there is not much awareness about our prehistory among archaeologists in the west. What, According to you, are the reasons for this ?

Clark : The reasons are several. First, beginning with the work of de Terra and Paterson in northwestern India and that of Zeuner in Gujarat in the early part of this century the emphasis has been on the discovery of cultural material from secondary contexts such as those associated with river gravels and silts. This trend is strong even today. One must realize that in such contexts the materials are reworked by natural agencies like river action and therefore cannot give us much meaningful information about prehistoric lifeways. If today Africa holds a place of pride in Early Man studies : it is partly because the late L.S.B. Leakey and other workers concentrated on the discovery and investigation of primary or *in situ* sites like those found in the Olduvai Gorge in Tanzania. One is glad to know that in India too search has begun for such sites.

* Deccan College, Department of Archaeology, Pune

A second factor coming in the way of Indian prehistory is the lack of a firm chronology, as provided by potassium argon and other scientific dating techniques used in Africa. Ages assigned to sites on the basis of typological and technological features of stone tools and the nature and types of sediments yielding these can at best serve as estimates. I personally doubt if Peninsular India has sites older than the Middle Pleistocene.

An additional consideration is the paucity of biological (palaeontological and palaeobotanical) remains on the Indian sites which are so essential for reconstructing both past human lifeways and their environmental settings.

Paddayya : Which are the potential areas in the country where primary sites are likely to be found ?

Clark : As I mentioned earlier, prehistorians in India have already started investigating such sites. The Bhimbetka group of cave sites near Bhopal studied by V.N. Misra is one such example. It is now necessary to go away from large rivers and take up source regions of their feeders. Special attention should be given limestone areas, as these are likely to preserve biological materials too. The Hunsgi-Baichbal valleys in Gulbarga district of North Karnataka where you are working and the Kurnool cave area investigated by M.L.K. Murty in Andhra Pradesh serve as good instances.

Paddayya : In which sedimentary contexts we could expect to find primary sites ?

Clark : I would attach much importance to the identification and investigation of paleosols, overbank deposits and levees.

Paddayya : What methodological changes would be called for by the shift in emphasis from secondary to primary sites?

Clark : You need to involve Quaternary geologist such more closely for understanding the palaeogeographical settings of stone Age sites. It is also necessary to initiate research on site formation processes for distinguishing primary sites from secondary sites. This research has both experimental and ethnoarchaeological aspects and calls for the joint efforts of archaeologists, geomorphologists, palaeontologists and other scientists.

Since dating is one of the weak aspect of Indian prehistory, efforts would be made to have bone materials and even sediments dated by uranium-thorium series, thermoluminescence and other methods. Detection of possible evolutionary trends in bovids, equids and other animal species also might be helpful for dating purposes.

There is no harm if you depend on foreign expertise initially but in the long run Indian prehistorians have to shoulder the entire responsibility. Your Department in Poona is already a good place for prehistoric research and other universities in the country can benefit from this example.

Finally, I think it is much more useful to have smaller, problemoriented seminars or discussions periodically so that workers actively engaged in prehistoric research could exchange views and redefine problems.

Paddayya : Most of the stone Age sites in Peninsular India are surface or subsurface occurrences. What, according to you, should be our strategy for studying of such sites ?

Clark : A regional approach involving both surveys and excavations is necessary. This is what we have done in the Son valley. One or a few sites give only fractional knowledge of the cultural system; even small sites have their place. The late Glynn Isaac called this approach the study of 'scatters between patches'.

Paddayya : Do you think we could identify on our sites features like the reuse of localities by the same or other hunter-gatherer groups ?

Clark : Yes, this feature is seen at Isimila, Olorgesailie and other African sites. Criteria such as those provided by differential bone weathering are very helpful for this purpose.

Paddayya : Our major handicap is the paucity of biological materials. How can one overcome this ?

Clark : To start with, you could safely project the present-day environmental diversity in the subcontinent back into the prehistoric past. You have to provide for the presence of many minor ecosystems within a larger ecosystem. One might also consider taking cores in areas like the Nilgiri hills for establishing pollen sequences.

Paddayya : Finally, what is your reaction to the latest wave of views by Binford and others who tend to consider the early hominids as scavengers rather than hunters in the regular sense of the term ?

Clark : I basically agree with the argument that animal foods were only a minor component of Early Man's subsistence. I think it is the plant foods, as provided by the riparian settings of sites, which were really important. Here again the staple items could have been limited in number.

Paddayya : What you say probably holds good even in the case of our Palaeolithic cultures.

Paddayya : Professor Binford, what, according to you, is the place of Indian prehistory on the world scene ?

Binford : There is a lot of curiosity now in the West about the Indian Stone Age record. For a long time there has been quite a bit of pessimism among the Indian workers that one cannot learn much about the Stone Age past from mere scatters of stone tools. But planned investigations like yours in the Hunsgi-Baichbal valleys should put an end to this pessimism.

Paddayya : Is the lack of hominid remains a factor in the indifference to the Indian materials among the text-book writers in the U.S.?

Binford : I would not think so, because sites like Torralba in Spain and Kalambo Falls in Africa also do not have hominid remains but are nevertheless very famous in world prehistory. These sites have produced evidence of site structure, as for example the co-occurrence of stone tools and animal bones at Torralba. It is this sort of evidence which is lacking on the Indian sites. Text-book writers after all write about what the researchers report on.

Paddayya : What is the scope for Stone Age research in the country ?

Binford : My first-hand experience with your materials is limited to the study of some of the collections housed in your Department in Poona and visits to sites near Bhimbetka and those you are working on in the Hunsgi-Baichbal valleys. All the same the scope is tremendous.

It will be useful to concentrate efforts in rain-collecting basins, since in such areas Stone Age sites are likely to be preserved in a better condition. The Hunsgi-Baichbal valleys form a good example. (At this stage the author drew Professor Binford's attention to the fact that many such areas exist in Peninsular India and await work.) Unlike in Europe and elsewhere, the Pleistocene events in Peninsular India were far from dramatic. As a result the ancient landsurfaces are preserved well and the sedimentary cover over the Stone Age sites is very thin. Such situation are a distinct advantage and should be fully exploited by the Indian archaeologists.

Once such areas are selected intensive surface surveys should be carried out. These surveys alone, and not digging a few holes, will provide meaningful data for making inter - and intra regional comparisons. Non-site approach should be adopted in these surveys. That is, the entire area should be treated as one unit and one must try to locate not merely big sites but even small occurrence and isolated artifacts.

Paddayya: You have visited some of the Acheulian sites in the Hunsgi-Baichbal valleys and have also seen the stone tools and other cultural remains from the recent excavation at Yediyapur in this area. Where would you place these sites in the context of ongoing debates about primary versus secondary sites in Old World prehistory ? I consider this question very important because what can be said about these sites will be true of many other areas as well in Peninsular India.

Binford : I have a strong feeling that in your area the cultural material and the rubble horizon on which it occures have different origins.

The rubble-strewn patches were already there as a part of the palaeo-landscape and prehistoric groups simply used some of these spots for their activities.

In my view these cultural levels are deflation surfaces. These were originally covered with thick black soil or some such fine sediments which have been stripped away subsequently, thereby exposing the cultural material to surface.

Paddayya : In the light of your current views based on taphonomy that Early Man was not a great hunter of large animals, as has been held for a long time by many prehistorians but was merely a scavanger of their death sites and/leftovers at kill sites of predatory animals, what are your impressions about the cultural status of the animal bones which you have examined from the Acheulian sites of the Hunsgi-Baichbal valleys ?

Binford : These bones are quite old and interesting. Some of these have a crystal-like, crunchy structure which suggests that the pieces originally lay in a brecciated sedimentary context.

I recall in particular the collections from two sites. One of these (from Hebbal Buzurg) contains vertebrae of wild cattle, and the other place (Teggihalli) has rib bone fragments of the same animal species. These bones obviously represent the meal remains of Stone Age groups. These two assemblages are very important in the sense that Lower Palaeolithic sites yielding rib bones and vertebrae are rare in the Old World. That these places have yielded only a limited number of stone tools along with animal bones is not surprising because a similar situation obtains at other sites such as Hope Fountain in Africa and Hoxne in England.

Paddayya : The recent discovery of a skull fragment of *Homo erectus* (or, Archaic Nenanderthal ?) group at Hathnora on the Narmada in Madhya Pradesh has served to generate much fresh interest in hominid remains among prehistorians in India. Do you have any comments to make about this discovery and its implications ?

Binford : The distribution of hominind remains in the Old World is staggering. In Western Europe these come mostly from cave deposits, while in central Europe these are found in fluvial sediments. There is no reason why human skeletal remains cannot be found in India. One has only to look for old deposits with favourable conditions for the preservation of organic remains. Hominid materials could in some cases be expected from deposites devoid of archaeological remains.

Paddayya : One last question. Both M.A. and Ph. D. students were highly inspired by the personal discussions with you and by your lectures at the summer institute in the New Archaeology organized by Deccan College last year. What message have you for them.

Binford : The real challenge in archaeology is one of addressing our igorance.... to get rid of the inadequacies in our knowledge of the human past. Our students have to realize that as science progresses more inadequacies will be noticed and attended to. This is not to be taken as a weakness of science but forms its very essence.

BOOK REVIEWS

Stone Age Hunter-Gatherers An ethno-archaeology of Cuddapah regions, South east India. By D.R. Raju, Ravish Publisher, Pune, 1988. Price not mentioned

Andhra and Tamil-Nadu were the first regions in India where evidence of a Stonce Age Stage in the history of India was found. Later Bruce-Foote found similar evidence in Gujarat. However for more than 150 years this research was confined to collection of stone tools. However, first in Eurpoe, U.S.A., the methods were defined, because the goal now was not merely a collection of tools and their statistical analysis. Attention was now paid to ecological and ethnographic data for understanding the past human behaviour.

Dr. Raju has done such a work. Gunjan valley in the Eastern Ghats region of Cuddapah district of Andhra Pradesh. After discovering undisturbed sites (as essential requisite for such a study), he collected artefact using scientific sampling method to obtain maximum information on patterning of industrial and economic activities of Stone Age group. The Upper Palaeolithic sites, first identified by the reviewer in the Sagileru river of Kerala, are the richest and best preserved in the country.

Dr. Raju then made a detailed study of the substistence strategy of the Yanadis, a primitive hunter-gatherer group in the area, and has utilized this information in interpreting the archaeological data.

Raju's study, should be guide to University students as well as teachers.

H.D. Sankalia

The Cultural History of Goa From 10,000 B.C. - 1350 A.D. By Anant Ramkrishna Sinai Dhume with a preface by the Vice Chancellor, B. Sheik Ali, Published by Dr. Ramesh Anant Dhume, Kamala Niwas, Santa-Cruz, Panaji-403001, Goa, Price Rs. 150/-

The publication of this book was most timely, when Goa was on the eve of becoming one of the States of India. It has been writtten by a person who has spent nearly 50 years in various administrative capacities in the Land Survey Department. Dr. Dhume has put to excellent use his experience so that the book gives a good idea not only of the geography, but the early settlements with their cultural trends. Dr. Dhume discusses the theory of the occupation by Sumerians. Then follows the account of Parsurama, and the immigrants from the Deccan Plateau, (Later) called Maharashtra.

Reliable history starts in the 5th - 6th century, when the Kadambas, the Western Chalukyas, and the Rashtrakutas tried to establish their sovereignty over Goa.

The name Goa is said to be derived from Gubi in the Sumerian records (2143-2124 B.C.) Latter Ptolemy called it Gouba, the city name Govapuri appears in *Suta-Samhita*, and letter in the inscriptions of Goa Kadambas.

The word "Goa" is said be derived from the Mundari word, "Goen-Bab" meaning "inclined ear of paddy", And the cultivation of paddy was first introduced by Kolis. From the word Goen-Bab, came the contracted Goa-ba. This later gave the word Goen from which arose the word Goa-Gowe.

The Sumerians who are supposed to have settled in Goa in 200 B.C. are said to have started the preparation of cloth-first wool and then cotton (p. 307-08). Later came people from Konkan and were called "Marang". This came to be pronounced as "Mhar".

Later came people who knew domestication of buffaloes and goats and lived in mud and stone cottages, and covered them with "kalvan", the smell of which drives away white-ants. These people who came from the south were matrilocal.

Then came Asuras, from - Mundari - from Chhotanagpur and were skillful agriculturist as well as well versed in iron technology. However they were overpowered by the Kolis. Between 1500-2500 B.C. came a wave of Aryans - Bhargavas and Angirasas.

Then came the Sumerians. They constructed large square or rectangular houses with a central courtyard and these people always insisted on entering the house after washing their feet and hence kept a huge water pot at the entrance.

The last chapter (No. 8) is most interesting from the point of view of the general reader as well as a scholar. For here Dr. Dhume weaves together all the various trends - physical (geographical), historical, archaeological and linguistic, and presents to us Goa as it is today.

With regard to the initial data 10,000 B.C. it is based on the discovery of three stone tools, handaxes, and one scrapper (pp. 29-30 and photo No. 3). This is too slender an evidence for making a large conclusion. Doubtful also is the Neolithic tool (p. 31).

Dr. Dhume does not seem to know that the Goa island was once - in the 12th century - known as Simhala or Lanka, as the very recent evidence - an inscription of Rattaraja, a Silahara king of Saka 930 (A.D. 1018) tells us that he belongs to the foremost family of Simhala, whereas the Dugamve inscription (*JBBRAS*, Vol. IX, p.266) calles the Kadamba king Jayakesi as the conqueror of Lanka, that is Goa, because being an island it was called Simhala. And a Copperplate found at Belgaum in the last centruy, *JRAS*,Vol. IX (1867-72), Bombay earliest evidence not only for the name of Goa, but that Goa was a famous port (pattana).

Further, I consulted "Sumer, the Dawn of Art", by Parrot. In this there are no doubt long oval stones (stelaes, p. 12, fig. 11) with engraved writing. But these are quite different from Goa stone stelac.

Of course it is now well known that there was a flowring trade between the Indus Civilization and Sumer, and Goa could have served as a port, as Bombay today. But so far there has been no trace of the Indus civilization in Goa. However, further careful search is necessary.

H.D. Sankalia

Iconography of the Hindu Temples in Marathwada, By Deshmukh, B.S Publication scheme, Jaipur, 1987 pp. 207 excluding Illustrations Price Rs. 375.

The cave temples of Maharashtra are well known while the structural temples of this region are still in dark. For the first time Dr. B.S. Deshmukh undertook an intensive study of the Hindu temples of the Marathwada region, a part of Maharashtra. This region consists of the following districts - Aurangabad, Parbhani, Bhir, Nanded, Jalna of Latur and Osmanabad. During the medieval period a large number of temples were built in this area either on the trade routes or in the vicinity of the Godavari vally. Most of them are located in the districts of Bhir, Osmanabad and Latur. These are commonly known as "Hemadpanti temples." They reflect several contemporary styles of the medeival period, i.e. Chalukya, Kakatiya, Hoysala, Yadava, etc.

For the first time thousands of sculptures lying loose or still *in situ* on the walls of these temples have been properly documented. The author has taken into account almost all the important forms of Siva, Vishnu, Mother Goddess and a number of minor deities mentioned in ancient literature. He considers all the relevant details, literary as well as archaeological, pertaining to them. Several unique images have been brought to the light for the first time. These are properly catalogued and illustrated in this book, for example the Matsya incarnation of Vishnu. As Matsya and Kurma incarnations of Vishnu have very little significance in comparison to other incarnations, these two are usually depicted in their animal forms and in group of incarnations. But in Marathwada temples these two forms have great symbolic significance. *Matsya* incarnation has been shown here in unique form - Vishnu seated in *yogasana* with *matsya* or fish as an emblem below. Similarly, Lakshmi and Narayana, standing and embracing each other, is also very unusual form of depiction, found on the exterior wall of Kedareswar temple at Dharmapuri. A number of other such images have been added to our knowledge by the author.

The books consists of seven chapters along with a separate introduction. While chapter one introduces the region, the subject and source material, chapters two to five are devoted to the iconographical studies of Vishnu, Siva, Mother Goddess and other minor deities. Chapter six conists of the details of drapery, ornaments, *mudras, asanas* and *ayudhas*. Chapter seven is devoted to conclusions.

The most complex problem of this region is that while majority of the icons belong to the Vaishava cults, there is hardly any temple dedicated to Vishnu or some other Vaisnavite deities. Surprisingly, the exterior walls of siva temples which are in hundreds here, are adorned with Vaisnavite icons. The author suggests that these temples were originally Vaisnavite with Vaisnava icons as presiding deity and latter were replaced with Sivalingas in the garbhagriha.

We may, however, indicate a few points for improvement in future edition; spellings of same of the words are not consistent throughout the book, like Nrsimha and Narsimha on page 53. Due to the lack of diacritical marks one faces great inconvinience in going through the book. Line drawings depicting *asanas, mudras, ayudhas*, ornaments etc. provide neither any separate explanation nor these are referred to in the text of chapter six to correlelate the text and illustration. In our opinion, the value of the book will be enhanced by adding a map of the Marathwada region and some views of the structural temples and a small caption to the illustrations below the photograph.

Shashi Asthava

Origins of the Gandharan Style - A study of the contributory influences by Lolita Nehru, Oxford University Press Delhi, 1989, Page 139, Plates 174. Price Rs. 700.00

The Gandharan art received much appreciation from early European scholars on account of its Occidential elements. It has variously been styled as Greaco - Buddhist, and Indo-Romanesque by most foreign experts who generally overrated its artistic value in comparison to the sculptural quality of the art idioms of the main land of India. However, there was also a school of art historians who considered it inferior and less original to early Indian art out of their sympathy for the main stream of Indian culture. Both these views have been regarded as subjective and academically illogical.

Basic contribution to Gandharan art has been made by foreign scholars Burgess, Foucher, Marshall, Smith, Buchthal, Rowland, Rosenfied, Bieber, Dobbins and many other scholars. What is most puzzling is that only very few Indian art historians have undertaken detailed and original researches on Gandhara art and Dr. Nehru deserves our thanks for carrying out indepth study successfully on the genesis of Gandharan sculpture, a most debated subject. The work was originally submitted as a Ph.D. dissestation in 1982 by the author to the University of Cambridge under the guidance of Prof. F.R. Allchin, a well-known archaeologist and Indologist.

The author clarifies in her perface her methodology. I decided to begin by 'separating' the different stylistic traditions present within Gandharan sculpture and to examine each one of these in turn...." Consisting of eight chapters besides the preface, preliminaries etc. and the notes, bibliography, index, and illustrations at the end, the main contents of the book include the introduction, covering background of the subject, objective and scope of study, discussions on the artistic sources and process of emergence and early development of the Gandharan style of sculptures and the conclusions drawn by the author. The main areas the author's researches pertain to three structural schemes viz; (i) systematic analysis of the artistic elemetns, which contributed to the formation of the Gandharan school, from other art idioms : Hellenistic-Bactrian, Parthian and Indian; (ii) the assessment of the surviving Hellenistic, cultural and artistic traits in parts of India, Afghanistan and Central Asia and varying process of their intermixture and (iii) emergence of Gandharan style as a result of a blend of already existing cultural and artistic traditions within its own conceptual and stylistic format in the first century A.D. and afterwards.

On the basis of the available data especially the excavated material (Ai-khanum) of recent decades, Lolita Nehru opines that Hellenistic (Greek) Bactria served as the major source of the Gandharan sculpture, thereby supporting Foucher's views expressed in the earlier part of the present century. she also admits the presence of the elements of Roman art in the Gandharan figures but feels that these travelled to Indian borderland on account of Parthian trade connexions with Western world along with conventional Achaemenid traits to form Gandharan compositions. Nehru tries to clarify (p.46) the role of Parthian art in Gandhara with these words : "The possibility cannot of course overrule the working of a direct Parthian influence upon Gandharan sculpture. The frontal representation of figures in the narratives, and the compositional treatment of some reliefs, are directly related to Parthian concepts."

About the impact of the art of the main land of India on Gandhara sculpture, the writer states that Gandhara art had drawn considerably upon the first phase of early Indian art, but like the Hellenistic, the Indian elements in Gandharan art of Kushana period become gradually duffused. She in fact notes an outflow of artistic elements from Gandhara into interior of India.

Lolita Nehru has termed developed Gandhara sculpture with a stylistic identity as Kushana Gandharan art and has logically traced its origins and formative stages. She concludes : "The research conducted here has revealed the two broad stylistic stages which preceded the emergence of the formulated Gandharan style. During the first stage, which lasted through the Mauryan, Greek and early Saka-Parthian period, till about the end of the first century B.C. or the beginning of the first century A.D. Hellenistic and Indian idioms in Gandhara evidently followed more or less independent stylitic expressions. The second stage lasted for about a century, fomr the close of the first stage till the end of the first century A.D., spanning the late Saka-Parthian and early Kushana period. During this stage, and from the later Parthian decades onwards in particular, and extending into the early years of Kushana rule, Gandhara underwent a major phase of stylistic and iconographical flux. This phase culminated, by the end of the first century A.D., in the crystallization of the mature Gandharan style, in the early years of the reign of Kanishka," (pp. 104-105).

She has also analysed the stucco, terracotta and clay sculpture of Gandhara region particularly of Taxila in relation to the growth of Gandharan art. She rightly feels that stucco as a sculptural medium was introduced into Gandhara during Greek rule and it continued subsequently in Gandhara and other region of India. Dr. Nehru has not only pointed out stylistic inconsistencies of Marshall's chronology of Gandharan art but has also attempted its revision on rational grounds.

What is more interesting in the book is that the author accepts revised dates (A.D. 20-30 onwards) for swat (Butkara Isculptures and she also agrees with Prof. Van Lohuizen in regard to their association with Mathura especially for the iconographical format of the Mathura Buddha.

Now the question arises whether Buddha's iconography in the Indian main land including Mathura was well settled in the first half of the first century AD and if so why the early Gandharan artist including that of Swat (Butkara I) sculpture failed to depict the Bodhi tree in the terms of Hellenistic realism. the logical inference of such a feature is that the Gandharan artist was not at all familiar with the *Pipal* (Bodhi) tree. Secondly the treatment of Buddha's head-dress and seat in the Swat figures is also different from Mathura. It may not be out of place to mention here that the most important pre-Kaniska figure of Buddha (MM-12) from Mathura shows him on a seat designed like a fire-alter with two loins below. This it is not unlikely that Gandharan sculptor under the formative stages of Mahayana Buddhism developed his own concept of the Buddha image in human form. Yet, certainly, there is evidence to show interaction between Gandhara and Mathura during the early centuries of Christian era in areas art and culture.

Dr. Nehru also refers to the outflow of Gandharan art current to the interior of India but she does not take any note of Gandhara sculptures in Mathura red sandstone. A comparison of such figures with original Gandharan examples may have been useful for the present study. Further an analysis of head-gears, ornaments, dresses, poses and mudras of figures, furniture, etc., depicted in Mathura and Gandhara art is also likely to yield good result for the verification of their chronology.

Lolita Nehru holds the view that most of the narrative scenes pertaining the life of Buddha in Gandharan art follow a chronological sequence, inspired by Hellenistic models, using a single moment. Thus Buddha's life cycle is visualized there as linear progression within formal compartments. But many art-critics may not agree with her as such elements can also be located in the Bharhut, Amaravati and Sanchi sculptures.

Another point where most scholars may differ with her is use of the term in 'India'in the context of Gandharan art. No doubt she considers Gandhara region to be within the traditional limits of ancient India but whenever she talks of art idioms she regards Indian art styles to be outside the area of Gandharan art. The book has some repetitions introduced most probably for the sake of stressing a particular point; otherwise it is supreb research work-well written and well produced. The author has carefully surveyed and objectively assessed the vast mass of archaeological material distributed in various collections of Asia and Europe besides published references.

On the whole the book deserves to be classed as valuable contribution to Indian art in recent years. The author has shown considerable maturity and a remarkable insight in interpreting her sources. A detalied bibliography, index and maps showing Gandhara, Bactria and area between India and Rome in the end-leaves are of much utility for any researcher. The scholarly community both within India and outside would welcome this book.

M.C. JOSHI

Archaeological Survey of India

MEETING OF THE WORLD ARCHAEOLOGICAL CONGRESS EXECUTIVE

HELD AT THE UNIVERSITY OF SOUTH DAKOTA, VERMILLION, USA ON 6 AUGUST 1989

MINUTES

Present :

Micheal Day	(Chair)
Jerry Bear Shield	
Susan Bulmer	(Southeastern Asia and the Pacific)
Christos Doumas	(Southern Europe)
Jim Everett	
Carol Gartside	
Angela Gilliam	(Northern America)
Jan Hammil Bear Shield	
Hirini Matunga	
Patrick Mbunwe-Samba	(Central Africa)
Irina Podgorny	(Southern America)
Gilbert Pwiti	(Eastern and Southern Africa)
Bettina Schmidt	(Northern Europe)
Petter Ucko	(Secretary)
Elizabeth Williams	(Southeastern Asia and the Pacific)

Present, as non-voting observers, at the request of the Chair :

Alicia Eugenia Silva (Director, Foundation for the Promotion of Culture, Bogota, Colombia)

Solly Simelane (ANC representative. New York)

Larry zimmerman (Organizer, WAC Inter-Congress, Vermillion, South Dakota)

Jane Hubert	(Secretariat)
Peter Stone	(Secretariat)

Apologies :

Ibeanu Anselm	(Western Africa)
Joseph-Marie Essomba	(Central Africa)
Clare Fawcett	(Northern America)
Ana Roca i Fontanals	(Southern Eurpoe)
S.P. Gupta	(Southern Asia)
Derek Hayes	(Treasurer)
Ian Hodder	(Treasurer)
Majeed Khan	(Near and Middle East)
Gustavo E. Politis	(Southern America)
Dashu Qin	(Eastern Asia)
Wu Rukang	(Eastern Asia)
Lesley Suttyt	(Central America and the Caribbean)
Abier H. Ziadeh	(Near and Middle East)

The Secretary reported that the representatives of the World Council for Indigenous Peoples had faxed the day before to say that its representatives were unable to attend the meeting due to lack of funds. The International Indian Treaty Council had therefore agreed to co-opt representatives of indigenous peoples : Australian Aboriginal (Jim Everett and Carol Gartside); American Indian (Jerry Bear Shield and one other); Maori (Hirini Matunga); Saami (one); and possibly one other, as they arrived for the Inter-Congress - as full voting members. In introducing Executive Members, the Chair explained proxy arrangements (Draft Statutes, Article 9.7) : I. Hodder to R. Layton; L. Sutty to Chair or Secretary; J-M Essomba to Secretary; M.Khan to Secretary; G. Politis to I. Podgorny.

Minor adjustments were made to the circulated Agenda as follows :

3(d) *One World Archaeology series*, 3(e) Support for Thrustan Shaw Nigerian Conference 1989. 4(c) ii Subscription renewals, 8(e) American Anthropological Association meeting, 8(f) WAB 4, 8 (g) Reprinting stationery, 8(h) WAC 3.

Item 1 : Report on WAC Membership.

The Secretary reported on the number of Members per Electoral Region, as follows :

Central Africa	11
Eastern and Southern Africa	28
Northern Africa	1
Western Africa	21
Central America and the Caribbean	7

Northern America	47
Southern America	18
Eastern Asia	5
Southeastern Asia and the Pacific	44
Southern Asia	76
Near and Middle East	10
Eastern Europe and Central Asia	6
Northern Europe	117
Southern Europe	35
	426 Members

It was noted by the Secretary that somewhere in the region of 25% of the Membership had been unable to pay their subscriptions, but had been granted discretionary Membership. It was further noted that 'Eastern Europe and Central Asia' had not nominated any Members for election to the Executive, that there had been no nomination of a Junior Representative for 'Northern Africa', and that those Members elected for 'Central America and the Caribbean' were perhaps not from the mainstream archaeological community.

In the following discussion it was further noted that while some Regional Colleges (especially 'Central Africa' and 'Southern Asia') had been very successful in recruiting Members, others had been considerably less so. Executive Members were urged to recruit new Members within their Regions. It was suggested that many people were still unclear about the aims and organization of WAC, and that others had not heard of it at all. It was therefore agreed that an information leaflet should be produced to help Members of the Executive with their recruitment of new Members - the Senior Representative for 'Southeastern Asia and the Pacific' offered to assist in the production of such a leaflet.

Item 2 : Financial Report.

As of May 9th 1989 WAC held L 1774 in the 'M.H.Day No. 3' account in England and c. 9000 Rupees (approx. L 360) in a special account held in India by M.Lal. The Secretary reported that by the end of the Inter-Congress the English account would be reduced to c.L300, and that part of the Southern Asia account had already been used for postage and xeroxing within Southern Asia.

2a: Relationship with previous WAC organization.

The Chair and Secretary explained that the 1986 Southampton WAC Congress had been organized by a Company Limited by Guarantee, which was also a Registered Charity. This Company is still in existence and although it has a zero bank balance at the moment it expects to receive income in the form of royalties from the sale of the *One World Archaeology* series. The Publishers, Unwin Hyman, had originally paid L30,000 to WAC, to pay for the precirculation of papers, and almost all of this had now been paid off through sale of the books.

The 'new' present WAC is not yet a legal body with formal Statutes, but could become such at the next Council meeting. At a recent Board meeting of the existing WAC Company the Directors had 'agreed to offer the WAC Company to the 'new' WAC Executive or to offer it places on the Directorship of the company...' The Directorship had empowered the Chair, Treasurer and Secretary to negotiate on its behalf and to report back to it for a final decision.

After considerable discussion it was *unanimously agreed* that the Executive would ask the Company Directors to operate with three Executive members - the Chair, Secretary and Treasurer and one other member to be elected by the Executive - and three further Directors to be nominated by the country that is to host the next WAC. The Executive *recommended* that these seven Directors should be in the majority.

The Executive wished the Company, for the present to continue to be registered in England. It further suggested that the Company should use any income for the continuation of WAC central services and as 'seed-corn' for future WAC meetings. However, it was noted that the major funding of all Congresses and Inter-Congresses would have to remain the responsibility of the host countries concerned.

2b : Future financial support.

The Secretary outlined the extremely precarious financial situation of WAC. The central office in Southampton was only able to function though the voluntary work of the secretariat, with very limited 'bought-in' secretarial support. As a result of WAC's position regarding the South African issue numerous funding bodies, which would normally be expected to fund such an organization, had refused support. The Secretary had been successful in negotiating isolated specific grants. However, the pursuance of such grants was extremely time-consuming, and the could not be relied on for the long-term survival of WAC. The Executive were urged to explore all possible sources of funding both for specific projects and for the administration and functioning of WAC.

Item 3 : Report on activities since WAC Steering Committe meeting.

3a : Inter-Congresses.

The first scheduled Inter-Congress, which was to have taken place in conjunction with the Waigani Cultural Seminar in Papua New Guinea, had to be cancelled due to the collapse of the Waigani Seminar through lack of 'promised UNESCO funding' at the last minute. The cancellation, reported in WAB 3, had been completely outside WAC's control.

The second scheduled Inter-Congress, now known as the First Inter-Congress, was about to take place here in Vermillion. The Secretary reported that despite the overall WAC financial situation, WAC had neverthless managed to make a significant contribution to the First Inter-Congress - namely, L1000 each from the Onaway Trust and The Royal Anthropological Institute respectively for the distribution of free copies of '*Who needs the past ?*' and '*Conflict in the archaeology of living traditions*' to Third and Fourth World participants;

L1500 from the Onaway Trust to assist with American Indian participation, and L15,000 from Lord Alistair McAlpine to assist with Australian Aboriginal participation. In addition WAC had been able to assist with some of the costs of some Third World Executive Members, and it had helped to gain a grant from the World Council of Churches.

3b : WAC had agreed to officially sponsor and/or be represented at :

i) The conference on 'The Use of the Past : Administration of Resources and Management of Archaeological Cultural Heritage at La Plata, Argentina, from June 13th - 16th 1989.

ii) The Indian Council for Historical Research's symposium on 'New Archaeology and India', in October 1988.

iii) The first joint archaeological congress at Baltimore, in January 1989, which had resulted in the formation of a new bulletin : 'Archaeology and Education'.

3c : The World Archaeological Bulletin.

WAB 3 was tabled. Copies have already been circulated to all WAC members. It was suggested that future WABs should contain a short and simple tear-out membership form. It was also suggested that the date of each WAB should appear on the inside front cover as customary in many journals.

The Executive expressed its thanks to Kate Golson for having acted as Honorary Editor for WAB 3.

3d : The One World Archaeology Series.

The Secretary reported on the progress of the series. Of the twelve volumes published to date, each had sold between 300 to 400 copies in under six months. Unwin Hyman had more or less agreed to produce paperback editions of any volume that sold 1000 copies in hardback within one to two years of publication.

The Executive congratulated the Secretary, in his capacity as Series Editor, on the excellent standard of the volumes published to date, and on the remarkable achievement represented by the series.

3e : Provision of computer to Nigeria.

The Secretary reported that WAC had supplied a microcomputer to the organizers of the 75 Year Birthday Conference for Professor Thurstan Shaw, to be held in Ibadan, Nigeria in November 1989. This gift had been made possible through the sale of an original painting donated to WAC by Yashodar Mathpal.

Item 4: Draft Statutes.

4a : Additions and alterations to countries within Regional Electoral Colleges.

i) The Secretary noted that the following countries had been inadvertently omitted from the list of countries comprising the Regional Electoral Colleges : Botswana, Swaziland and Mozambique. It was *unanimously agreed* to add these countries to the 'Eastern and Southern Africa' Region.

ii) The Secretary referred to a tabled letter from Professor Wu Rukang criticising the listing of Taiwan and Tibet as independent countries. Professor Wu Rukang suggested that the Regional listing could state 'China (including Taiwan)', After considerable discussion it was *agreed* that WAC would follow the policy of the UN in these specified cases, and that a letter would be sent to Professor Wu Rukang informing him of this decision.

4b: Transfer of individuals from one Regional Electoral College to another.

The Secretary drew the attention of the Executive to a tabled letter from Dr. L. Raposa and colleagues regarding the nomination of Dr. J. Morais as a Representative for Southern Europe. This case highlighted the question of whether the Draft Statutes should be altered in any way regarding nominees who, although residing in one region, practised archaeology in another. After discussion it was *agreed unanimously* (a) that Dr. Morais had been correctly assigned to Southern Europe, (b) that he had every right to stand for election for that Region, and (c) that Article 5.5. of the Draft Statutes should not be altered. The Executive further noted that Dr. Morais had made no approach for his Regional Membership to be transferred to another Region.

4c : Membership Registration fees - appropriate currencies and renewals.

i) It was *unanimously agreed* that article 4.4 of the Draft Statutes should be amended to read: *'The rates of membership subscription shall be determined by the Executive ...'* i.e. 'Council' is replaced by 'the Executive'.

ii) After discussion of the problem of continual variations in international and national inflation and exchange rates the Executive *agreed* that there should be no change in the membership fee at present.

iii) It was *agreed* that the arrangement whereby the Junior Representative for Southern Asia had been collecting membership fees in rupees should continue, and furthermore that Representatives of other regions should propose suitable regional arrangements to the Executive and Council meetings in 1990 for the simplification of membership fee collection.

iv) Renewal for membership.

It was noted that many members' renewals were overdue, or about to become so. It was *agreed* that separate 'reminder' mailings would not be made, because of the cost and lack of secretariat, but that renewal reminders could be sent out with notices about the next Congress.

4d: Life Membership.

i) In the light of amended Draft Article 4.4 it was proposed, and *unanimously accepted,* that Life Membership of WAC be made available with the payment of a single membership fee at a rate to be decided from time to time by the WAC

Executive. In the first instance the fee would be US $ 400

ii) It was further proposed, and *unanimously accepted,* that a four-year (non-student) membership registration fee be made available. This would be at a rate to be decided from time to time by the WAC Executive. In the first instance this fee would be 10% less than four times the annual membership fee, i.e. US $ 72.

It was *agreed* that these new arrangements would be announced in WAB 4.

4e : Head Office.

With reference to Draft Article 3. (a) it was *agreed* that the Head Office of WAC would remain in England until the first meeting of Council, where the matter should be discussed further again.

4f : Honorary Members.

With reference to Draft Article 4.3. it was agreed that the Statutes should contain reference to Honorary Members of WAC, and that Draft Article 4.3 should be amended to read: *'The Council may elect Honorary Members on the recommendation of the Executive. Honorary Members shall not be required to pay any subscriptions.'*

4g : Length of service on the Executive of representatives of indigenous peoples/Fourth World.

After a long discussion it was *agreed* that Draft Article 9.2 (c) be retained unaltered.

4h : Length of service of half the Executive.

With reference to Draft Article 9.5 it was *agreed* that owing to the cancellation of the Executive meeting scheduled to have taken place in Papua New Guinea in September 1988, resulting in the present situation whereby this Executive has only met for the first time at the Vermillion Inter-Congress, it was *agreed* that the Draft Article should be amended to read :

'Members of the Executive (other the officers of the WAC whose term on the Executive shall be determined by their period in office) shall be elected for a term of eight years save that one half of the members of the first Executive to take office after the ratification of these Statutes *(i.e. those meeting for the first time at the Vermillion Inter-Congress in 1989)* shall remain in office for a term of four years only *(i.e. until 1994).* The Council shall decide at the next International Congress *(i.e. 1990)* which members of the Executive are to retire at the end of four years (i.e. 1994). Thereafter half the Executive shall retire four years and a new Executive will take office immediately after each International Congress *(i.e. at an Executive meeting convened immediately following the last Council meeting during a Congress.).*

(In effect, elections for the vacant 14 posts on the Executive which meets immediately following Council in 1994, will have been conducted (in accordance with Draft Article 9.4. (d)) during the first half of 1994. Thereafter, elections for the vacant half of the Executive will take place in the months preceding each meeting of Council).

4i : Vacancies on the Executive.

With reference to Draft Article 9.9. it was *agreed* that the Officers continue to attempt to fill any vacancies on the Executive. After considerable discussion it was further *agreed* that Officers could co-opt members to fill vacancies on the Executive, provided all reasonable steps had been taken to elicit nominations from a Region, but none had been forthcoming. It was *agreed* that the term of office of Executive Members appointed by the Officers and not elected after nomination fiom the Regional Electoral College concerned, should be until the next meeting of the Council only, but for this period they would be full members of the Executive, with full voting rights.

4j : Correspondence with Professor Carmel Schrire.

Mr. Solly Simelane (ANC New York office) clarified the ANC policy regarding the academic boycott of South Africa. While the ANC still required a 'comprehensive mandatory boycott' of the apartheid regime, clearance for individual academics to attend international academic gatherings could be obtained from the National Liberation Movement (NLM) and the Mass Democratic Movement (MDM). To qualify for such clearance individual academics would have to be approved by the NLM/MDM.

The Chair raised specific points, and a number of conclusions were reached. It was *unanimously agreed* that while the apartheid regime continued to govern South Africa :

i) WAC will not use South Africa as a venue for any meetings.

ii) If any organizing committee for congresses or Inter-Congresses receive an application to participate from a resident South African, or from an individual in receipt of South African funding, the organizing committee should refer the application, via the Secretary of the Executive, to the ANC, who would then ascertain the status of the individual with the NLM/MDM. If the individual is approved by the NLM/MDM then s/he would be welcome to attend the meeting in question.

iii) No individual resident South African or individual in receipt of South African Government funding should be allowed to become a Member of WAC without the approval of the NLM/MDM.

iv) With regard to the specific case of Professor Schrire's tabled letters, it was now clear that neither Professor Schrire nor her South African colleagues could become Members of WAC unless they are approved by the NLM/MDM. The Secretary was asked to reply, correcting his letter to her of 29.6.89, and outlining WAC's policy, as above.

Mr. Simelane further emphasized that the general statement against the apartheid regime in South Africa issued by the UISPP did not in any way satisfy the terms of the ANC academic boycott of South Africa.

It was *agreed* by the Executive that WAC's position on the South African academic boycott be published in WAB 4.

Mr. J. Everett then claimed that the Tasmanian Aborigines felt themselves to be in the same situation as the black population of South Africa. He argued that this parallel procedure be considered. The Secretary pointed out that both the Plenary Session of the Southampton WAC Congress, and the Steering Committee set up by that Plenary session, had isolated the South African situation as being unique, as did the United Nations. It was agreed that Mr. Everett's view be minuted, and that the issue would be discussed further at a later meeting.

Item 5 : World Archaeological Congress 2.

The Secretary outlined the detailed negotiations that had recently taken place in an attempt to continue to hold WAC 2 in Merida in Venezuela in 1990, as had previously been agreed with Professor M. Sanoja and Jacqueline de Briceno. It was now clear that it was impossible for the Venezuelans to host WAC 2 because of the present economic and social situation in their country. Parts of relevant correspondence and telexes were read out.

According to the draft Statutes, the choice of venue for a WAC Congress is the responsibility of Council. However, given the present situation, and the fact that Council would not be meeting until a Congress was held, the Officers had to take on the responsibility of finding an alternative venue, preferably within South America. They *recommended* to the Executive that should Colombia offer to host WAC 2 in 1990, such an offer should be accepted.

To this end a provisional programme had been drawn up, including co-ordinators of five important themes, who had agreed in principle to organize sessions, whether in Venezuela or Colombia.

The Chair asked Ms Alicia Silva to outline the facilities that could be available in Cartagena, Colombia, if the Congress were to be held there

The Executive *unanimously endorsed* a motion from the chair that since Council could not meet until there was a WAC Congress, the Executive should take the initiative and accept an offer from Colombia, should one be forthcoming.

Ms Silva asked for further consideration of this item to be deferred to the next meeting of the Executive.

Item 6 : Membership subscriptions : special cases.

It was agreed that the Officers should continue to act with discretion regarding the waiving or deferring of individual WAC membership fees.

Item 7 : Membership of the 'Active Museum of Fascism and Resistance in Berlin' (correspondence tabled).

This item was deferred until the Executive had been circulated with fuller background details.

Item 8 : Future WAC activities.

8a : Inter-Congresses.

i) A WAC Inter-Congress concentrating on Urbanism was provisionally offered by the Junior Representative for Eastern and Southern Africa, to be held in either Kenya or Zimbabwe in 1992.

ii) A WAC Inter-Congress - without a specific theme - was provisionally offered by the Junior Representative for Southern America, to be held in Uruguay in 1991. Further discussion of this proposal was deferred to a later Executive meeting.

8b : Training fellowships.

It was agreed that WAC should pursue the possibility of initiating training fellowships when finances became available.

8c : Dissemination of literature.

It was *agreed* to continue to facilitate exchanges and distribution of literature as funds allowed.

8d : International free passes to archaeological sites.

It was *agreed* that free passes to archaeological sites should be negotiated for WAC Members wherever possible, as soon as the level of secretarial support would allow.

8e : American Anthropological Association.

The Officer's decision for WAC to co-sponsor the AAA meeting on 'The Social construction of the past : representation as power' from November 15th to 19th 1989, was *ratified.*

8f : WAB 4.

It was agreed that WAB 4 should be produced as soon as finances allowed, to give the utmost publicity to decisions taken in South Dakota - not least, news about WAC 2, and renewal of subscriptions.

8g : Reprinting stationery.

The Executive agreed to the printing of WAC stationery, as soon as finances allowed.

8h : WAC 3

This item was deferred to a later Executive meeting.

Item 9 : Data Protection Act.

The Secretary brought the Data Protection Act to the notice of the Executive and requested Regional Representatives to inform their Members, when appropriate, that their names, addresses and subscription details were held on computer at the WAC office, and could be open to public scrutiny.

Item 10 : Any Other Business.

i) Letter from Ms. A. Ziadeh (tabled) - the Executive

expressed sympathy for the circumstances reported, and resolved to consider the matter further at its next meeting.

ii) Professor Michael Day and Jan Hammil Bear Shield each circulated documents about the 'reburial issue' which they hoped would be endorsed by the Executive and the Inter-Congress Plenary Session - the Executive decided to return to both documents at future meetings.

Item 11 : Place and date of next meeting.

The next meeting of the Executive was fixed for 19.00 on August 9th 1989.

MEETING OF THE EXECUTIVE ON 9 AUGUST 1989 MINUTES

Present : Michael Day (Chair)

Jerry Bear Shield	
Susan Bulmer	(Southeastern Asia and the Pacific)
Robert Cruz	
Christos Doumas	(Southern Europe)
Jim Everett	
Carol Gartside	
Jan Hammil Bear Shield	
Makkhan Lal	(Southern Asia)
Robert Layton	(Proxy : Northern Europe)
Hirini Matunga	
Patrick Mbumbe-Samba	(Central Africa)
Inge-Maria Mulk	
Irina Podgorny	(Southern America)
Gilbert Pwiti	(Eastern and Southern Africa)
Bettina Schmidt	(Northern Europe)
Peter Ucko	(Secretary)
Elizabeth Williams	(Southeastern Asia and the Pacific)

Present as non-voting observers, at the request of the Chairman :

Alicia Eugenia Silva (Director, Foundation for the Promotion of Culture, Bogota, Colombia)

Larry Zimmerman (Organizer : WAC Inter-Congress, Vermillion, South Dakota, USA)

Jane Hubert (Secretariat)

Peter Stone (Secretariat)

Apologies :

Angela Gilliam

Bili Means

(Others as for 6.8.89 meeting).

Proxy arrangements remained as for 6.8.89 with the addition of A. Gilliam to Secretary.

Item 1 : Matters arising : Life membership - India

The prohibitively high cost of life membership of WAC (at the sum agreed by the WAC Executive on 6.8.89) for those from the developing world, was raised by the Representative for Southern Asia, and was discussed at some length. The Executive *agreed* to allow the Officers to make individual arrangements for specific countries as and when they could agree such arrangements with the Regional Representatives.

Item 2 : Format of Plenary Session on August 10th 1989.

It was agreed that the Chairman and Secretary, with three Executive Members drawn from the Indigenous Representatives should be seated on the dais, and that the format of the Plenary Session would be :

a) Formal opening (Michael Day)

b) Thanks to Inter-Congress staff (from Larry Zimmerman)

c) Resolutions to the Plenary Session from the Executive

d) Resolutions tabled from Inter-Congress participants

e) Resolutions from the Floor

f) Any Other Business

g) Formal thanks to the Inter-Congress Organizers

h) Closure of Inter-Congress.

It was confirmed that all Inter-Congress participants were eligible to vote on all resolutions of the Plenary Session. Such Inter-Congress Plenary Session resolutions would then be considered by the WAC Executive.

Item 3 : Future appointment of Indigenous Representatives to the Executive.

The Secretary requested the Executive to discuss this

item further, recognizing the need for both flexibility and continuity with regard to the representation of Indigenous Peoples on the Executive. He reaffirmed that one of the first calls on any WAC finance was to enable the full Executive to meet.

After much discussion the Chairman put two motions to the Executive :

a) That the Indigenous Representatives on the Executive form a Sub-Committee of the Executive,

b) That this Sub-Committee draft a policy paper with regard to the eight places for Indigenous Representation on the Executive that could, if necessary, be recommended by the Executive to council to replace or amend Article 9.2 (c) of the Draft Statues.

Both motions were *agreed unanimously*, and Mr Matunga agreed to co-ordinate the exchange of ideas and discussion of the Sub-Committee.

It was further confirmed that the present Indigenous Representatives would continue to serve as full members of the Executive until the next meeting of the Executive (when they might or might not be replaced under the present Draft Article 9.2 (c).

Item 4 : WAC 2.

Ms Alicia Eugenia Silva, Director of the Foundation for the Promotion of Culture formally offered to host WAC 2 in Cartegena, Colombia in September 1990. The offer was unanimously accepted by the Executive.

The Secretary tabled a draft 2nd Announcement for WAC 2, including the titles and suggested co-ordinators for several major themes, some based on precirculated papers, some on precirculated papers and oral addresses, and others as verbal contributions only. The draft of the 2nd Announcement included a message from the President explaining the change of venue, and gave some details about Cartegena as a town. A timetable was proposed, of February Ist 1990 for the receipt of abstracts and manuscripts for precirculation; April Ist for the mailing of the Final Announcement; July Ist for early registration fees. With Ms Silva's agreement, full registration was suggested as US $ 200 (WAC Members US$150) with various special 'early' and 'student' rates.

Simultaneous interpretation for Spanish/English was proposed.

The academic programme would consist of various specialist symposia, as well as some nine major themes. The first day, however, would be on 'Current developments in the archaeology of Latin America and the Caribbean', to be co-ordinated by Dr. G. Politis (Argentina) - this first day would act as orientation and briefing about Latin American archaeology.

Subsequent thematic meetings would include: 'Computers and Archaeology : a global view of the impact of Information Technology (co-ordinated by the IBM UK Scientific Centre); 'Education and Archaeology' (co-ordinated by the Centre for the 'sensibilization' of the European Cultural Heritage, Barcelona, Spain): 'Tropical Agriculture' (co-ordinator Professor J. Golson, ANU, Canberra, Australia); 'Landscape Archaeology' (co-ordinators: Messrs. D. Austin, A. Fleming (UK) and others); 'Management of the Archaeological Heritage' (co-ordinator : ICAHM). In addition a thematic meeting would be co-ordinated by the Gold Museum, Bogota. A further theme, following up the Inter-Congress on 'reburials' would almost certainly also be organized.

After some discussion of the proposed overall programme and after considering a tabled statement by Ms Schmidt and Dr. Pwiti it was proposed, and accepted, that an additional major theme should be devoted to 'The Social Contexts of the Practice of Archaeology', to be co-ordinated by Dr. Gilbert Pwiti, (Harare, Zimbabwe) and Ms. Bettina Schmidt (University of Mainz, W. Germany).

Item 5 : Future WAC activities (continued from 6.8.89)

a) 1992 Inter-Congress on Urbanism.

The Secretary wished to inform the Executive that the Junior Representative for Eastern and southern Africa might have been ultra-cautious at the last Executive meeting regarding the proposed 1992 Inter-congress. Both he and Dr. Pwiti had every reason to believe that generous finances would be provided for the Inter-Congress by SAREC.

b) Proposed Inter-Congress in Uruguay. Given the strong probability of the Urbanism Inter-Congress in 1992, and the Executive's acceptance of the offer to hold WAC 2 in Colombia in 1990, the Executive *agreed* that the feasibility and success of a further Inter-Congress in 1991 - just one year after WAC 2 and also in South America - was unrealistic. The Executive asked the Secretary to write to Uruguay pointing out that WAC 2 would be discussing Latin American archaeology for its first day, and suggesting that an Inter-Congress in Uruguay might be more appropriate at a later date.

c) WAC 3

Dr. Lal reported that discussions that he had held in India could lead to an offer to host WAC 3 in Delhi in 1994, with specialist symposia being held in other Indian towns. The Executive *unanimously agreed* to ask Dr. Lal to continue negotiations with a view to his presenting a formal offer to Council at WAC 2 in 1990.

Item 6 : Appointment of one additional Director of WAC

The Executive agreed to the nomination of Dr. Gustavo Politis for the third Directorship position on the WAC Company.

Item 7 : Recommendations to the Executive

7a) The AOB item (of 6.8.89) from Ms Ziadeh regarding the isolation of some archaeologists from their professional colleagues as a result of the political situation on the West Bank, Israel.

The Chairman suggested that Ms Ziadeh be asked whether she wished to contribute an article to a future WAB on this subject. It was further suggested that the topic be included within the WAC 2 programme, within the theme 'The Social Contexts of the practice of Archaeology'. The executive also requested the Secretary to write to Ms. Ziadeh reporting on the Inter-Congress and Executive meeting, in order to decrease her isolation.

7b) From the Inter-Congress:

i) A memorandum had been received from Kent Schneider, Muriel Crespi and Evan 1, DeBloois recommending WAC to seek sponsorship from government agencies, international motel chains, airline companies etc. for WAC 2. The Executive *agreed* that any ideas of gaining sponsorship were valuable, and that once a secretariate could be established, such ideas should be followed up. Meanwhile the Secretary was asked to write to Kent Schneider et al asking them to act on WAC's behalf on this matter.

ii) A letter of 2.8.89 to WAC Members from the Chairperson of the Mwekma Tribe was read out, regarding the recent return of skeletal material by Stanford University to American Indian groups. A paper on the subject had been read at the Inter-Congress. The Executive *unanimously approved with acclamation* a suggestion that the WAC should write to the Vice President and Provost of Stanford University expressing its strong support for this action.

iii) Mr. Jim Everett tabled a document which, as amended by him, read:

'Motion : That this conference recommends that WAC resolves to determine firm decisions to the following :

A. That applicants from Australia seeking membership and/or to attend WAC Conferences will be referred to the appropriate aboriginal body for assessment and recommendation of action for WAC to consider,

B. That WAC commit itself to assist in acquiring adequate funds to employ an aboriginal person to be responsible to organize a nationally represented conference of aborigines to :

(i) establish a national aboriginal body to specifically deal with the rights of the dead,

(ii) open discussions on aboriginal structures for aboriginal community determinations and control of aboriginal culture and heritage,

(iii) work towards a Statement of aboriginal community rights in matters of their respective customs, practices and lifestyle.

C. That the Foundation for Aboriginal and Islander Research Action Organization be the sponsor and administrative body to implement A and B aforementioned motions.

The Executive discussed (A) at considerable length. (A) was then withdrawn by its proposer. In the discussion of (B) there was a general concensus that some mechanism that could 'seive' and identify archaeologists who were working in an unethical manner would be a major step forward. The danger of the 'oppressed' themselves becoming the 'oppressors' was also noted. It was eventually *agreed* that the sub-Committee of the Executive, set up under Agenda Item 3 above, should be requested to draft an acceptable code of ethics for archaeologists, which all archaeologists would be required to accept on joining WAC. It was further noted that this would then necessitate the creation of a disciplinary procedure for any WAC Member identified as breaking such an agreed code. It was *agreed,* given the above decisions regarding (A) and (B), that suggestion (C) was no longer relevant.

iv) A document received from Mr. Michael Aird was read out, which proposed :

'That all Aboriginal people in Queensland :

a) should have rights of access to all documentation on Aboriginal sites; and

b) should have the right to control all future archaeo logical material in Queensland.

After some discussion of the problems regarding the safe keeping of sacred/secret Aboriginal material it was agreed that the new Sub-Committee (Agenda Item 3, above) should also bear this item in mind while considering a proposed ethical code, and that Mr Aird should be asked to re-submit a revised motion to the next meeting of the Executive.

(v) A proposal was received from Celia Gunn, that WAC should send a letter, based on the following draft, to the Minister of Municipal Affairs, Recreation and Culture, Victoria, British Columbia, Canada, (and others) regarding the request of the Arrow Lakes Band for the return of ancestral remains and burial goods for reburial :

'The WAC held the first Inter-Congress on "Archaeological Ethics and the Treatment of the Dead" at USD on August 7 - 10 - 1989.

It has come to our attention that the Arrow Lakes Band of WA State have been given a delayed and conditional response to their request for the return of ancestral remains and burial goods for traditional reburial at the Vallican site, DjQji, B.C. Canada.

Our understanding is that these materials were received from the site under Ministerial authority without knowledge or consent of the descendants, namely the Arrow Lakes Band, and were analyzed and then stored under unsatisfactory conditions in the Royal British Columbia Museum, Victoria, B.C.

Despite a pledge, the Museum has apparently has no authority to make decisions concerning release of the remains and in fact has no policy to deal with a request of this kind.

We understand that determination as to the disposition of ancestral remains and burial goods rests with the Minister responsible for the B.C. Heritage Conservation Act, namely yourself, Ms. Johnson.

We wish to inform you we stand in total support of the request of the ALB and urge you to return these materials for rightful reburial unconditionally and as soon as possible.

Also we would suggest that any policy to be drafted concerning future requests of this kind include substantial Native input and consultation. We recommend immediately opening lines of communication with Native Bands on this issue.

It is desirable, that if such materials are to be stored, that the Museum should have suitable facilities so that such material is treated with honour and respect.

We request and official response.'

The Executive *agreed* that a letter should be sent, using the above draft as a basis.

Item 8 : Recommendations to the Plenary Session.

i) Page 1 of the Agenda Item 10 (ii) document (6.8.89) from Jan Hammil Bear Shield on behalf of the international Indian Treaty Council was *accepted for recommendation* to the Plenary Session as follows :

'POSITION PAPER OF THE INTERNATIONAL INDIAN TREATY COUNCIL BEFORE THE FIRST INTER-CONGRESS ARCHAEOLOGICAL ETHICS AND THE TREATMENT OF THE DEAD, WORLD ARCHAEOLOGICAL CONGRESS.

'The International Indian Treaty Council in conjunction with and on behalf of American Indians Against Desecration hereby proclaims the following, TO WIT :

1. That the sacred burial ground of indigenous peoples have been desecrated with the bodies and sacred items thereof scattered throughout the world and stored in universities, laboratories and museums, AND

2. That with few exceptions, said treatment of sacred remains and burial items is sacreligious, and contrary to the religious beliefs, practices and customs of those affected, their friends, relations and allies, AND

3. That said treatment is, as a normal course, the result of anthropologist, archaeologist, paleontologist and/or physical anthropologist desires to further research, AND

4. That said treatment, in isolated cases, includes the display of sacred burials and items therein for public viewing, AND

5. That said display is, as a normal course, contrary to the religious practices, beliefs and customs of the individuals involved, their relatives, friends and allies, AND

6. That said treatment of sacred remains, in numerous cases, includes preservation, casting, scraping, core sampling and otherwise destruction of said sacred remains and burial items therewith, AND

7. That said treatment is, as a normal course, contrary to the religious practices, beliefs, and customs of the individuals involved, their relatives, friends and allies.'

Page 2 of the document (with the minor amendment of 'consider' for 'include') was referred for consideration to the WAC Sub-Committee (Agenda Item 3 above) as follows :

'NOW THEREFORE LET IT BE RESOLVED THE FOLLOWING, TO WIT :

That the world Archaeological Congress initiate and draft an International Code of Ethics which will consider but not be limited to the following :

In research, anthropologist primary responsibility is to those he studies, their relatives, friends and allies. When there is a conflict of interest, these individuals must come first. The anthropologist must do everything within his power to protect their physical, social and physiological welfare and to honor their dignity and privacy, AND

There is an obligation to reflect the foreseeable reprecussion of research and publication on the general population being studied, AND

It is axiomatic that the rights, interest and sensitivity of those studied must be safeguarded, AND

That a thorough and continuous effort be made in locating and soliciting from friends, relatives and allies of the ancestors whose graves are threatened and/or have already been desecrated; said solicitation being for the purposes of appropriate disposition thereto, AND

That the World Archaeological Congress condemn and seek educational enlightenment to decision makers thereof affecting the display of human remains in cases where the wishes of the deceased is contrary to said display, AND

That the World Archaeological Congress call for a moratorium on preserving, casting, scraping, core sampling and otherwise destruction of human remains until such time as consultation occurs with the relatives, friends and allies for purposes of determining to the best of one's ability the appropriateness of said destruction on the religious beliefs, customs and traditions of the individuals affected.'

ii) A considerably amended 'Vermillion Accord' *(Agenda Item 10 (ii) 6.8.89)* was tabled. The Chairman informed the Executive that this document had received approval and support from Dr Tom King. The proposed accord read :

'Human remains

1. Respect for the mortal remains of the dead shall be accorded to all irrespective of origin, race, religion, nationality, custom and tradition.

2. Respect for the wishes of the dead concerning disposition shall be accorded whenever possible, reasonable and lawful,

when they are known or can be reasonably inferred.

3. Respect for the wishes of the local community and of relatives or guardians of the dead shall be accorded whenever possible, reasonable and lawful.

4. Respect for the scientific research value of skeletal, mummified and other human remains (including fossil hominids) shall be accorded when such value is demonstrated to exist.

5. Agreement on the disposition of fossil skeletal, mummified and other remains shall be reached by negotiation on the basis of mutual respect for the legitimate concerns of communities for the proper disposition of their ancestors, as well as the legitimate concerns of science and education.

6. The express recognition that the concerns of various ethnic groups as well as those of science are legitimate and to be respected, will permit acceptable arrangements to be reached and honoured.'

After lengthy and detailed discussion the Executive *agreed* to accept the 'Vermillion Accord', while also acknowledging that some positions existed that went further than that proposed in this document. Nevertheless, the Executive considered the Statement - coming as it did from an international archaeological organization with significant 'Fourth World' membership - to be a significant contribution to the debate on the archaeological treatment of skeletal remains. In this context, some Executive Members saw the 'Accord' as a most significant step forward in the clarification of issues and the possibility of future co-operation between groups with apparently different philosophies.

The motion to accept the 'Vermillion Accord' was *approved nem. con.*

Item 9: Membership of the 'Active Museum of Fascism and Resistance in Berlin' (Agenda Item 7 of 6.8.89).

The Executive *agreed* to the Chairman's suggestion that WAC give all possible moral support to this organization, but that WAC could not afford to pay any membership fees. He also asked for enquiries to be made regarding the possibility of the AMFRS becoming a WAC Institutional Member.

Item 10 : Any Other Business

There was no other business.

Item 11 : Next meeting of the Executive.

The Executive agreed to meet on August 10th, after the Plenary Session.

MEETING OF THE EXECUTIVE ON 10 AUGUST 1989 MINUTES

Present : Michael Day (Chair)

Jerry Bear Shield

Susan Bulmer (Southeastern Asia and the Pacific)

Robert Cruz

Christos Doumas (Southern Europe)

Jim Everett

Carol Gartside

Jan Hammil Bear Shield

Makkhan Lal (Southern Asia)

Robert Layton (Proxy : Northern Europe)

Hirini Matunga

Patrick Mbunwe-Samba (Central Africa)

Iange-Maria Mulk

Irina Podgorny (southern America)

Gilbert Pwiti (Eastern and Southern Africa)

Bettina Schmidt (Northern Europe)

Peter Ucko (Secretary)

Elizabeth williams (Southeastern Asia and the Pacific)

Also present, at the invitation of the Chair :

Alicia Eugenia Silva (Director, Foundation for the Promotion of Culture, Bogota, Colombia).

Jane Hubert (Secretariat)

Peter Stone (Secretariat)

Apologies and proxy arrangements : as for 9.8.89. meeting.

The Chair indicated that the main business of this meeting was to respond to the motions supported by the Plenary Session.

Item 1: Motions put to the Plenary Session by the Executive.

i) Document put forward by Jan Hammil Bear Shield on behalf of the international Indian Treaty Council (Agenda Item 10 (ii) of 6.8.89.; Agenda Item 8 (i) of 9.8.89.)

Some Clarification of various points on page 2 had been requested at the Plenary Session, followed by a unanimous vote in favour of accepting page 1, and of referring page 2 to the new WAC Sub-Committee (Agenda Item 3 of 9.8.89).

ii) The Vermillion Accord (Agenda Item 10 (ii) of 6.8.89., Agenda Item 8 (ii) of 9.8.89.)

This document had been discussed at length by the Plenary Session, and then approved with an overwhelming vote in favour of adopting it as WAC policy.

Item 2: Motions Put to the Plenary Session from the floor.

i) From Jim Wilson and Celia Gunn :

'We request that the WAC Executive attempt to establish a two to three year fellowship providing for the livelihood and research costs of an individual to locate, inspect, and document the conditions of human skeletal collections and associated burial goods with a view to possible repatriation and/or reburial.'

This motion had been passed unanimously by the Plenary Session.

The Executive *accepted* the motion.

The Secretary then moved a second motion :

'That funds should also be sought for Indigenous Peoples to visit such collections once they had been identified.'

This motion was also *accepted* by the Executive.

ii) From Gordon Briscoe and Robert Layton :

'After four days of intense discussion, within a world wide context, on the subject of "Archaeological Ethics and the Treatment of the Dead", the Australian Aboriginal participants, joined by the other Australian participants, urge the WAC Executive to :

Communicate with relevant Australian authorities with a view to raising the necessary funds to enable a national conference to be held for Aboriginal people to be able to come together to fully discuss the question of the treatment and disposal of the dead. This is a consideration vital to the interests of all Aboriginal people.

The proposed meeting should allow for the full participation of Aboriginal people of all backgrounds and needs, to allow for full consideration of all the complexities of the issue.

It is now timely and urgent for a consistent national Aboriginal view to emerge. Only by facilitation of genuine inter-Aboriginal consultation of this kind, will it become possible for Aboriginal people to develop a meaningful strategy with regard to the disposal of the dead, and thus to gain control of this own people's past and future.'

This motion had been accepted *nem.con.* by the Plenary Session.

Dr. Layton now suggested two amendments to the document :

- Line 5 : insert' if requested' after'....urge the WAC Executive' and before 'to:';

- Line 6 : delete 'Australian' before 'authorities' and after 'relevant'.

The document was *accepted* by the Executive *in this amended form*.

iii) From the World Indigenous Congress (with 38 names attached):

'We, the World Indigenous Congress, congratulate the World Archaeological Congress for providing a forum for discussing these pressing matters and we thank the individual members for their sensitivity in considering this issue. Indeed the world Archaeological Congress's action shows an unprecedented degree of sensitivity towards the world's indigenous peoples and their religious beliefs and cultural diversity. The forum helps the international community to have diverse cultural perspectives on the complex ethical issues that arise during archaeological investigation. Growing concerns for morality, human decency and cultural pluralism among the world's society will gradually compel other institutions to follow your example.

It is our understanding that certain members of your profession have chosen to boycott the conference. The refusal to participate in our discussions at the World Archaeological Congress does not give authority to continue the desecration of out ancestors' resting places. Permission to work with the sacred burial and ceremonial sites and human remains and grave goods of our ancestors must be obtained from the appropriate indigenous group. We therefore recommend that the World Archaeological Congress adopt the following :

1. that grave robbing and pot hunting done in the name of scientific inquiry, academic freedom and professional development be ended immediately,

2. those individuals, institutions or governments responsible for the disinterment and curation of indigenous remains and grave goods bear the full cost of reburying same,

3. advocate the passage of enforceable laws which protect indigenous cemeteries, grave sites, and burial mounds,

4. return all curated indigenous remains and associated sacred burial possessions to appropriate indigenous groups.

When your organization has implemented these recommendations, it will then have truly taken a lead in breaking down a major barrier dividing academic and indigenous communities.

Respectfully,

The World Indigenous Congress.'

The document had been accepted by the Plenary Session with only 11 votes against.

The Executive had some problems with the wording of parts of the four recommendations. It welcomed the spirit of the motion yet felt unable to accept it as it stood becuase of a number of (presumed unintentional) ambiguities. The secretary suggested the following possible wording of the recommendations :

1. that grave 'robbing' and pot-hunting be ended immediately.

2. those individuals, institutions or governments responsible for the disinterment and curation of indigenous remains and grave goods bear the reasonable cost of reburying same.

3. advocate the passage of enforceable laws which would protect indigenous ceneteries, grave sites and burial mounds,

4. if requested, return all curated indigenous sacred remains and associated sacred burial possessions to appropriate indigenous groups.

The Executive was prepared to accept the amended wording of (2), (3) and (4) but remained concerned about (1). After further discussion it was *decided* that the document should be further considered by the Executiver Sub-Committee (Agenda Item 3 of 9.8.89), and re-addressed at the next meeting of the Executive.

Item 3: Documents presented directly to the Executive.

i) Recommendation from Philippe Soulier :

'That WAC should :

1 publish the main resolutions of the congress in a special paper ;

2. send this paper to all the participants and to the main important archaeological organizations;

3. translate these resolutions into French, Spanish, German etc. because it must be an iternational project.'

The Executive noted that the main resolutions would be published in WAB 4 and would be sent to all members, but not to all Inter-Congress participants. It was suggested that if Larry Zimmerman was mailing all participants he could be asked to include the resolutions in that mailing.

It was *agreed* that as much as possible of the report of the Inter-Congress, and certainly the motions from the Plenary Session and the Executive should be translated into, at least, Spanish (by Irina Podgorny), German (by Bettina Schmidt), French (by Philippe Soulier).

ii) Proposal from Mark Price :

'Dialogue and communication between aboriginal communities and scientific and educational communities is important to resolve inter-ethnic issues, including that of reburial. Failure of communication is frequent, even in the context of dialogues between well-intentioned people. Further, the question is often raised, "How do the aborigines benefit from a particular study ?" Mutual understanding would be enhanced by the presence of more aborigines trained in anthropology.

I am in the process of establishing a scholarship at the University of Missouri - Columbia to benefit Indian students interested in anthropology. The scholarship will be funded by all royalties I would otherwise receive from the sales of my doctoral dissertation and from private donations. During this congress the thought occurred that WAC might support (or at least encourage) national scholarships to benefit indigenous students interested in anthropology, these scholarships to be funded by donations of royalties from published works of scholars in respective countries. If such a national fund should be established in the United States I would be glad to attempt to restructure my present scholarship and even remove my name from the title, to which I have presently (immodestly) fixed it.'

The Executive *welcomed* this suggestion and the Secretary was asked to write to Mr. Price asking him to try and encourage others to establish such scholarship Funds through WAC. another

iii) Item 7(iv) of 9.8.89.

Mr. Michael Aird aksed for this matter to be withdrawn pending further consideration by him.

Item 4: Any other Business.

i) Information leaflet outlining WAC principles and activities (Item 1 of 6.8.89)

The production of the proposed leaflet was discussed further, and Ms Susan Bulmer agreed to draft a text and have the pamphlet designed. A 'master' copy would then be sent to all Executive Members for duplication and distribution within their own Regions.

ii) Payment of Membership by Credit Card.

The Executive discussed the benefits associated with payment by credit card and the Secretary agreed to look into the possibilities, and, if this method of payment was indeed possible and advantageous to WAC, to announce details in WAB 4.

Indian Archaeology Society
C/of National Museum, Janpath, New Delhi 110 011
Life Members

Mr. Ravindra Nath Aggrawal
Department of A.I.H.C. & Archaeology
Dr. Hari Singh Gaur Vishwavidyalaya
Sagar 470 003
Madhya Pradesh

Prof. D.P. Agrawal
Physical Research Laboratory
Navrangpura
Ahmedabad 380 009
Gujarat

Mr. M. Shafiqul Alam
Department of Archaeology
Deccan College
Pune 411 006

Dr. F.R. Allchin
Ancient India & Iran Trust
Brookland House
23, Brooklands Avenue
Cambridge CB2 2BG
England

Dr. I. H. Ansari
P.G. Department of History
Government Roza P.G. College
Rampur 244 901
Uttar Pradesh

Dr. Arun Kumar
Archaeological Survey of India
Lucknow Circle
Lucknow
Uttar Pradesh

Dr. Shashi Asthana
National Museum
Janpath
New Delhi 110 011

Prof. K.D. Bajpai
H-15, Padmakar Nagar
Makronia
Sagar 470 004
Madhya Pradesh

Prof. Shiva G. Bajpai
Department of History
California State University
Northridge, Los Angeles
California 91330
U.S.A.

Mr. S. R. Bharadwaj
'Saroj', G-62, Dhaka Colony
Delhi 110 009

Dr. D.K. Borah
Deputy Director Research (H)
Ita Nagar
Arunachal Pradesh

Prof. D.K. Chakrabarti
Flat 20, Uttaranchal Housing Society
Plot No. 5, Patparganj
Delhi 110 092

Dr. P.K. Chattopadhyaya
Training Centre
Alloy Steel Plant
Durgapur
West Bengal

Mr. Sumant Chowdhary
297, Tilak Ganj, Gala Mand'
Sagar 470002
Madhya Pradesh

Prof. G.F. Dales
1025, Keeler Avenue
Berkeley, CA 94708
U.S.A.

Mr. B.P. Das
Sunder Villa
Chukan Ghat
Varanasi
Uttar Pradesh

Mr. Bijan Bihari De
Department of History
Gauhati University
Guwahati 781 014
Assam

Mrs. Devangana Desai
'Shanti', 30-19, Peddar Rd
Bombay 400 026
Maharashtra

Mr. M.N. Deshpande
D-25, Press Enclave
Saket
New Delhi

Mr. K.N. Dikshit
Archaeological Survey of India
Janpath
New Delhi 110 011

Mr. Hemendra Nath Dutta
Registration Officer
Department of Archaeology
Jorhat 785 001
Assam

Dr. D.P.S. Dwarikesh
Department of Linguistics
Michigan University
Kalamazoo 49008
U.S.A.

Mr. H.P. Francfort
CNRS, URA No. 10
23, Rue du Maroc
75019 Paris, Cedex 19
France

Prof. R.C. Gaur
4/16, Kelanagar
Marris Rd Extension
Aligarh 202 001
Uttar Pradesh

Ms. Geeta Dharmarajan
A-3, Sarvodaya Enclave
New Delhi 110 017

Mrs. Geeta Narvare
C/O Dr. Giriraj Kumar
Dayalbagh Educational Institute
Dayalbagh
Agra 282 005
Uttar Pradesh

Prof. A.K. Ghosh
16B, R.K. Chatterjee Road
Calcutta 700 042
West Bengal

Prof. N.C. Ghosh
Department of A.I.H.C. & Archaeology
Visva-Bharati
Santiniketan 731 235
West Bengal

Mr. G.K. Ghosh
Flat No.4
5 Ruwwell Street
Calcutta 700 016
West Bengal

Mr. Gopal Shesh
Juna Killaward
Bilaspur 495 001
Madhya Pradesh

Dr. C.S. Gupta
Department of A.I.H.C. & Archaeology
Nagpur University
Nagpur
Maharashtra

Dr. Jagdish Gupta
181-A/1, Nagavasuki
Allahabad 211 006
Uttar Pradesh

Mr. Mahendra Kumar Gupta
Department of A.I.H.C. & Archaeology
Banaras Hindu University
Varanasi 221 005
Uttar Pradesh

Dr. P.L. Gupta
J-12/15-R, Bowliabag
Ram Katra, Varanasi 221 002
Uttar Pradesh

Dr. S.P. Gupta
Allahabad Museum
Allahabad
Uttar Pradesh

Mr. Shyam Sharan Gupta
Archaeological Survey of India
Prehistory Branch
Old High Court Building
Nagpur 440 001

Dr. H. Haertel
Museum of Indian Art
Berlin - 33
Taku Street
Federal Republic of Germany

Mr. Hemraj
Department of Archaeology
Jawhar Bhawan, 9th Floor
Lucknow 226 001
Uttar Pradesh

Ms. Kirti Jain
Department of Archaeology
Deccan College
Pune 411 006
Maharashtra

Mr. Ramesh Jain
6/25, MACT Colony
Bhopal
Madhya Pradesh

Mr. Achyutanand Jha
Archaeological Survey of India
Janpath
New Delhi 110 011

Mr. Jeetendra Nath
National Museum
Janpath
New Delhi 110 011

Dr. Krishan Kumari
Department of History
Andhra University
Waltair 530 003
Andhra Pradesh

Mr. K. Kumar
19, MIG, Shah Ganj
Agra
Uttar Pradesh

Dr. Kumar Anand
Shivapuri, Beur Road
P.O. Anisabad
Patna 800 002
Bihar

Dr. Krishna Murari
Faculty of Social Science
Department of Ancient Indian Studies
Magadh University
Bodh Gaya
Bihar

Prof. B.B. Lal
C/O Wing Cdr. Rajesh Lal
Officer Commanding 21 Squadron IAF
c/o 56 A.P.O.

Dr. Makkhan Lal
Department of History
Aligarh Muslim University
Aligarh 202 001

Mr. H. Laven
Institute of Genetik
University of Mainz,
Mainz (West germany)

Dr. Lokesh Chandra
J-22, Hauz Khas Enclave
New Delhi 110 016

Ms. K. Madgavkar
41/42, Lucknow road,
Delhi 110 007

Dr. Sudha Malaiya
Vijay Oil Mills,
Damoh
Madhya Pradesh

Dr. S.C. Malik
5/90 Connaught Circus
New Delhi 110 001

Dr. Man Mohan
Dept. of History
M.D. University
Rohtak 124 001
Haryana

Yashodhar Mathpal
Folk Culture Museum
Bhimtal, Nainital
Uttar Pradesh

Dr. C. Margabandhu
Archaeological Survey of India
Janpath
New Delhi 110 011

Dr. Richard Meadow
H-48 Elm Street Canton
Mass. 02021
U.S.A.

Mr. K.K. Mohammad
Department of History
Aligarh Muslim University
Aligarh
Uttar Pradesh

Dr. Ravi Moorti
Department of Archaeology
Deccan College Pune 411 006
Maharashtra

Mr. K.S. Murthy
Department of Anthropology
Andhra University
Waltair
Andhra Pradesh

Dr. Malti Nagar
Department of Archaeology
Deccan College
Pune 411 006
Maharashtra

Prof. A.K. Narain
Usha Kiran
Nand Nagar
Banaras Hindu University
Varanasi 221 005
Uttar Pradesh

Mr. S.B. Ota
Prehistory Branch
Archaeological Survey of India
Nagpur

Dr. J.N. Pal
Dept. of A.I.H.C. & Archaeology
Allahabad University
Allahabad

Dr. J.N. Pandey
Dept. A.I.H.C. & Archaeology
Allahabad University
Allahabad

Mrs. Sandhya Pande
K.R.G. College
Gwalior
Madhya Pradesh

Dr. P. C. Pant
Dept. of A.I.H.C. & Archaeology
Banaras Hindu University
Varanasi
Uttar Pradesh

Dr. V.S. Parikh
M.S. University of Baroda
Baroda
Gujarat

Dr. ASKO Parpola
Untuvasetie 5.B.64
00820 Helsinki-82,
Finland

Dr. K.H. Patel
M.S. University of Baroda
Baroda
Gujarat

Dr. G.L. Possehl
Department of South Asian Studies
University of Pennsylvania
33rd and Spruce Streets
Philadelphia PA. 19104, U.S.A.

Mr. Ajit Kumar Prasad
Sunder Bhavan
Gardani Bagh, Kacchi Talab
Patna 1
Bihar

Mr. G.C.Rai
10A/4 Shakti Nagar
Delhi 110 007

Dr. K. Rajan
Dept. of Archaeolgoy
Tamil University
Thanjavur 613 001

Mr. Ravinder Kumar
B-13/78 Sonarpura
Varanasi 221 001
Uttar Pradesh

Mr. S.B. Roy
B-20, Sujan Singh Park
New Delhi

Dr. M.D.N. Sahi
Department of History
Aligarh Muslim University
Aligarh 220 001

Dr. K.S. Saraswat
Birbal Sahni Institute of Palaeobotany
Lucknow 226 007
Uttar Pradesh

Mr. Jinendra Sema
c/o Malwa Sugar Mills
Below Dhuri
Dist. Sangrur
Punjab

Ms. Aparna Sengupta
c/o Dr. P.K. Sengupta
Rattanpalli Post
Dist. Bhirbhum 731 235
West Bengal

Mr. Vinod Kumar Seth
H-17, Maharani Bagh
New Delhi 110 014

Mr. R.P. Sharma
Institute of Archaeology
24, Tilak Marg
New Delhi

Mr. Sharad Kant Sharma
Neelambar Prachiya Vidya Path
24, Gangwal Bagh
Jaipur 302 004
Rajasthan

Mr. S.R. Sharma
Village & P.O. Pahargarh
Dist. Morena
Madhya Pradesh

Prof. T.C. Sharma
Department of Anthropology
Gauhati University
Guwahati 781 014
Assam

Prof. A.M. Shastri
23, Vidya Vihar
Ranapratap Nagar
Nagpur 440 022
Maharrshtra

Prof. K.M. Shrimali
155, Vaishali, Pitampura
Delhi 110 034

Dr. Pradeep Kumar Shukla
Studio Manoj
Parkota Hills
Sagar 470 002
Madhya Pradesh

Dr. Amrendra Kumar Singh
Department of Ancient Indian History
A.P.S. University
Rewa
Madhya Pradesh

Dr. Bhagwan Singh
J3/227, DDA Flats
Kalkaji
Delhi 110 047

Mr. Birendra Pratap Singh
Kabir Chaura
C23/15, Ayodhya Bhawan
Varanasi
Uttar Pradesh

Dr. Bhupendra Pal Singh
Block 19, Flat 4
Kabir Nagar Colony
Varanasi 221 001
Uttar Pradesh

Prof. Purshottam Singh
Department of A.I.H.C. and Archaeology
Banaras Hindu University
Varanasi 221 005
Uttar Pradesh

Dr. R.C.P. Singh
Department of A.I.H. and Asian Studies
Magadh University
Bodh Gaya
Bihar

Mr. Ravi Pratap Singh
Chandra Bhawan
Alajatapur
Gorakhpur
Uttar Pradesh

Dr. S.B.Singh
Department of A.I.H.C. and Archaeology
Kurukshetra University
Kurukshetra
Haryana

Dr. Y.B. Singh
Department of History
Jammu University
Jammu 180 001
J & K

Mr. K.K. Sinha
Archaeological Survey of India
Janpath
New Delhi 110 011

Dr. Prakash Sinha
2, Malaviya Nagar
George Town
Allahabad
Uttar Pradesh

Prof. U.V. Singh
Department of A.I.H.C & Archaeology
Kurukshetra University
Kurukshetra
Haryana

Prof. W.G. Solheim II
Department of Anthropology
University of Hawaii
2550 Campus Road
Honolulu 96822
U.S.A.

Dr. V.H. Sonawane
Department of Ancient History & Archaeology
M.S. University
Baroda 390 002
Gujarat

Mr. J.P. Srivastava
Archaeological Survey of India
Purana Qila
New Delhi

Mr. K.C. Srivastava
'Gokul', H.No. N-11/58, M-11-C
Mohalla Ranipur, P.O. Bazardiya
Varanasi
Uttar Pradesh

Mr. S.K. Srivastava
Grukul Kangri
Hardwar
Uttar Pradesh

Dr. V.C. Srivastava
Department of A.I.H.C. & Archaeology
Banaras Hindu University
Varanasi 221 005
Uttar Pradesh

Prof. A. Sundara
Department of A.I.H. & Epigraphy
Karnatak University
Pawte Nagar
Dharwad 580 003
Karnataka

Prof. K.K. Thapalyal
C/3 University Flats
Lucknow University
Lucknow - 226 007

Prof. Romila Thapar
School of Historical Studies
Jawaharlal Nehru University
New Delhi 110 067

Dr. Rakesh Tiwari
Department of Archaeology
Roshanadaula Kothi
Kaisarbagh
Lucknow
Uttar Pradesh

Dr. V.K. Tiwari
Department of Archaeology
27/2, Kaisarbagh
Lucknow
Uttar Pradesh

Prof. P.K. Tiwari
288/63, Arya Nagar
Aish Bagh Road
Lucknow 226 004
Uttar Pradesh

Prof. Maurizio Tosi
Italian Embassy Cultural Centre
D-27, N.D.S.E., Part 2,
New Delhi 110 049

Ms. Gayatri Tripathi
Department of A.I.H.C. & Archaeology
Banaras Hindu University
Varanasi 221 005
Uttar Pradesh

Mr. Alok Tripathi
Archaeological Survey of India
Khajuraho
Madhya Pradesh

Mr. L. Tripathi
Department of A.I.H.C. & Archaeology
Banaras Hindu University
Varanasi 221 005
Uttar Pradesh

Dr. Vibha Tripathi
B 31/35-22, Sankat Mochan Colony
Varanasi 221 005
Uttar Pradesh

Mr.P.K. Trivedi
Archaeolgocial Survey of India
Jaipur Circle
Jaipur
Rajasthan

Mr. G.S. Tyagi
c/o AGE (I), Amla
P.O. Amla 460 553
Dist. Betul
Madhya Pradesh

Dr. V.D. Tyagi
D.S. College
Aligarh
Uttar Pradesh

Prof. R.K. Varma
'Samarpana', 18 C, Hastings Road
Allahabad
Uttar Pradesh

Note : All the Life Members who have paid only a part of the membership fee are requested to clear the dues. Othervise they may find their names deleted in the next print out.

Rakta Lokeswara 9th-10th Century A.D. Kashmir, National Museum, New Delhi (Shashi Asthana).

Plate 1. Persian Wheel with pin-drum gearing from *Khamsa of Nizami* (Afzal Khan).

Plate 2. Another painting showing pin-drum gearing from *Khamsa of Nizami* (Afzal Khan).

Plate 1. Vedic brick altar, Purola (K.P. Nautiyal).

Plate 2. Central chamber, Purola (K.P. Nautiyal).

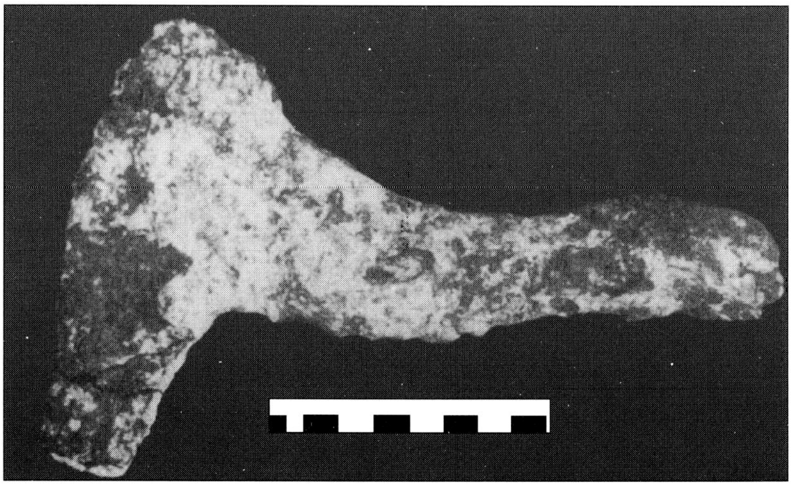

Plate 3. Iron-axe, Purola (K.P. Nautiyal).

Plate 1. Vedic brick altar, Purola (K.P. Nautiyal).

Plate 2. Central chamber, Purola (K.P. Nautiyal).

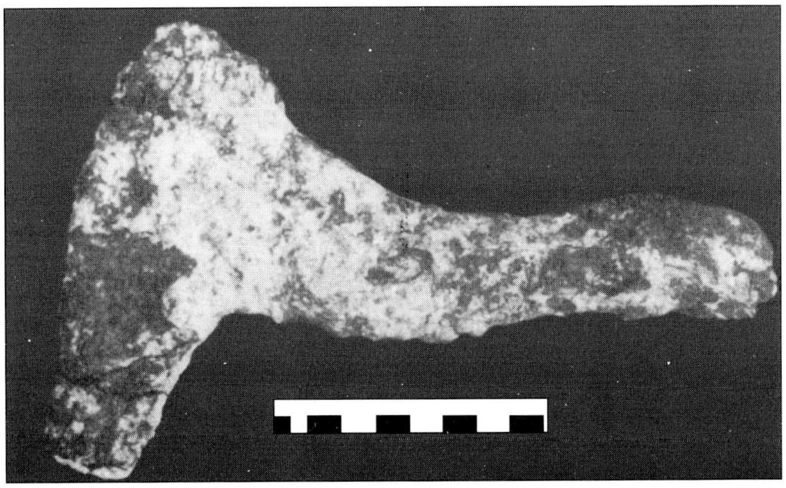

Plate 3. Iron-axe, Purola (K.P. Nautiyal).

Plate 1. Persian Wheel with pin-drum gearing from *Khamsa of Nizami* (Afzal Khan).

Plate 2. Another painting showing pin-drum gearing from *Khamsa of Nizami* (Afzal Khan).

Plate 1. Persian Wheel with pin-drum gearing from *Khamsa of Nizami* (Afzal Khan).

Plate 2. Another painting showing pin-drum gearing from *Khamsa of Nizami* (Afzal Khan).

Plate 3. Building of Fatehpur Sikri, from *Akbarnama* (Afjal Khan).

Plate 4. Akbar being welcomed at Fatehpur Sikri after this victory in Gujarat, from *Akbarnama* (Afjal Khan).

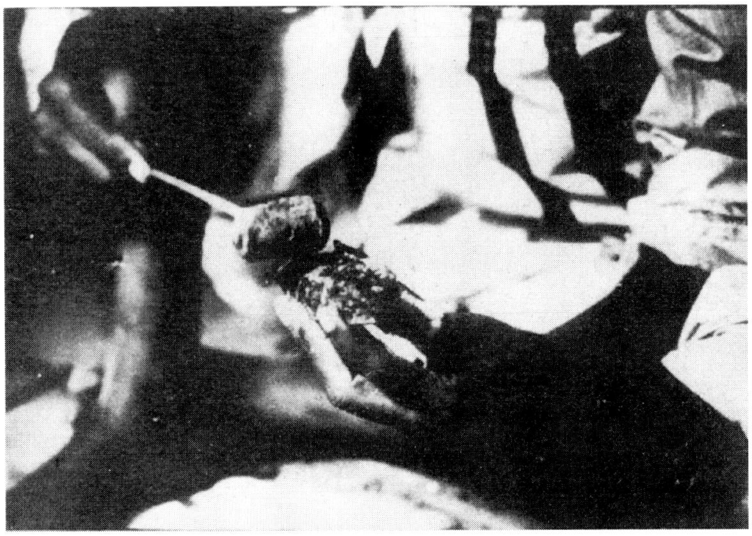

Plate 1. Indirect-reverse percussion (Roux and Pelegrin).

Plate 2. Knapping workshop (Roux and Pelegrin).

Plate 1. Apping of beads by children in the street (Roux and Pelegrin).

Plate 1. St. Augustine church complex, old Goa general view before excavations (A.K. Sharma).

Plate 2. Main hall of church after celearance (A.K. Sharma).

Plate 3. Chappels after clearance, reconstruction and conservation (A.K. Sharma).

Plate 4. The Inscription on Slab (A.K. Sharma).

Plate 1. Vedic brick altar, Purola (K.P. Nautiyal).

Plate 2. Central chamber, Purola (K.P. Nautiyal).

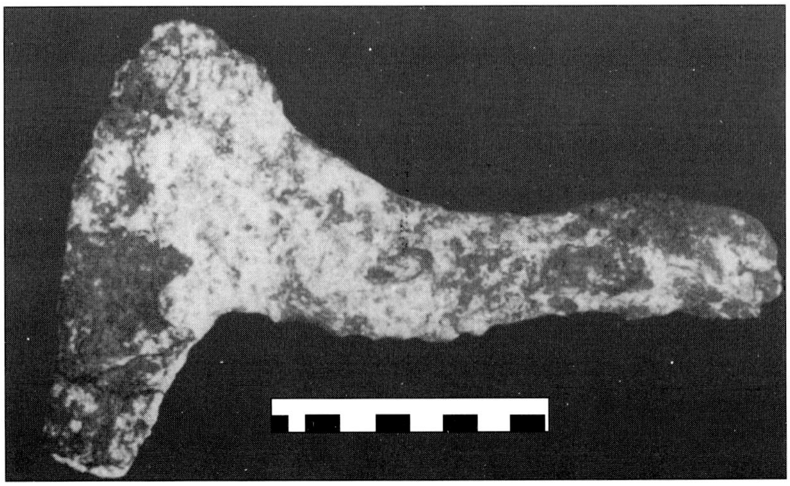

Plate 3. Iron-axe, Purola (K.P. Nautiyal).

Plate 2. Details of horoscope writting of Buddha ? Nagarjunkonda, 3rd Century A.D. (Anamika Pathak).

Plate 1. Complete slab depictiing scenes from Buddha's life, Nagarjunkonda, 3rd Century A.D. (Anamika Pathak).